DANCES AND STORIES OF

THE AMERICAN INDIAN

DANCES
AND STORIES
OF THE
AMERICAN
INDIAN

➤➤➤◄◄◄

By BERNARD S. MASON

➤➤➤◄◄◄

Photographs by PAUL BORIS
AND OTHERS

Drawings by FREDERIC H. KOCH

➤➤➤◄◄◄

A. S. BARNES AND COMPANY

NEW YORK

To
THE CAMP FAIRWOOD DANCERS
with happy memories of
those inspired Grand Council nights
when together we donned
our moccasins and plumes.

Contents

Part I
PROLOGUE

Part II
DANCE STEPS AND MOVEMENTS

Part III
DANCES

Part IV
STAGING THE DANCES

Acknowledgments

The author expresses his appreciation:

To James C. Stone whose artistry is reflected in the many photographs of him which adorn these pages, for posing for these pictures and for carefully checking the manuscript.

To Robert Raymond, Lawrence Ratliff, and John Landis Holden for their co-operation in dancing these routines and in posing for certain photographs.

To Ernest Thompson Seton for inspiration during youthful years, and for permission to include his "The Lone Scout," "The Courtship of the Eagles," the "Zuni Call to Council," and the ritual of Council.

To Julia M. Buttree Seton for permission to use the "Winnebago War Dance," the "Yei-be-chi" and the "Apache Devil Dance."

To Julian Harris Salomon for permission to include the "Plains War Dance" and the "Sioux Buffalo Dance."

To Dr. William D. Heintz for his notes on the "Cheyenne Buffalo Dance."

To all of the dancers who appear in the photographs. In keeping with the purpose of presenting the dances in such form that they can be re-enacted by us today, these photographs are all of white interpreters of the Indian's dance art whom it has been the author's privilege to train.

To the photographers who made these pictures: to Ralph Haburton for taking those facing pages 134, 135, 182, 183, 247, and 263; to Arthur C. Allen for taking those facing pages 87, 151, 214, and 262 (top); to Homer Jensen for taking those facing pages 167 and 262 (bottom); to Paul Boris for taking all the others.

Acknowledgment is hereby made to Harper and Brothers for

permission to use material from *The Book of Indian Crafts and Indian Lore* by Julian Harris Salomon; to Hale, Cushman and Flint for permission to use material from *Indian Story and Song from North America* by Alice C. Fletcher; to E. P. Dutton and Company, Inc., for permission to use material from *Manito Masks* by Hartley Alexander; to Theodore Presser Company for permission to use Zuni Sunrise Call by Carlos Troyer; to A. S. Barnes and Company for permission to use material from *Rhythm of the Redman* by Julia M. Buttree.

PART I

PROLOGUE

RED WINE IN THE WHITE DESERT

The gap that often exists between popular conception and truth is nowhere better exemplified than in the treatment of the dance-drama of the American Indian. "A crude jumping about," "a mere hopping up and down," "a leaping about in the most comical manner imaginable," "a frenzied expression of uncontrolled passion"—with comments such as these the memoirs of early travelers among the Indians have indicted the dance. After some such fashion as this the entertainment profession of years past has often depicted Indian dances. With expressions such as these the average person today is inclined to dismiss the subject as unworthy, interesting only as an example of the bizarre customs of savagery.

Truth rests somewhere near the opposite pole. A brief moment of study of an Indian dance will convince that it is far indeed from a mere hopping up and down, for its movements are intricate and highly skilled, its routines often involved and complicated. The seeming simplicity is after all a tribute to the artistry of the dancers, for it is the eternal way of the skillful artist to make that which is intricate appear simple and easy. That which is labeled as an impulsive leaping about is more apt to be a deeply significant ritual moving under the edicts of long-established tradition. Instead of a wild frenzy of uncontrolled emotions the dance is characterized by a peculiar reserve which gives the feeling, even in its most violent forms, that the dancer is using only a fraction of its latent power. Those who see comic antics in such seriousness of purpose and striving for perfection bespeak their own lack of horizon, the degree to which their own conventions have imprisoned them.

Our lack of understanding and appreciation of the Indian's dance-art is as abysmal as our lack of understanding of his personality. The distance is far between White and Red and the passing of the years has shortened it but little. The depths of the Indian's soul has never been explored, indeed its very surface is difficult to see in full vision. The barrier of reserve that he has erected to withstand the onslaught of the whites can be scaled only by years of intimate living, and even then the view beyond is hazy and obstructed.

But however great our lack of understanding the Indian, the fact still remains that we appreciate the worth of the other manifestations of his personality better than we do his dancing. In the excellence of his crafts,

3

for example, he is accorded the full stature of an artist. The supremacy of his blanket weaving, his basketry, his pottery, his jewelry making, his beading, to mention a few, and of his design as it manifests itself in all of these, is well-established. Similarly, his music has been credited with a unique quality of special interest. Again, his legendary lore is acclaimed both for its richness of quality and its amazing quantity. As compared to these, little effort has been made to assay his dancing. It has just been assumed to be relatively lacking in significance.

And yet, it is in his dancing that the height of the Indian's artistic attainment is reached, the peak of the aesthetic expression of a truly aesthetic people. Here all of the elements of his other arts are combined, as integral parts of an animated design in which the movement of the human body is the dominant means of expression. The voice of the drum is the controlling factor that brings order out of chaos, commanding as the Chief controls his warriors. It is the song that expresses verbally the human hopes and aspirations, and addresses them to the All One. It is the spectacle of painted bodies, of shimmering feathers, of urgent design and potent symbol, that expresses again in different form these same emotions. But all of these combined—drum rhythm, song, ornamentation—do not define the dance-form. Nor do the supplementing legends as related by the older folk complete the understanding. It is movement of rhythmic bodies that is the dance's central characteristic, its animated essence. It is

"Brown limbs lifting, brown limbs falling, lifting, falling, all together." *

All this combines into a dance-drama that is addressed to no idle purpose but to the worship of the One Great Spirit. It may be purely such, a ritual of praise and thanksgiving, a supplication for life's needs and for success in human ventures. Again, it may be secular, even for sheer fun and satisfaction of appetite, but always the relation to the spiritual is present. Indeed, the dances of the people become more than a dramatic representation of life activities, they reflect and symbolize the full scope of their philosophy. Like the Bantus of Africa who asked of a stranger, "What do you dance?" and thereby learned all that was essential to know about the visitor's people,** so the Indian embodies in his dances the representation of all phases of his life, his ideals and his values.

To the extent that the Indian dance has been adequately analyzed, its related or marginal elements have received the most attention—its music, its instruments, its symbols, its costuming—and not the dance movements themselves. Whether in pursuit of dance steps as done by the individual or the pattern of dances as done by groups, one can often read for weary days through book after book of Indian customs without finding the slightest ray of light. One envies the opportunity of the anthropologists

* Hartley Alexander, "The Singing Girl of Copan," *Theatre Arts Monthly*, Vol. XVII, No. 8, page 595.

** Havelock Ellis, *The Dance of Life*, page 38. Boston: Houghton Mifflin Company, 1923.

of the past who lived long among the Indian tribes in the study of their culture, and whose findings are recorded in voluminous reports. In attempting to visit these tribes vicariously through reading these reports, one is often amazed at the dearth of material on dances, even in cultures where a wealth of dance-art is known to exist.

The same fate awaits one in delving into the works of the highly skilled and specially trained musicians who have spent long lives in study of the songs of the various tribes, and whose reports occupy long shelves in the libraries. The songs have, indeed, been well-recorded. So closely related are the song and the dance that the Indian often uses the terms interchangeably, speaking of the dance as the song and the song as the dance— yet, it is only in rare instances that any detailed mention is made of the dance that accompanies the song. After all is said and done, the scientists, regardless of type, have done little better for the dance than the early travelers, explorers and missionaries.

One cannot watch the meticulous chorus perfection of a group of Hopi Katchina dancers in their amazingly dramatic costumes without feeling that the best of chorus performance on the modern stage and screen is somehow wanting. One cannot watch a Pueblo Eagle dancer without sensing an innate capacity for imitation, a oneness in spirit with the being that is portrayed, that is wholly superior. One cannot behold the eager dramatics of a dynamic, forceful story-dancer of the northern Plains without labeling it as the manifestation of a native dramatic genius. One cannot even witness a conventional chorus dance in which the dancer's only function seems to be to fill a space for the sake of symmetry, as a feather occupies its place in a warbonnet, without feeling that here are beings wholly absorbed in a task that to them is supremely significant. One cannot watch a dancer pulsating and throbbing in every cell and corpuscle without realizing that here is more than mere movement of limbs, mere quiver of muscles—that here is a being who is dancing with his very soul.

One cannot enter the "powwow" arena of the Woodlands or Plains, moccasins afoot and bells on ankles, joining as one with the vibrating forms, obeying the booming commands of the mighty drum, without a forthright admission that here is a conception of dancing that, for solid fun, ours cannot match.

These impressions combine to leave one with an insistent conviction that in the dancing of the Indian is a consummate artistry, a vital, living dance-art that finds no exact counterpart in our own conception and use of dancing. Indeed, it leaves us with a feeling that if it is not preserved our own culture will be the loser. Until the time comes that an American dance-art evolves that has meaning to all the people, participated in by all as exemplifying our life philosophy, fulfilling our desires and satisfying our needs—until that time comes we must sit at the feet of the Indian as our teacher. Here is Red Wine for the parched lips of those who travel the White Desert.

ANCIENT MOCCASINS ON MODERN FEET

"Are these dances authentic?" The question seems to arise whenever Indian dances are presented outside their native tribal homeland, whether danced by Indians or by interpreters of the Indian way, whether seen as dances or read from the printed pages. The attitude it reflects is welcomed by the sincere interpreter, for the virtue of authenticity is none other than the virtue of truth, and it looms as more significant still against the background of untruth and misconception that has beclouded the Indian's dance-art in years past. Important as it is, however, there are other considerations.

The purpose of this book is to preserve the dances of the American Indian, but to preserve them *in action*, not merely in printed word . . . to preserve them as dances that we ourselves may use and enjoy. It presents the dances in such manner that they can be re-enacted for stage or campfire entertainment.

In the light of these facts, the question of authenticity is already answered in part, if by "authentic" one implies an exact reproduction of the dances as the Indians did them. To be of practical use a dance must bring enjoyment and aesthetic satisfaction to the audience and to the dancers. Many dances, if reproduced exactly, would not accomplish this for either group, for what we speak of as dances are often ritualistic ceremonies in which the same movements are repeated over and over, and may continue thus for hours. In their native setting such ceremonies captivate the Indian audience, because there the audience is in fullest harmony with the motion-language, and has vital concern with the purpose for which the dances are an instrument in achieving, whether it be rain for the crops, thanksgiving for the harvest, success in the hunt, tribal propagation, or whatnot. But the non-Indian audience, holding no such concern for the purpose, would find them hopelessly monotonous. From a practical standpoint all that is possible in such cases is to lift out a segment of the dance for reproduction, as an orchestra might select one movement of a symphony, or to re-enact the general movements so as merely to give an impression of the dance.

Not all dances are of this repetitious type and so do not offer such complications. Indeed, some are brilliantly dramatic and admirably suited in

JAMES C. STONE

JAMES C. STONE

their exact form, and still others need only minor omissions and adaptations.

In the handling of these dances, two pressures have relentlessly influenced every thought and move: The first has been an intense desire for truth and accuracy. The second has been a flair for showmanship that has insisted that these dances be given the full advantage of proper presentation, lest their beauty and artistry be needlessly lost. Only the necessity of transporting the dances in time and space, from one culture to another, has brought the two pressures into conflict, and when this has happened, the former has been too potent to permit needless meddling.

The barriers to learning the full truth of any dance are often such that no one can scale them completely, the difficulties such that any recording of it is apt to be only an approximation. Literature throwing needed light is often scanty, in some cases non-existent. No more has been possible than to record the dances as they are understood and conceived, so altered as to adapt them for acceptable re-enactment. These dances are presented with a full awareness of their inadequacy as precise recordings but with full confidence in their usefulness for the purpose for which they are intended.

In approaching these dances, therefore, we are putting ancient moccasins on modern feet. We are true to the gloriously artistic and dramatically beautiful tradition of these moccasins, true to the conventional movements that the ages have established as appropriate for them, but the very fact that they are on modern feet imposes certain limitations and demands that certain liberties be taken with them.

To what extent are these modern feet of non-Indian dancers capable of filling these ancient moccasins? That is to ask, "Will not the inability of our dancers to perform the typical movements result in an obviously unauthentic performance?" Much has been said on the point that there is an indefinable something about the dancing Indian that no other seems able quite to duplicate, an intangible element in style that is distinctively, inimitably Indian. Some have thought that this arises from postural characteristics of the Indian, from straight shoulders, flat back, etc., but, to the extent that it exists at all, it is more apt to be the result of long-established differences in attitude and in concept of dance movements. This margin of the supposedly unattainable is narrow and fleeting, and may doubtless be more a matter of individual differences than of racial ones. It is no more possible for a non-Indian to duplicate exactly the style of a certain Indian than it is for one Indian to duplicate that of another. Many a sincere and thorough interpreter of the Indian way has entered the Redman's dance arena and blended with the dancing Indians so harmoniously that even the practiced eye could not label one as Indian and another as not.

In one word: The steps and movements can be learned with reasonable exactness, and the rituals or routines can be reproduced. Many of these are suitable in their original form and others need adaptation. When this has been necessary the right of dramatic license has been invoked. Those few numbers that have been included that are Indian in theme and spirit, yet not based on authentic originals, are so labeled.

Dance Without Song

In the scheme of dancing set forth in this book no songs are used. The dances are accompanied by percussion only.

This break with dance tradition is one that an Indian would scarcely be able to comprehend, for to him dance movement and song are merely different phases of the same thing. Moreover, most of the adaptations of Indian dances that have appeared in the past have made much of the songs, often to the point where the songs seem to become the primary consideration ... with complete song arrangements and very sketchy directions for the dances.

Why, then, this departure? The reason is, first of all, one of expediency. To insist on the use of songs would mean to prohibit dancing in many situations where otherwise it might be used. Indian songs are very difficult for non-Indian vocalists to sing with anything approaching a true native quality. The difficulty in finding a drum-singer would, more often than not, erect an insurmountable barrier. Even if one were found capable of singing the songs properly, his efforts could not be heard above the ringing of many bells in the vigorous group dances—a *chorus* of drum-singers would be needed as in the Indian's dances. Viewed practically, this could seldom, if ever, be achieved.

Concern over the songs might be justified were it not for the fact that the dances do not need them. Whether or not they are used, the interest centers primarily in the dancing. Whatever symbolic meaning the Indian may attach to the song, or however important it may be considered in accomplishing the religious or other purpose of the dance as he sees it, the fact still remains that the spectator is usually only vaguely aware of the song because of the consummate appeal of the dance.

The present-day tendency to use orchestra music as accompaniment to Indian dances is still more to be discouraged. However beautiful it may be in itself, it seems wholly incongruous in the Indian setting, a foreign element that robs the dance of its true Indian flavor.

Good dancing, whether Indian or other, is capable of standing on its own without symphonic or vocal accompaniment. Percussion is essential, and in this case is all that is desirable.

The drum is indispensable. It is to the dance as the bow to the arrow. It is the spring to action. And in the scheme of dancing here presented, the man behind the drum is of greatest importance. His is the task not only of beating the rhythm, but of directing the dance, of commanding all movements. He is at once rhythm-maker and dance director, and to repeat— he alone rules the scene.

Scope of the Dances

Out of the maze of countless dances from the many tribes, the task of selecting has presented itself. Four principles have guided this selection: The *first* is the ever-present one of usefulness, preference being given to those that lend themselves best to reproduction. Every dance in this volume has been danced many times, and found to be practical and within the capacity of the average group, and to possess adequate dramatic quality and audience appeal. Dances that have not met these standards have been omitted.

Second, the dances selected are confined largely to those with which I have had personal experience. Most of them have been witnessed first hand and recorded as seen; many have been actually danced with the Indians. Some have come from the notes of other observers, and still others, particularly the ancient ones, have been taken from the literature and checked with the present-day dance customs of the tribes that used them.

Third, effort has been made to represent the various main cultural areas, with a few dances from each. The one conspicuous omission is the Pacific Northwest, with the dances of which area I have not had sufficient personal experience.

Fourth, effort has been made to include as many of the themes, motifs and types of dances as possible. These types are many. There are religious dances and secular dances; there are dances for the accomplishment of serious life-purposes and others for sheer fun. There are comic dances and tragic dances, social dances and mourning dances. There are dances built on the war theme, on the hunting theme, and on the agricultural theme. There are dances of mimicry, some in imitation of spirit bodies and others in imitation of nature, as in the animal and bird dances. There are dances in which masks and other disguising costumes are worn to aid in this mimicry and others that rely only on the art of pantomime without special costuming. There are dances that tell stories, some with obvious overt dramatics and others with conventionalized symbolic movements, understandable only to the informed. There are dances for men only, others for women only, and still others for mixed groups. There are solo dances, some that can be done by any dancer and others that are personal property of a single individual. There are dances limited to certain societies which own them, and there are dances open to everybody.

The Indian Style

In the light of tribal variations in dances the question arises, is there a basic Indian dance style? In all Indian dancing, regardless of tribe, there is a certain similarity of movement that identifies it unmistakably as Indian and that can rightly be called a basic Indian style. There are several fundamental steps or movements, such as, for example, toe-heel dancing, flat-heel dancing, stomp dancing, trot dancing, etc. These appear in practically all areas, although some tribes may make greater use of some types than others, and may accent the movements in slightly different fashion and use variations of them that are not universal. The shade of difference between these various basic steps and movements is slight and all are done with much the same characteristic style. The basic steps and movements are therefore presented as Indian rather than tribal.

Dancing for Men

Both psychologically and physically, the dancing of the Indian is peculiarly adapted for American young men. They like it. Its appeal is deep-rooted. They accept it with enthusiasm. A contributing factor may be the glamour that surrounds the Indian himself, but more basic is the inherent masculinity of the dancing. In historic background it is man's dancing; in its typical movements it is an expression of masculine qualities. The type of vigorous muscular action involved is accepted by men as the sphere of men alone. The dramatic themes it employs are of the type that challenge the male mind. It reflects life with a man's slant.

This whole-hearted acceptance plus this intrinsic appropriateness lifts it far and away above other available types of dancing as ideally suited for young men.

American boys need dancing. Their craving for rhythmic expression is seen in the eager response and the solid joy they manifest once they find a type in which they can engage whole-heartedly, without laying themselves open to the charge of possessing a fondness for that which is sissified. Along with the many priceless contributions the Indian has made to American youth, he has given boys and young men that type of dancing.

Many of the dances in this book are, therefore, designed primarily for men and boys. As in all athletic effort some will possess more talent than others. The very vigorousness of the movements, the need for perfect co-ordination and for muscular power, will limit full attainment to those youth who are mature, and will give advantage to those with athletic talent. But joy will be found by all.

Dances for Women

The dances in which women will find their greatest joy are those which were actually danced by Indian women. For the most part these are the group dances of the chorus type. Four chapters of group dances are included in this book, not all of which were engaged in by Indian women, but all suitable for use by women. The dancing commonly thought of as man's dancing is the go-as-you-please type, the "powwow" dancing with its robust action and its mannish movements. This may be imitated by women, as is often done in interpreting the story dances, but a full approximation of it as done by Indian men, is not to be expected. Aside from occasional use of it for dramatic purposes, it is recommended that women use the delightful and appropriate group or chorus routines.

Stage or Council Ring

An atmospheric something is lost in transplanting the Redman's dances from their native setting to the modern stage. The dances in this book are therefore described for the outdoor dancing arena or council ring, the nearest approximation to their original setting, with the hope that such a location will be sought out whenever possible. When necessity demands the use of a stage, the routines are still applicable as described. Only in rare instances have separate directions been necessary for stage and council ring. In all other cases the director of the dances will have no difficulty in adjusting the council-ring directions to the stage.

PART II

DANCE STEPS AND MOVEMENTS

Chapter I

INDIAN DANCE STEPS

In the dancing of the American Indian there are three characteristic foot movements or steps. These appear to greater or less degree in all areas, although one of them may find more frequent use in any given area than the others. These steps are the *toe-heel*, the *flat-heel* and the *flat-foot*. These three steps are here regarded as basic movements.

An analysis of the three will indicate that they are very similar, seeming to differ one from another more in accent than in the use of widely different movements. Yet each is sufficiently different as to form the basis for a distinctive style of dancing.

Each of these steps is also done with a sort of double foot action, with both feet participating on each step, which immediately results in a different movement and one which has a different aesthetic effect on the observer. The double movements also constitute basic dance styles.

In this chapter these three steps, the toe-heel, the flat-heel, and the flat-foot, together with the double form of each, are described as fundamental movements. Each has many variations, and there are many related steps that are employed with each for the sake of variety. After the descriptions of the fundamental steps themselves, these other movements suited for use with them are discussed.

These steps are characteristic of go-as-you-please dancing in which each individual is permitted to dance in any way he chooses, unregulated by specific ritual. There is another very prevalent dancing style, called *stomp dancing*, that finds its greatest use in ceremonial dances. This and other such steps are described at the end of the chapter. Many ceremonial dances require specific steps and movements that cannot be called general and do not find use in other dances. In such cases the steps are described in connection with the discussion of the dances in question, rather than in this chapter.

UNDERSTANDING THE TERMS USED

The terms used in describing dance steps are words which are used in everyday conversation with various shades of meaning, and so it is necessary that we understand the meaning of these words as this book uses them. These are as follows:

Toe—the ball of the foot—not the toe itself. For example, the expression "Place the toe down, with the heel raised" means to place the ball of the foot down with the heel raised off the floor.

Step—a step as in walking, the stepping foot touching the ground before the other foot is raised. (In running the advancing foot is still in the air when the other foot is raised.)

Trot—a short spring from one foot to the other as in relaxed running, in which the advancing foot is still in the air when the other foot is raised.

Hop—a short spring on one foot. A hop is made by standing on one foot, making a short spring and landing on the same foot.

Jump—(1) a spring from one foot to the other; (2) a spring on both feet at the same time.

Skip—a low, short spring on one foot in which the foot is barely raised off the ground—a sort of push or scrape in which the ball of the foot "brushes" the ground.

Tap—(1) a pat on the ground with the ball of the foot, the foot being immediately raised again; (2) a pat on the ground with the heel, the heel being immediately raised again.

Beat—one beat of the drum.

Count—a unit of drumming that would be expressed as one count. In unaccented drumming it is one beat of the drum. In two-time drumming, accented *loud*-soft, it is the unit of loud and soft beat, counted *one*-and, etc.

Powwow dancing—dancing in which each dancer is free to dance as he chooses, using whatever appropriate movements he desires, without following a fixed routine.

Group dance—a dance with a fixed routine, in which each dancer performs essentially the same movements at the same time.

Story dance—a dance depicting a story.

"I Saw" dance—a story dance re-enacting an exploit or happening, presumably one that the dancer saw or experienced.

Fundamental Steps

The basic steps of the three common dance styles are here described, first in their simple form and then with the two-foot action.

THE TOE-HEEL STEP

(soft beat) &   Place left toe down, heel raised
(loud beat) 1   Drop left heel, simultaneously raising right foot
(soft beat) &   Place right toe down, heel raised
(loud beat) 2   Drop right heel, simultaneously raising left foot

This universal movement is particularly characteristic of the dancing of the northern Woodlands and northern Plains. It is the best foundation for the other dancing styles and is recommended as the first step to be learned.

To achieve the proper movement the feet must be kept under the body at all times. Figure 1 illustrates both the right and the wrong positions of the feet. When the foot is extended far forward as in B the heel cannot be brought down gracefully and naturally, and the step will seem awkward and strained.

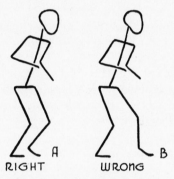

Figure 1. Toe-heel Step

With the feet in the proper position, lower the body a little by bending the knees to the angle shown in A. The knees remain bent at approximately this angle at all times in doing the step. They are never straightened out.

With the weight on the right foot, place the ball of the left foot down about six inches forward, keeping the heel elevated at a natural height. Drop the left heel down, and simultaneously lift the right foot for the next step. As the left heel is brought down, *the left knee bends or gives a little—* to use the dancing term, the knee is *soft.* The heel is not forced down by the leg muscles but by dropping the weight of the body on it. In placing the left toe forward the weight is on the right foot; then it is suddenly transferred to the left, thus dropping the heel down hard, the knee flexing to take up the jar. To the extent that the legs are kept relaxed and the knee soft the step becomes easy, natural and fluid. The movement is thus more of an up-and-down one than a forward or gliding one. Relaxed as it should be, the whole body shakes up and down a little on each step.

The step is done to two-time drumming, accented loud-soft. *The toe is placed down on the soft beat and the heel dropped on the loud beat.* The accent of the loud beat is an aid to bringing the heel down emphatically. The step is counted "and-*one*, and-*two*."

Here, then, are the pitfalls of the beginner:

1. Long straddling steps
2. Stiff knees
3. A tendency to drop the heel stiffly, using ankle and leg muscles only

And conversely, the correct movement involves the following:

1. Feet under the body with the knees slightly bent always
2. Steps short enough so that the knees can be kept bent at approximately the same angle constantly
3. Soft knee, flexing when the weight is placed on it
4. Heel lowered by dropping weight of body on leg

Once the step has been learned certain liberties may be taken with it. It is not necessary, and indeed not typical, to keep the toe in place after it is put down. It may be picked up and moved a little as desired, either forward, backward, or sidewards, and the foot brought down *flat* on the hard beat. This shifting of the toe gives greater freedom and flexibility to the step, eliminates all probability of getting off balance, and facilitates a natural, flowing style.

The variations and amplifications of the steps are described on page 22.

THE FLAT-HEEL STEP

(soft beat)	&	Step forward with left foot flat on floor
(loud beat)	1	Raise left heel and drop it down on count
(soft beat)	&	Step forward with right foot flat on floor
(loud beat)	2	Raise right heel and drop it down on count

The difference between this step and the toe-heel is largely one of emphasis, but the effect it produces is different. The feet hug the ground. They are raised no higher than necessary in stepping and are brought down flat; the heel is raised but very little in making the heel tap. The weight stays on the heels all the time. It is the step used in the *close-to-ground dancing* so characteristic of the Indians.

As in the toe-heel step, the knees are kept a trifle bent constantly, thus keeping the feet directly under the body, and the steps are short so as not to straighten out the legs.

The heel is raised for the heel tap, not by the ankle alone, but by an upward movement of the whole body, and is lowered by dropping the weight of the body on it. There is an up-and-down motion from head to foot, including the shoulders which are kept relaxed and are bobbed up and down a bit. To get the idea, stand with the feet side by side and shake the body up and down by flexing the knees a little. When this movement is accentuated it lifts and lowers the heels. This is the movement that raises and lowers the heel for the heel tap, and that raises the foot in stepping forward. The knee is soft and flexes with each impact.

If the toes are turned up so that they touch the top of the shoe or moccasin it is easier to put the foot down absolutely flat. Many experienced dancers make a habit of this whenever they step flat.

To repeat the essential points to watch:

1. Feet flat, hugging the ground
2. Knees bent to keep feet under the body
3. Soft knee, flexing when weight is placed on it
4. Heel raised by an upward lift of the body
5. Heel lowered by dropping weight on it

The flat-heel is a favorite step of older men who in their youth may have danced on their toes in springing style but now have settled down on their heels. It must not be dismissed as the resort of old men only, however, for this close-to-ground dancing with the whole body pulsing and aquiver is a good and favored dance style. Often a dashing youthful dancer will drop down from the high-springing double toe-heel to a moment of earthy accent with the flat-heel and its variations and thereby achieve the most brilliant moments of his dance.

The variations are described on page 34.

THE FLAT-FOOT STEP

(loud beat)	1	Step on left foot flat
(soft beat)	&	Skip on left foot flat
(loud beat)	2	Step on right foot flat
(soft beat)	&	Skip on right foot flat

A step and a skip with each foot suggests the skipping of children, but as the Indians do it the accent is not the same, and the appearance and the feeling produced are widely different. The feet are flat at all times; they are brought down flat on both the step and the skip, and when raised the sole of the foot is flat or parallel to the floor. The knees are kept slightly bent so as not to permit the advancing leg to straighten out in front.

Keeping the feet flat, step forward on the left, raising the right, skip forward on the left as the right advances, then repeat with the right. On the skip the foot is barely raised off the floor, brushing the floor as it goes forward, but on the step the foot is raised to a height of perhaps six inches. At all stages, however, it is flat to the floor. The body is erect and sways from side to side naturally with the step.

This movement differs widely from that of the flat-heel step. There is no heel action, no pounding of the floor, no hugging the floor with the feet. Although the foot is flat it does not give the close-to-ground feeling.

Although the body is relaxed there is less of the up-and-down shaking that characterizes the heel steps. The step is light, the accent forward.

The flat-foot is a much used and very characteristic Indian dance movement. On the southern Plains and among the Southwest tribes it finds greater favor than does the toe-heel.

The variations of the step are found on page 35.

THE DOUBLE TOE-HEEL STEP

This sparkling step is an amplification of the toe-heel step and is one of the most brilliant of Indian movements. It enjoys widespread use by accomplished dancers. It is found wherever toe-heel dancing is used. Old men from whose legs the spring of youth has departed may confine themselves to the simple toe-heel but men in their vigor find their best expression here. It is particularly characteristic of the Indians of the Great Lakes area and the northern Plains.

As quickly as possible a dancer should shift over from the toe-heel to the double toe-heel as his basic step.

Place the left foot in natural walking distance in front:

(soft beat)   &   Jump on both toes, heels raised
(loud beat)   1   Drop left heel and raise right foot forward
(soft beat)   &   Jump on both toes, heels raised
(loud beat)   2   Drop right heel and raise left foot forward

The step is best learned by approaching it in four stages:

1. Do it first with both feet side by side: Jump with both feet, landing on balls of feet. Drop left heel and raise right foot; then jump on both feet again, drop right heel and raise left foot. Do this on the spot, without making progress.

2. When this can be done, put the left foot at normal walking distance in front and perform the same motions in this position, dancing forward, first with one foot leading, then the other (Figure 2).

AND   ONE   AND   TWO

Figure 2. Foundation of the Double Toe-heel Step

3. This simplified version now evolves into the actual movement: Jump forward on both feet as usual, but instead of dropping the left heel, hop up with the left foot and bring it down flat. As the left springs up for this hop the right foot is raised and carried forward for the next step. This hop is just high enough to get the foot off the ground and the foot comes down on the same spot.

4. When this can be done, jump forward on both feet as before, hop on the left but instead of bringing it down absolutely flat, allow the ball of the foot to hit a split-second before the heel. The ball of the foot thus comes down just before the drumbeat and the heel on the beat. This really constitutes a little toe-heel step on one beat of the drum. If the feet are kept flexible and springy it is more natural to do it this way than otherwise. When the third stage has been learned one finds himself drifting into this movement unconsciously.

As in the toe-heel step the knees are slightly bent, keeping the feet directly under the body (Figure 2).

The accent is up and away from the ground, the feet springing up with exceeding lightness. It differs from the toe-heel in this respect. The advancing foot rises to a height of perhaps a foot off the ground, cutting a semi-circle in the air as it goes forward. The feet rebound, as if they touched the ground for the purpose of springing away from it. They spring up on *every* step. However, it is only the *advancing foot* that goes high, the hops lifting the feet only two or three inches. But they do add sparkle.

The steps and movements best-suited for use with the double toe-heel are described on page 31.

THE DOUBLE FLAT-HEEL STEP

Stand with left foot in advance of right:
(soft beat)   &   Jump on both feet flat
(loud beat)   1   Raise and lower left heel, simultaneously raising right foot forward
(soft beat)   &   Jump on both feet flat
(loud beat)   2   Raise and lower right heel, simultaneously raising left foot forward

It is the same general motion as the double toe-heel except for accent and style. Once the double toe-heel has been learned it can be given the flat-heel accent without difficulty.

The steps are very short and the feet are brought down flat. The weight is on the heels. The feet are raised with the up-and-down motion of the body characteristic of the flat-heel step. Having jumped on both feet, an upward bob of the body raises the heel of the forward foot for the heel tap and also raises the back foot which advances while the heel tap is being made.

It must be remembered that this is close-to-ground dancing, with none of the high springs and the light rebounds that characterize the double toe-heel. The one dance is up and away from the ground, the feet touching the earth for the purpose of springing away from it; the other is down and onto the ground, the soles of the feet hugging the earth and leaving it reluctantly.

THE DOUBLE FLAT-FOOT STEP

Stand with the left foot in advance of the right:

(loud beat)   1   Jump on both feet flat
(soft beat)   &   Skip on left foot flat, simultaneously raising right forward
(loud beat)   2   Jump on both feet flat
(soft beat)   &   Skip on right foot flat, simultaneously raising left forward

The double flat-foot is to the flat-foot as the double toe-heel is to the toe-heel. It represents the movement at its most appealing level. If anything it is easier and less fatiguing than the flat-foot itself.

The movement is essentially as in the double toe-heel except for the flat-foot accent: Jump forward on both feet, bringing them down flat, then skip forward with the advanced foot and raise the back foot, carrying it forward while the skip is being made.

As soon as the feet hit the floor they rebound, but coming down flat as they do, they do not spring to any such height as in the double toe-heel. It is nevertheless an upward and forward motion with none of the hugging of the floor seen in the double flat-heel.

Toe-Heel Variations

The following are the steps and movements appropriate for use in toe-heel dancing. They are employed to add variety and color to the toe-heel step, not to replace it. Using the toe-heel step as the basic pattern, such steps as these are introduced on occasion. The toe-heel is a favorite step in go-as-you-please dancing when each individual is free to dance as he chooses, without following any ritual or routine. In such situations these variations may be inserted at will.

In all cases the drumming should be in two-time, accented *loud*-soft. The toe is always placed down on the soft beat, the heel on the loud beat.

CROSSED TOE-HEEL

&   Cross left foot over right and place toe on floor
1   Drop left heel and at the same time swing right foot to the right
&   Cross right foot over left and place toe on floor
2   Drop right heel and at the same time swing left foot to the left

Photograph by Paul Boris

JAMES C. STONE

Photograph by Paul Boris

JAMES C. STON

This is the regular toe-heel step except that the feet are crossed on each step. This gives an interesting zigzag appearance to the leg motion (Figure 3). If the knees are bent a little more than usual it permits the legs to

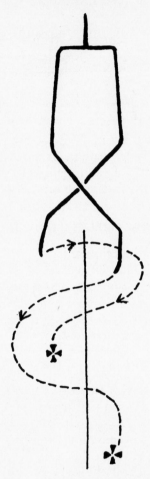

Figure 3. Crossed Toe-heel Step

cross more easily. The step lends itself admirably to a swaggering body style with the shoulders swaying from side to side in harmony with the leg motion. Indeed it is difficult to do it without a sidewise sway of the shoulders.

TOE-HEEL DRAG BACK

& Place left toe down in front
1 Drag back to position and drop heel
& Place right toe down in front
2 Drag back to position and drop heel

The toe is placed down about six inches farther forward than normal, then dragged back to place in contact with the floor and the heel dropped. It is best adapted for dancing on the spot although slow, inch-by-inch progress may be made with it. Its favorite use is as a rest step.

ROCKING STEP

&   Place left toe forward, heel raised
1   Drop left heel down
&   Place right toe back, heel raised
2   Drop right heel down

This step results in a rocking motion, forward and backward, with the body called into action to accentuate it. As the left steps forward the body is bent forward slightly, to straighten again as the right steps back.

It is a common maneuver for dancing on the spot and makes a good rest step.

TOE-HEEL-HEEL-HEEL

&   Place left toe forward, heel raised
1   Drop left heel and raise right foot
&   Tap left heel
2   Tap left heel
&   Place right toe forward, heel raised
3   Drop right heel and raise left foot
&   Tap right heel
4   Tap right heel

This is the toe-heel step with two extra taps of the heel thrown in. It means that the raised foot stays in the air twice as long as usual. This raised foot is not held stationary but moves slowly forward so as to be in position for the next step, following a semi-circular course as it does so. This results in a change in the speed at which the raised foot moves forward, taking twice the usual time in making the step. As a variation for the toe-heel step, it is this very change in speed that adds interest. Usually only one of these steps is thrown in at a time, to be repeated by another a little later. Again four such steps are used in succession.

The toe-heel-heel-heel is a much-used step in hoop dancing (Chapter XII).

This step is sometimes carried to double its length, that is, the heel is tapped *seven* times instead of three, which means that the raised foot is in the air for seven beats of the drum. In this case the treatment is entirely different: the raised foot is kicked straight forward on the first heel tap, its knee straight, its foot about 10 inches from the floor; the dancer bends well forward at the waist and remains in this position until the taps are completed. Then the step is repeated with the other foot.

HEEL TAPS

Stand with left foot slightly in advance of right:
8 beats—Tap left heel eight times
8 beats—Tap right heel eight times
8 beats—Tap both heels eight times
About-face, putting right foot in advance, and repeat.

Such heel taps are often employed for the sake of a rest. Again they are much used in the story dances where the acting demands that a stop be made. As a general principle it can be said that whenever a stop is made, one heel must be kept in motion.

These taps are made by an up-and-down motion of the entire body, not by leg action alone. There is much animation of the body from head to foot. Often the number of taps by each foot is doubled to 16; indeed the number depends entirely upon the fancy of the dancer.

TOE-TAP-TAP-HEEL

&   Tap left foot forward and raise parallel to floor
1   Tap right heel down
&   Tap right heel down
2   Drop left foot flat
&   Tap right foot forward and raise parallel to floor
3   Tap left heel down
&   Tap left heel down
4   Drop right foot flat

In tapping the foot forward the ball of the foot is tapped down, then the foot is raised three or four inches and held parallel to the floor. The steps are short, keeping the feet under the body. The heel taps are done with the usual up-and-down motion of the entire body.

THREE-COUNT TAP

&   Tap left toe
1   Tap left toe
&   Place left toe down
2   Drop left heel down
&   Tap right toe
3   Tap right toe
&   Place right toe down
4   Drop right toe down

The only difference between this and the regular toe-heel step is that the toe makes two preliminary taps before being placed down for the toe-heel step. These taps do not need to be made on the same spot but the foot may move a little on each, either forward or to one side. A favorite way of doing it is to turn the body to the left, tap the left foot to the left side, then tap it farther front, then place it down in front for the usual toe-heel step; then repeat to the right (Figure 4).

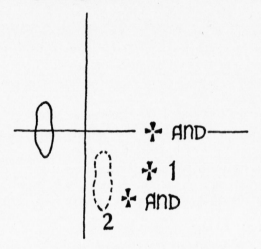

Figure 4. Three-count Tap

This step is sometimes amplified by making four preliminary taps instead of two (Figure 5).

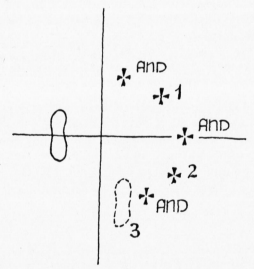

Figure 5. Five-count Tap

GLIDES

    &   Cross right foot in front of left and place toe on floor—skip back on both toes

1-&-2   Skip back, back, back on both toes

This constitutes a backward gliding motion and should be done as smoothly and evenly as possible. The number of backward skips can vary depending upon the space and the mood of the dancer, four to six being the usual number. The legs are straight and are held in contact with each other above the knees; the body is bent forward at the hips as necessary to relieve all strain.

A very effective variation of this glide is as follows:

    &   Cross right foot in front of left and place toe on floor, skip back on both feet

1   Skip back on both feet

    &   Skip back on right foot and swing left forward

2   Skip back on right foot and swing left foot across in front of right

    &   Place left toe on floor and skip back on both left

3   Skip back on both feet

    &   Skip back on left foot and swing right leg forward

4   Skip back on left foot and swing right foot across in front of left

Repeat all

The leg is kept straight with knee unbent as it is swung forward and across in front of the other leg. This is accomplished by swinging it out to the side in carrying it forward.

FORWARD GLIDES.—The forward glides are done with the feet in the same position as for the backward glides.

LEAPS.—A forward glide is often terminated with a long leap forward. Having glided four to six counts, raise the right leg with the knee high in front, skip twice on the left foot to gain momentum, then leap forward with the right leg straight as in jumping the hurdles. As soon as the right foot hits the floor go into toe-heel dancing again. The most difficult part of this leap is to time it so that the foot hits the floor on the drumbeat.

PIVOTS

The quickest method of turning around is by doing an about-face, as a soldier would in drilling. This turns the dancer instantly and starts him off in the opposite direction.

There are three pivot turns or spin-arounds, however, which are much more colorful. Of these, the *tap pivots* are good, the *push pivots* are better and the *kick pivots* best of all.

TAP PIVOTS.—Stand on ball of left foot, right foot raised:

&   Tap right toe
1   Tap right toe
&   Tap right toe
2   Drop left heel down

While doing this, spin the body around to the left, pivoting on the ball of the left foot. By the time the three taps are completed the dancer should be facing in the opposite direction.

To turn completely around, tap *five times* instead of three.

In turning to the right the directions for the feet are reversed.

PUSH PIVOTS.—Stand on ball of left foot, right foot raised:

&   Tap right toe
1   Tap left heel
&   Tap right toe
2   Tap left heel
&   Tap right toe
3   Tap left heel

All the time that this is being done the body is being turned to the left, pivoting on the ball of the left foot. The impression given by the tapping of the right foot is that the body is being pushed around by it. When the step is completed the dancer should be facing in the opposite direction.

To turn completely around continue the movement for *five counts* instead of three.

To turn to the right, reverse the instructions.

KICK PIVOTS.—The kick pivot is the most spectacular of all. It is done exactly like the push pivot except that the right foot is *raised high and is stamped down hard*, like a horse pawing the ground. Raise the knee high in front, pull the foot up under the leg until the heel almost touches the thigh, point the toe down—from this position stamp the toe down on the floor to the count and immediately pull it up again, all the time spinning to the left, pivoting on the ball of the left foot. Lean well to the left, drop the head, and pivot fast and with abandon. This is one of the most colorful flourishes in toe-heel dancing.

Three kicks should spin the dancer completely around and five kicks should take him around twice.

TOE-HEEL-TAP-HEEL

&   Place left toe down
1   Drop left heel down, lifting right foot
&   Tap right toe behind

2   Tap left heel down
&   Place right toe down
3   Drop right heel down, lifting left foot
&   Tap left toe behind
4   Tap right heel down

This is a valuable step which finds its best use in a spectacular moment of dancing in a low crouch. Bend far forward at the hips, place the left toe down as in the toe-heel, drop the left heel and extend the right leg out behind as far as it will go conveniently, strike the right toe down hard, then lift and drop the left heel as the right leg is brought back under the body. Then repeat with the right foot stepping. All motions are emphatic, with the feet striking the floor hard. Four to six steps are made without progress, then the body straightens for the regular toe-heel step again.

TOE-HOP STEP

&   Step on left toe, raising right
1   Hop on left toe
&   Step on right toe, raising left
2   Hop on right toe

In this step the heel is not dropped down but a little hop is made with the toe instead. The weight is taken on the advancing foot as soon as it is placed down. This step is not as graceful and appealing as the toe-heel, and is more fatiguing.

TAP-TAP-HEEL

This is an advanced step of interest to mature performers:

1. Jump on left foot flat, and simultaneously tap right toe in back oblique position
2. Tap right foot at side with a forward scuffing motion
3. Bring right heel down in front with foot turned sharply up, knee straight
4. Jump on right foot flat, and simultaneously tap left toe in back oblique position
5. Tap left foot at side with a forward scuffing motion
6. Bring left heel down in front with foot turned sharply up, knee straight

This step is interesting and the movement not difficult for an experienced dancer. On Number 1 the body must be turned to the right to permit tapping the right foot at the back oblique position. On Number 2 the right foot is tapped to right side as it swings forward, scuffing or brushing the floor without stopping. On Number 3 the right heel strikes the floor in front with the foot turned up so as to form a right angle to the leg, the

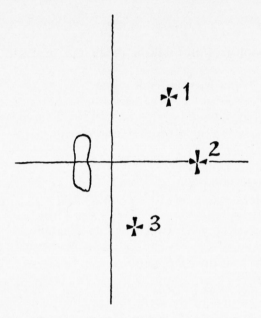

Figure 6. Diagram of Foot Positions in the Tap-tap-heel

right leg fully extended and the knee straight (Figure 7)—this position is made possible by bending the left knee to lower the body and bending forward at the hips. The effect of the step is created by the Number 3 position and so there is a slight pause here, holding the position, then a quick jump to make the next step on time. The body sways naturally to the side as the side taps are made and bends forward at the waist when the heel is brought down. The arms are relaxed and the hands joined in front of the chest.

Figure 7. Tap-tap-heel Step

The drumming is in 3-4 time, with the accent of the drum on one, counted *one*-two-three. When the step is thrown into a toe-heel routine with its two-time drumming, it is better to use a variation of the step, called the tap-tap-tap-heel. This is done in exactly the same way except that the foot is scuffed twice at the side as it goes forward instead of once.

TAPPING FIGURES

This series of tapping figures will be of interest primarily to advanced dancers.

To start, stand on right foot with left raised:

&   Hop on right, crossing left over right
1   Tap left at right oblique
&   Hop on right, swinging left to left, uncrossing
2   Tap left to left oblique
&   Hop on right, crossing left over right
3   Tap left at right oblique
&   Hop on right, swinging left to left, uncrossing
4   Tap left at left oblique
&   Hop on right, kicking left back toward right shin
5   Jerk right back and step on left (left now becomes supporting foot)
Repeat with right foot now tapping

The trick in performing the step comes on the Number 5 count—the left leg is kicked back toward the right shin as if to kick the right foot out from under the body. Just before the left hits the shin, the right leg is jerked back as if it were kicked out, and is then swung forward to start the figure over, in which case the right foot does the tapping.

A series of three related figures are used in succession. The first is as described. The second is done in the same way except that the taps are made to the rear. With the left foot doing the tapping, tap back right oblique, then back left oblique, etc. Having completed the taps the left foot is kicked forward against the right calf, as if to kick the foot out of place.

In the third the taps are done at the side. With the left foot tapping, tap first to the left front, then to the left back, etc., then swing the foot forward and kick it back against the right shin as before.

The complete series is danced in the following sequence:
(1) front taps, first left foot, then right foot; (2) back taps, first left foot, then right foot; (3) side taps, first left foot, then right foot.

Double Toe-heel Variations

One and all, and without exception, the toe-heel variations as already given can be used with the double toe-heel, the only difference being that they are done with the double toe-heel movement.

The following movements are also particularly suited to double toe-heel dancing.

ZIGZAG

This is not a step in itself but rather a maneuver in which the double toe-heel is danced along a zigzag course. With the left foot advancing, dance two steps in a left oblique direction, then turn sharply to the right and dance two steps in a right oblique direction, then two to the left oblique, and so on.

Such zigzag dancing is popular among the Chippewas, and when done with dash and zest, creates a striking picture with true primitive flavor.

FLAT-FOOT TROT

One of the favorite means of adding variety in dancing the double toe-heel is the use of the flat-foot trot (page 37). The Chippewas use it much in this connection. While dancing the double toe-heel, go into the trot for four steps, then immediately go back to the original step again. In the trot the foot is brought down flat, thus making strong contrast to the toe springs of the step itself.

SKIPS FORWARD

Let us suppose that the right foot is advancing in dancing the double toe-heel: Bring the toe down as usual, then lift it immediately and hold it in the air while skipping forward for four skips on the left foot. Then drop the right toe and continue dancing as usual.

Again, with the right foot advancing: Bring the toe down as usual but instead of dropping the heel, hold it there at a point, toe touching the floor, and heel up. In this position skip forward on *both* feet for four counts, then drop the right heel and proceed as usual.

The third form is a combination of these two: Bring the right forward as before and tap it down, raise it and skip forward with the left for one count, tap the right down on the next skip, raise it on the next, etc., continuing thus for six skips. The left foot thus skips forward for six skips and the right toe taps down on every other count.

These steps can be done with either foot leading.

STI-YU

This is perhaps the most spectacular of all Indian steps. It is an advanced movement that will be of particular interest to those who dance the double toe-heel well. The following directions assume a mastery of the double toe-heel step.

One will catch on quicker if it is approached in stages:

1. Do the double toe-heel on the spot, without making progress. Note that in each step the advanced foot is pulled back under the body.

2. Repeat the double toe-heel on the spot but swing the leg *out to the side* in carrying it forward. It is the lower leg only that is swung out; the thigh and the knee remain in close—see C in Figure 8. Lift the feet up high and swing them out wide. Kick the foot up behind sharply as in B to get it high off the floor at the start. Note, however, that the knee is not raised

forward on this kick but remains beside the other knee. This stage is the foundation of the step and should be practiced long.

3. Lean forward at the hips and swing the advancing foot *far forward* as in D—the knee straight and the foot flat to the floor. To get the leg out in this position the knee of the supporting leg must be bent to lower the body and the body must bend well-forward at the hips.

4. In swinging the leg forward let it straighten out with the knee flat with the foot parallel to the floor and about three inches above it. Then the foot is allowed to drop flat to the floor. The leg is thus kicked to its farthest extent in front and as it jerks on reaching its extremity, it is relaxed and allowed to drop limp to the floor, the foot falling flat.

5. As soon as the advancing foot hits the floor it bounces up and is drawn back under the body as in E for the next step.

This whole movement is based on the double toe-heel step. It begins with that step, and differs from it in (1) the high kick behind as in B, (2) the wide leg swing out to the side, as in C, (3) the kick far forward as in D, (4) the bringing of the foot down flat to the floor, and (5) the stooped position of the body.

The hands are held in front of the chest, lightly joined, with elbows pointing out to the sides, and the arms fully relaxed.

While this step is strenuous it is done in a completely relaxed manner with the body limp and flowing. In fact, it could not be done if the body were not limp. There is no hard banging on the floor, the advancing foot expending its force as it reaches its limit of motion while still in the air and before it touches the floor. It is this lightness that is one of the chief characteristics of the dance.

The effect created by the dance is one of strong, free action, with the legs thrown to their fullest extent and with complete abandon, yet with the body limp and fluid, giving that feeling of reserve, in spite of full-bodied action, so characteristic of good Indian dancing. When done without bells, the feet touch the floor so lightly that they scarcely can be heard, this in spite of unreserved leg effort. Were the arms permitted to swing with the same freedom as the legs, the step would have the atmosphere of wild exertion, but with the hands in front of the chest and the elbows held in, the feeling of reserve and unexpended power results.

The tempo of the drumming must be slower than for the double toe-heel to give time for the movements—a medium-fast, accented two-time.

The name of the step, *Sti-yu* (pronounced Stī'-you'), is the Cherokee word for "Are you strong" and is used as a dance call by these Indians to mean "Dance hard." The step was characteristic of good Cherokee dancers of the Smoky Mountains whenever the *Sti-yu* call was heard. However, it turns up now and then with slight variations and individual interpretations by good, youthful dancers among the Chippewa of the Northwoods, and again, movements resembling it are seen on the Plains.

STI-YU VARIATION.—An interesting variation results if the forward foot is not dropped to the floor flat but is brought down on the heel with the toe pointed sharply upward. The toe is turned up as the foot is carried forward and is kept in this position as the heel is dropped to the floor.

Another valuable use of the Sti-yu is to do it in *flat-foot style*, bringing the feet down heavily, flat to the floor but with the accent on the heels. In this case the leading foot contacts the floor as soon as it straightens out instead of expending its energy in the air. There is emphatic pounding of the floor on every step. It is done with a deep bend at the waist, and finds its greatest use as a spectacular moment of low dancing.

Flat-Heel Variations

All of the toe-heel variations as already described are at once applicable to the flat-heel also, the only difference being that they are done with the flat-heel accent. Whenever the instructions state to place the toe down, the foot is placed down flat instead.

In addition to these, the following two steps are particularly useful with the flat-heel.

HEEL-TOE STEP

&   Place left heel down, toe pointed up
1   Drop left toe flat
&   Place right heel down, toe pointing up
2   Drop right toe flat

This is the direct opposite of the toe-heel. The heel is brought down first, with the toe pointing up and then the toe is dropped. To do this step comfortably the body must be bent forward a little at the hips. The knees are very soft and bend deeply when the toe is dropped.

This emphatic use of the heel fits in admirably with the heel accent of the flat-heel step.

HEEL BRUSH

&   Turn left toe up and brush left heel forward
1   Drop left foot flat
&   Turn right toe up and brush right heel forward
2   Drop right foot flat

The heel does not stop as it brushes the floor, but merely strikes the floor with a scuffing motion and goes right on forward. It hits the floor on the beat, then is raised and the foot brought down flat farther forward.

This is an excellent step. It gives ample opportunity for strutting body style. Stand straight up, lean the shoulders back and sway them from side to side with style.

Flat-Foot Variations

The following are the movements most characteristic of and best-suited to the flat-foot style of dancing. These are used both with the flat-foot or the double flat-foot.

FLAT-FOOT WITH BACKWARD SKIP

1 Step on left foot flat
& Skip backward on left foot
2 Step on right foot flat
& Skip backward on right foot

This differs from the standard flat-foot step in that the skip is backward instead of forward. The skip is only three or four inches in length. Progress is made possible because the step forward is longer than the backward skip. This is a much-used form of the flat-foot, although lacking the widespread favor for brilliant dancing enjoyed by the forward skip.

This backward skip is a useful step for dancing on the spot or marking time: standing with the feet side by side, step forward on the left, skip backward with the left bringing it back to position, then repeat with the right.

CROSSED FLAT-FOOT

1 Cross left foot over right and step flat
& Skip forward on left foot flat and swing right foot to right, un-crossing
2 Cross right foot over left and step flat
& Skip forward on right foot flat and swing left foot to left, uncrossing

This is the standard flat-foot step except that the feet are crossed on each step. It is a very typical movement.

This step is also used with a backward skip instead of a forward one.

FLAT-FOOT KICK

1 Step on left foot flat
& Skip on left foot and kick right across in front of left shin
2 Step on right foot flat
& Skip on right foot and kick left across in front of right shin

The foot is kicked across close in front of the other leg by a twist of the thigh, the knee remaining bent to keep the foot in close. It is never carried

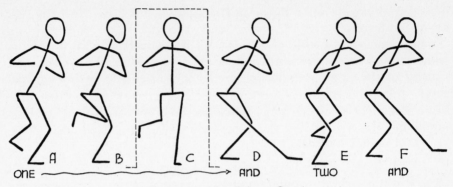

Figure 8. The Sti-yu Step

higher than the knee of the other leg. The toe of the kicking foot is not pointed.

This step appears often in the powwow dancing of the Chippewas and the Sioux, even when dancing in the toe-heel style.

FLAT-FOOT SKIPS

Step with left foot and skip, skip, skip forward, holding the right foot in the air, sole parallel to the floor and ready to step. In this very characteristic movement eight or ten skips are frequently made before the right foot is dropped to repeat the skips on that foot. Very little progress is made with the skips; often they are no more than flat hops on the spot, and again inch-by-inch forward progress is made. The body bends forward slightly at the hips and the knee of the skipping leg is hard. To fast tempo skips are effective and typical.

FLAT-FOOT SKIP AND KICK

1 Step on left foot flat

& Skip on left foot flat and kick the right foot across in front of the left shin

2 Skip on left foot and bring right foot back to side of left

& Skip on left foot and kick the right foot across in front of the left shin

This is a combination of the last two steps. Any number of skips are made in succession with the right foot kicking across on every other skip; then the step is repeated with the right foot skipping. The kick is made as in the flat-foot kick.

An equally attractive variation of this much-used step is done by kicking first in front of the leg and then *in back* of it. The front kick is across in front of the shin and the back one across behind the calf. Several of these are repeated in succession.

Trots and Stomps

Stomp dancing is a style of dancing all its own. Similar to it are the various trots. These movements find widespread use and are fundamental to many of the dance routines in this book, particularly the ceremonial dances.

FLAT-FOOT TROT

1   Trot on left foot flat
&   Trot on right foot flat

It is a trotting or easy running motion, altered as necessary to bring the feet down flat. The steps are shorter than in ordinary walking. There is no play in the ankles as would be the case in normal running; the ankles remain stiff and the foot flat even when it is in the air. (It is easier to keep the feet flat if the toes are curled up against the top of the moccasin.) The knees do not bend to lift the feet behind as in ordinary running but the feet are kept under the body constantly. The knees are very soft, however, flexing to take up the jar as the foot hits the floor. Indeed the step is done *very lightly*, there being no perceptible jar or sound. The body is thoroughly relaxed, bent forward naturally at the hips.

This step has many uses and appears frequently as a variation for the toe-heel and the double toe-heel.

Typical of this, and all other trots, as the Indians do them, are the occasional pauses for one step, holding one foot in the air for an extra count before bringing it down. These little pauses make an interesting and effective break in the dance.

SLOW TROT.—This is the flat-foot trot done in slow motion, bringing the feet down on every other beat of the drum. Changing from the fast trot to this slow motion is effective. It is often used as a variation in double toe-heel dancing. It should never be continued longer than four steps. The body should be bent well-forward and the feet raised high.

STOMP STEP

This is an important and widely used step, particularly in ceremonial dances. It is the basis of all the Cherokee dances in Chapter VIII. The style of dancing in which it is used is spoken of as stomp dancing.

It is precisely the same as the flat-foot trot except for accent. It is done with a definite stomp, accomplished by stamping the feet down, not with the legs, but by dropping the weight of the body on them. The steps are short, the feet are directly under the body. It is an up-and-down motion rather than a forward one. The body shakes and the shoulders bob a little with each impact. The knees are soft the body fully relaxed, so that there is absolutely no annoying body jar. While the flat-foot trot is a forward motion, this is an up-and-down one; while that step is light and silent, this is noisy.

As done in the stomp dances, it starts slowly and with gentle stamping, gains in speed and emphasis, and culminates in the double stomp step.

To repeat:

1. Body erect, feet directly underneath
2. Very short steps, feet brought down flat
3. Drop weight of body on feet, taking it on heels
4. Knees soft, legs relaxed, no stamping by means of legs
5. Accent up-and-down, shoulders bobbing for increased emphasis
6. Body fully relaxed, arms hanging naturally

DOUBLE STOMP

The feet are brought down flat on each step:

1   Jump forward on both feet, side by side
&   Jump forward on both feet, left foot slightly in advance
2   Jump forward on both feet, side by side
&   Jump forward on both feet, right foot slightly in advance

This step is included among the trots because it is a natural outgrowth of the stomp step and is often used as a climax for it. It is most effective when a group of dancers do it in unison, creating an interesting up-and-down effect with strong ringing of the ankle bells.

Progress is made slowly, the forward jumps being not more than six inches in length—the movement is an up-and-down one rather than a forward one, with the weight coming down on the heels. The body is completely relaxed and the knees are soft, flexing each time the feet come down. The body is erect except for a relaxed and natural give at the hips when the feet strike. The trunk and shoulders turn naturally to right or left, depending upon which foot is leading.

BACK TROT

1   Trot forward on left foot, raising right foot high in back
&   Trot forward on right foot, raising left foot high behind

This step is especially typical of the Southwest Indians and is often referred to as the Southwest Trot. It is a running motion with the feet raised high behind, but *the steps are short*, only a few inches of progress being made on each step. The feet are brought down flat, the ball of the foot hitting just a split second before the heel. The knees are kept soft, the body is erect with arms relaxed and hanging naturally.

As in all trots, there are frequent pauses with the foot kept on the floor for two counts rather than one, and the raised foot held high behind for the extra count.

FRONT TROT

1   Trot forward with left foot, raising right knee high in front
&   Trot forward with right foot, raising left knee high in front

This gives a prancing effect, up and away from the ground, like running in place. The weight is taken on the ball of the foot, both ankles and knees are soft, and all movements light and springy. The steps are very short. The body is kept erect and the arms hang naturally. Pauses should be employed occasionally, keeping the raised knee up for an extra count.

CROSSED TROT

1   Cross left over right, step on ball of left foot, and at the same time swing right foot to right
&   Cross right over left, step on ball of right foot, and at the same time swing left foot to left

Commonplace as it may seem, this step is spectacular. Its chief usefulness is in connection with toe-heel and flat-foot dancing, as a variation, and when so used it adds much flash. The step is done rapidly, the feet crossing on every beat of the drum. There is little forward motion but *much sideward motion of the legs*. The legs are swung as far across as possible on each step. The knees are hard and stiff, the legs are swung at the hips. The shoulders sway, or rather jerk, from side to side, in keeping with the sideward leg motion.

The result is a quick sidewise flutter of the legs and a corresponding sidewise jerking of the shoulders. When tossed into the forward, flowing motion of the toe-heel or the free springing of the double toe-heel, these jerky sidewise motions appear accentuated. Four to six steps of it in a series are enough.

Fear Steps

In the picturesque story dances these scare steps are much employed to show fear and retreat. There are three, often used interchangeably.

FEAR STEP NO. I

1   Step to left with left toe
&   Step to left with right toe
2   Step left with left toe
&   Step to left with right toe

The movement is thus a sidestepping to the left; the steps are reversed if progress to the right is desired. The knees are well-bent throughout.

Since this a fear step used in running away from danger, the dancer keeps the corner of his eye on the object from which he is retreating and holds his hands over his face, palms out, to protect himself from it. The steps are short and fast.

FEAR STEP NO. 2

1   Cross right over left and step on right toe
&   Step left toe to left, right still crossed
2   Step right toe to left
&   Step left toe to left, right still crossed

FEAR STEP NO. 3

1   Cross right in front of left and step on toe
&   Step to left on left toe, uncrossing
2   Cross right in front of left and step on toe
&   Step to left on left toe, uncrossing

SQUAW STEP

Stand with the weight on the left foot, the right leg hanging limply and resting gently on the toe.

1. Step forward on the right toe
2. Step flat on the left foot taking the weight on it heavily, at the same time allowing the knee to bend a little so that the body is lowered with a snap

The motion is much like one would make if he had a sore right foot. He limps with the right foot, taking as little weight on it as possible, and stepping heavily on the left.

By stepping on the right toe the body is raised, and then, as the left foot comes down flat, it is lowered suddenly. The left knee bends a little in the process to lower it still farther. The result is a very definite up-and-down shaking motion which quivers the body and rattles the tin-tinkles with which the Chippewa woman's dress is decorated, or the bone beads with which the Sioux woman's dress is adorned.

Progress is made forward with the step as described. If the dance calls for sidewise movement, as is so often the case, it is performed in the same way but with the left foot sidestepping to the left, thus making progress to the left.

This is the step used by the women of the Woodland and northern Plains tribes. It is also sometimes used by the men, particularly in the Giveaway Dances (Chapter XIV) and in Everybody's Dance (page 225).

Another woman's step is merely to trot forward flat-footed, or in its sidewise version, merely to sidestep to the left. This is usually done by old women who are unable to use the regular step as described.

Chapter II

BODY MOVEMENTS AND THE INDIAN MOOD

COME WITH ME to a little adobe-walled patio in the heart of some ancient Southwest village and sit entranced as fluid bodies flow effortlessly through figure after figure of unfolding dance-drama. Behold the consummate seriousness, yet the utter relaxation; the expressionless faces, yet the vividly expressive bodies. . . .

Come sit with me in some rickety roundhouse on the northern Plains, historic with memories of a glory that was, and absorb from stalwart figures a fresh vitality as they pulsate with full masculine power. Witness the unrestrained freedom, yet the dignified reserve; the conventionalized movements, yet the complete naturalness of motion. . . .

Come join me in some roundhouse tottering with age under Northwoods pines, reverberating with the jingling of a thousand dress-tinkles as women vibrate to the booming drum. Witness their passive calmness, yet their utter seriousness; their sedate footsteps, yet their quivering bodies. . . .

What of the steps these dancers are using over this wide frontier? The steps?—one glance at these pulsating forms reveals that more than "steps" is involved, for no mere movement of feet could create this mood. It is a projection of the entire body—ah, no, for flesh alone could not do it—a projection of the entire being, spirit as well as flesh.

It becomes clear that behind the visible dancing movements is a depth of meaning, a seriousness of purpose, a sense of responsibility, often a reverence, that comes only from deep concern for the purpose for which the ceremony is danced. Those of us who are foreign to Indian culture and possess no such understanding, find it difficult to cope with those intangibles of feeling and mood in our dancing, but the bodily movements are capable of analysis and reproduction. And in the study of these movements something of the feeling should evolve.

The Angular Characteristic

The dancing movements of the Indian are characterized by angles. Seldom is the arm thrown out to its full extent, or the fingers fully extended to flatten the hand, as is often seen in some forms of our present-day dancing. Neither is the leg kicked out straight with pointed toe. When on occasion the leg is fully extended the foot usually remains turned up at an angle. Should the body rise fully erect so as to straighten the hips, the arms remain bent at distinct angles, and should the arm be thrown overhead it is with a crook at the elbow. Thus it is with all parts of the body. Herein rests the explanation of the feeling of reserve, of unreleased power, that one gets in watching an Indian dance, even when exerting himself fully. Angles seem to hold the power in. To extend the arm and hand fully is as if to let all force escape.

This angular characteristic of the extremities must be maintained if a true Indian movement is to be achieved. The angles need not be sharp or extreme but their presence is essential. One of the extremities may be extended fully when occasion demands, but such is compensated for elsewhere, so that the general aspect of the body is angular.

Handling the Arms

The function of the arms is to move in harmony with the general body movement to bring it out more fully; they are never relied upon to create the dance by themselves. If the arm motions are appropriate and nicely done they accentuate, point up, and illuminate the body movement, whatever its nature.

ARMS AT SIDES.—The commonest use of the arms among the Indians is merely to allow them to hang naturally at the sides, fully relaxed. The only movements they make are the reflex motions that follow naturally upon the foot and body action. The hands, too, are kept open and hang naturally. When allowed to hang in this way the arms contribute to the feeling of complete relaxation one often gets in watching some Indians dance. This is always a safe use of the arms, and is better than deliberate but poorly executed flourishes with them. If the arms are inclined to flop about or pump up and down when held at the sides the hands should be lifted in front of the chest as next described.

HANDS IN FRONT OF CHEST.—Next to holding the arms at the sides, this is the commonest arm position among the Indians of the northern Woodlands and Plains. It is effective, pleasing and most useful. It is shown at A in Figure 9, with the hands in front of the chest, perhaps separated a few inches and moving in reflex fashion, perhaps with the fingers loosely joined, or perhaps with both hands fingering some small object that is being carried. The elbows hang close to the sides, the arms and hands completely relaxed. Should they be allowed to become tense the muscles of the back will bulge out in strain, the shoulders stiffen and motions become jerky and forced.

While the most characteristic position is that shown at A, the elbows may be raised so as to stick out at the sides a little farther as in B, or again the hands may be raised near the chin with the elbows extending straight out to the sides as in C. The effect of this latter is seen in the photograph facing page 230. The positions at B and C find only sparing use in certain showy moods; the standard position is that at A.

Figure 9. Arm Positions in Front of Chest

This use of the arms gives increased height to the dancer, making him appear taller than he is. Its upward accent is excellent for use with the springing, up-and-away-from-the-ground foot action of the double toe-heel step. Moreover, it is without equal in facilitating a relaxed style. It leads to graceful movement, and serves to cover up arms that otherwise might appear ungainly and to keep under control arms that are inclined to flop about.

HANDS ON HIPS.—Place the hands on the flat of the back just in back of the hip bone. The *knuckles* rest against the back with the hand so placed that the fingers point downward. The hands and arms are kept relaxed. One or both hands may be so placed.

This position is more important to the non-Indian dancer than to the Indian: The average Indian keeps his back straight while dancing, even when bending far forward in a low crouch, a feat that seems difficult for others to do, but when the hands are placed on the hips, the effect is to flatten the back and make it appear straighter than it is.

STRUTTING ARM MOTION.—This is not a common, and scarcely a typical arm style among the Indians but when it does appear in the story dances and "powwows" it is stunning in its effectiveness. It involves a forward swing of the arms that results from a swaggering shoulder style.

Assume a fully upright position with head high, shoulders back and chest out. In dancing forward swing the shoulders naturally as in walking but exaggerate the motion, swaying them backward and forward with emphasis and with style. This shoulder action throws the arms forward. The arms are held naturally at the sides and then made rigid so as not to flop about, and from this position are swung as far forward as the shoulder action carries them. The motion originates entirely in the shoulders and not in the arms themselves.

FLOWING ARM STYLE.—This motion is related to the weaving body style and will be described later in connection with body movements.

The Use of the Hands

The Indian holds his hands naturally and gives little thought to them. Popular ideas to the contrary notwithstanding, the fists are seldom clenched. Neither are the fingers fully extended, but rather are held in the position they normally take when the arm is hung at the side. The fingers thus create a slight angle, and angles are characteristic of Indian dancing. The hands will be ugly and attract attention undesirably if they are stiff and strained, with the fingers held tensely. They will blend into the dancing movements fully unnoticed if relaxed and held naturally.

There is one hand position, not necessarily Indian, that assists greatly in keeping the hands relaxed and in proper form. This is to bend the middle finger in until it almost touches the palm near the base of the thumb, allowing the other fingers to take the position they naturally fall into when the middle finger is thus bent. If this is learned so that it becomes habitual, a graceful hand will result that is thoroughly in accord with the general Indian tradition, that tradition being a naturally open, relaxed and flexible hand.

OBJECTS HELD IN THE HANDS.—It is a great help in dancing to have some small object in the hands—indeed, many Indians do not like to dance unless they are holding something. It gives them something to manipulate and seems to help them to relax. Moreover, an object in the hands often serves to emphasize and give increased spectacle to the arm motion. Eagle-wing fans are commonly used for this purpose, seen in the hands of the dancer in photos facing pages 6 and 23. Other appropriate objects are feathers and dance rattles.

Body Styles

Let us pick out the most colorful of the feather-bedecked dancers in the ring and see how he handles himself. He dances erect, not at all like the doubled-up, crouching figures we have always seen in the pictures; his body is relaxed, his arms hang quietly with his hands in front of his chest. But wait, now he *is* bending forward—just a little, not way down, a sort of semi-crouch, his back flat—but only for a few steps when up he comes again, stretching tall. Now he goes down once more, this time way down, the full crouch at last—he stops on the spot and bends way forward, his back parallel to the floor, shaking hard from head to foot. But before we get a good look he straightens again, tall, erect as before and dances on his way.

While he did use the crouch after all, it was only for a quick flourish.

These three body styles, the upright, the semi-crouch and the crouch, together with a fourth called the "weave," require careful attention.

THE UPRIGHT POSITION

The mood of the dance does much to determine the details of body style. The upright position changes as the mood changes from the quiet and passive to the dashing and bold.

The relaxed mood in the upright position is the most commonly seen basic style in Indian dancing. This is true not only in the quiet ceremonial dances but also in the dashing "powwow" dances. The brilliant flourishes in the "powwow" dances are used periodically against the background of the relaxed style.

Stand naturally with the upper body in about the same position taken in relaxed walking. Relaxed as they are, the shoulders may droop a little, the head may hang slightly forward, and the body may bend a trifle forward at the waist. The arms may hang at the sides, although the most effective arm position is with the hands in front of the chest (A in Figure 9). All muscles are kept relaxed so as to achieve fluid action. The body pulsates and vibrates to the rhythm of the feet.

As the mood changes to the boastful and challenging, the body style changes accordingly: Stand straight up, shoulders back, head high, chin up, chest thrown out. Dance forward proudly, swaying the body from side to side on each step, and swaggering the shoulders back and forth a little. Throw all of the personality of the body into play, as if to say "Is there a more striking figure present than I am?—if so, let him prove it."

The arms may be placed on the hips so as to throw the chest out farther, or may be held high in front of the chest to give increased emphasis to the shoulder play; again, the strutting arm motion may be used. The swaggering shoulder style described later in the chapter finds its greatest use in this mood, and is the basis of the arm action.

Often the change in the mood from the relaxed style to the boastful and showy is abrupt and startling.

THE FULL CROUCH

The full crouch is the climax or extreme of close-to-ground dancing. It is not used as a fundamental movement for all-the-time dancing but as a brief moment of spectacle, a splash of color, most effective when suddenly dropped into from the upright position. The abrupt contrast from way up to way down is much used by the dancing Indian.

No progress is made with the crouch—it is dancing on the spot, involving nothing more in the way of foot work than raising the heels and jarring them down. Go into the full crouch, bending the trunk forward parallel to the ground, spread the legs well apart, the knees sticking outward a little, as shown in Figure 10. Drop the arms between the legs, with the hands close to the ground, fists closed. Keep the back flat and the shoulders straight.

Figure 10. The Full Crouch

In this position shake hard up and down to the drumming, raising the heels and jarring them down. The heels are not raised by the feet alone, but more by an up-and-down motion of the entire body. When done strenuously the whole foot may be lifted off the ground and brought down flat. This action may cause the dancer to move sidewise a little, or more typically around himself in a small circle, but no effort should be made to cover ground.

As the body shakes, the arms join in the motion, the closed fists striking downward on each drumbeat as though pounding at the ground, yet not quite touching it. It is a great help in this dance to hold a rattle in each hand, shaking them down as though striking at the ground with them, going lower and lower, harder and harder, and nearer and nearer the ground. The rattles or fists may be shoved under the knees and out to the side, or one hand may be raised overhead for a few beats by turning the shoulders while the other is kept low.

THE SEMI-CROUCH

This very characteristic style of dancing is often found to be a little more difficult than either the upright style or the full crouch because of the position in which it is done.

Figure 11. The Semi-crouch

To get into the proper position, squat part way down and put the hands on the knees, assuming the pose of a backfield man in football, as shown in A, Figure 11. When in this position note that the knees are well-bent and that the back is straight and the shoulders back. Take the hands off the knees and you are in position to dance. The natural thing to do, once the hands are off the knees, is to bend the back and allow the shoulders to droop, thereby getting into a more comfortable position and one that permits the legs to move more easily, but *the back must be kept flat* ... otherwise the dance loses its character and its Indian style. To accomplish this with less strain, the hands may either be placed on the hips or held high in front of the chest as shown in B, Figure 11, both of which positions shove the shoulders back and make the back appear flat.

In dancing in this position it may be found that a strain is placed on the thighs and back which makes the position uncomfortable and tiring. This may be relieved by swinging the leg out to the side a little as it is carried forward and stepping a little farther forward than usual. It is the *lower leg* only that is swung out ... the knee is pulled in close to the other leg, and the foot thrown out by a twist of the thigh. The knee is not lifted up as the step is made and the foot is raised no higher than necessary.

There are three factors that contribute to the characteristic style: *First*, is the side swing of the legs, a movement that is distinctive and different. *Second*, is a sinewy, weaving motion of the back, achieved by keeping the back flexible and allowing the rump to swing from side to side, a natural movement arising from throwing the lower leg out to the side. *Third*, is a rolling of the shoulders in keeping with the willowy movement of the body, accomplished by grasping the hands firmly together in front of the chest and rolling first one shoulder and then the other, a movement that again seems to arise naturally from the foot and hip action. The protruding elbows accentuate this shoulder roll.

THE WEAVE

This movement consists of a graceful forward dip of the body in which the trunk moves around in a circular course. It is a recommended body style for advanced dancers.

To get the idea, do it while standing still in four counts:

and 1   Shove hips to left and lean shoulders to right and back, chest out
and 2   Shove hips to right and lean shoulders to left and back, chest out
and 3   Bend forward to left
and 4   Bend forward to right

The body flows along evenly and smoothly from one position to another. When this can be done add the foot action with the toe-heel step by stepping forward with the left foot on 1, the right foot on 2, etc. The body thus completes the circular movement on four steps.

The arm motions must now be coordinated with the body action. Hold the hands loosely in front of the stomach with the elbows close into the sides. As the shoulders lean to the right on 1 turn the right forearm forward with the palm up, keeping elbow and upper arm stationary. As the shoulders lean to the left on 2 the left arm makes a corresponding motion, while the right is pulled back to position. On 3 the right arm is extended forward from the shoulder with the palm of the hand up, the shoulder moving forward also; the arm is not extended fully but remains with a slight bend at the elbow. The elbow is not projected out to the side but moves forward in the same plane. On 4 the left arm makes the corresponding motion as the right is withdrawn. Throughout, the hand remains in a naturally relaxed position. The tempo of the arm motion is determined by that of the body movement with which it is blended as an integral and wholly natural part.

The chief characteristic of this body style is its graceful flowing movement, around and around, with the arms moving in complete harmony with the trunk. There are no jerks, no sudden movements to disturb the even, fluid, weaving motion. It is best achieved by practicing the trunk and arm movements in front of a mirror while standing still.

Shoulder Movements

One of the chief sources of dancing style is in the handling of the shoulders. There are several movements, each producing a different aesthetic effect upon the observer.

SWAGGERING THE SHOULDERS.—In normal walking the shoulders sway backwards and forwards a little. It is this movement when exaggerated that makes the shoulder swagger. The left shoulder is swung forward as the left foot advances and the right shoulder as the right foot steps. The action of the toe-heel step facilitates this movement. Stand erect with head high and chest out. As the left toe is placed forward swing the left shoulder far forward so that the chest faces to the right oblique, then as the heel is dropped snap the left shoulder back and the right forward, twisting the body correspondingly and carrying the right leg forward. It is a twist of the spine, of course, that moves the shoulders back and forth, rotating the entire upper part of the body. If done with zest and spirit the shoulders swagger so as to give to the toe-heel movement an entirely different appearance than when relaxed shoulders are used.

There are several ways this is used in the proud, boastful, challenging moods of the story dances and powwows. *First,* is to swing the shoulders on *every step* as described, with the hands either on the hips or held high in front of the chest (B or C in Figure 9). *Second,* is to hold the left shoulder forward for *two steps,* then the right forward for two steps. This produces a different effect. *Third,* is to hold each shoulder forward for *several steps,* before changing. To accomplish this, turn the left shoulder forward, place the hands on the hips, or in front of the chest with the elbows extending out in the same plane as the shoulders, hold the head

high and turn it to the left in line with the shoulders, and look down at the
ground behind the left shoulder with the eyes. The position of the head
and arms is seen in the photograph facing page 230. In this dramatic pose
keep the left shoulder forward for six to eight steps, then reverse the directions with the right leading.

DIPPING THE SHOULDERS.—In this the shoulders are dipped *sideways* instead
of being swung backward and forward. They are dipped to the left as the
left foot advances and to the right as the right foot steps, accomplished by
bending the body from side to side so as to tilt the shoulders. At the same
time the neck is relaxed and the head thrown from side to side. The accent
of the toe-heel step facilitates the movements, the shoulders and head going
down with a snap as the heel is dropped. This is a simple yet very pleasing
maneuver.

ROLLING THE SHOULDERS.—This movement is similar to the swagger except
that the shoulders are rolled instead of jerked back and forth. Each
shoulder makes a little circular motion, moving forward as the corresponding foot advances and backward as the other foot steps. It takes a limber,
willowy dancer to do it well. Between this and the swagger, the movement
should be selected that best fits the particular dancer.

SHAKING THE SHOULDERS.—The shaking of the shoulders is a most spectacular gesture and is used by many dancers as a finale. To exit from the dance
arena or the stage with shoulders rippling and aquiver is to say farewell
to the audience in the most glamorous of Indian fashions. It is purely a
shoulder action and should not be confused with muscle dancing.

There are two movements—shaking the shoulders up and down, and
shaking them back and forth. The first is the easier: Stand in front of a
mirror and practice the shoulder part only, shaking the shoulders up and
down, up on the soft beat of the drum, and down on the hard beat. Hold
the hands relaxed at the sides. When this can be done easily, try it while
dancing, shaking the shoulders up and down once on each toe-heel step.
The shoulder shaking should be emphatic and conspicuous, and in perfect
rhythm with the feet.

Having accomplished this, double the tempo with the shoulders and make
two shakes to each step, that is, one on *each beat* of the drum. This calls
for fast shaking and is a trick that is not bought cheaply if done in good
dancing form.

The forward-and-backward shaking should be practiced in the same
way. Shake the shoulders back and forth once on each step, and when this
can be done, twice on each step. This is a *shaking* of the shoulders and not
an emphatic twist of the whole spine. A limber body is required to do it
well.

These two shoulder-shaking methods are often used in the same dance, employing the up-and-down motion first and finishing with the back-and-forth one.

Head Action

In informal, go-as-you-please dancing, there is much nodding of the head to the rhythm. This is not done on every step but employed occasionally, perhaps on every fourth step—a sudden, quick nod of the head, often accompanied by a flash of the eyes. It is remarkably effective, attracting attention to the dancer and seeming to make his personality radiate.

Another use of the head is in connection with the shoulder shaking just described, a movement of the head that synchronizes with the shoulder action. In shaking the shoulders up and down the head also nods up and down, and in shaking the shoulders back and forward the head shakes sideways. A good dancer can mix his head and shoulder movements, shaking his head up and down when his shoulders go back and forth, and his head sideways when his shoulders go up and down. Three separate rhythmic motions are thus achieved, one with feet, one with shoulders, and one with head.

Facial Expression

Immobile and expressionless—such is the typical face in the Indian way of dancing. There are exceptions to all rules, and the exceptions will be noted, but by and large, the dancer's disinterested face shows no sign of emotion within or distraction without. He is seemingly oblivious to his surroundings and unaware of his audience. Relying on his body action to portray his mood, his face remains wholly natural, without scowl or smile, neither stern nor pleasant—immobile, composed, relaxed, natural.

More often than not, the eyes look downward toward the ground. Even when the head is held high and the chin up, the eyes turn downward, displaying the eyelids rather than the eyes themselves. This is effective and dramatic—especially so in those head-high, proud poses. We see it in the pictures of the dancers, facing pages 22, 70 and 86. The eyes are not closed in these pictures but are turned downward as if to look at the ground near the dancer's feet. To repeat, more often than not the eyes are used in this way, but again they look up, round and full and large, perhaps even flashing, but they do not look at anything in particular, seeming to focus in the distance.

The mouth is closed and expressionless, not turned downward in a scowl nor upward in a smile, not drawn nor twisted out of shape by the physical efforts of dancing. Hardest for the inexperienced to do is not to reflect his feelings in his face, be he frightened or worried, or tired or winded, and not to allow his face to become distorted as he makes the strenuous full-bodied effort of the dance.

Exceptions there are as already stated: Sometimes the dancer smiles, as for example in the "powwow" dancing of the jovial, good-natured Chippewas, or of their neighbors to the westward, the Sioux. But it is not the smile of the vaudeville actor, playing for favor and applause; the mouth opens a little, its corners turn up, the eyes sparkle, and the face takes on a pleasant expression, all of which is held throughout the dance and does not change or vary in degree. But, more often than not, these same people dance with an immobile face. Again, they may look directly at the crowd, or at someone in the crowd, playing upon him with all of the business described under "Playing on an Object" . . . nodding the head, waving the hand, flashing the eyes, smiling. But again, and more typically, these same dancers do not do this.

Story acting in the story dances involves a different situation. Here the dancer's eyes are employed as the plot dictates, looking for tracks, following the enemy, etc., but his face does not reflect his emotion except for an occasional startled look. The story is told primarily by body action.

The Looking Pose

Perhaps the commonest pose in which Indians are depicted in pictures is with the hand stiffly placed across the eyes to shade them from the sun. Suffice it to say this is not the way the dancing Indian does it! He puts his *forearm* across his forehead with the hand hanging down at the side of his head, relaxed and natural, as indicated in Figure 12. He holds it there for three or four steps, then drops it, later to raise it again; he raises one arm thus and then the other. He may hold his arm up for about ten or twelve steps, jerking his body from side to side to change the angle at which he looks, or jerking his arm back and forth to shade his eyes from different angles.

Figure 12. The Looking Pose

Were he to hold his *hand* over his eyes, the position would be stiff and the effect would not carry. The arm position is bold and obvious, and it harmonizes with general body action. It allows the hand to hang down at an angle, and as said before, angles are characteristic of Indian dancing.

This is one of the most frequently used of all dance gestures. It is employed constantly in story dances.

Playing on an Object

Let us suppose that the object in question is a spear stuck in the ground and that the routine calls for the dancer to discover it and pick it up. It could well be any other object. The dancer stops suddenly as he sees the spear, one heel only tapping to the drumming. He fixes his eyes on it as if to make sure of its identity, he leans down a little and looks, then rises up and looks again. He jerks his head from side to side, as if to get a better view. Then he turns sidewise to it and dances back and forth, going about six feet in each direction, always with his eyes focused on it, shading his eyes with his arm. He makes perhaps three such sidewise trips, then swoops up to it, makes a pass at it as if to pick it up, turns and runs away from it with the fear step (page 39), looking back at it over his shoulder. He repeats this twice, picking up the spear on the third time.

On these approaches to the object there is important arm action: He raises his right hand to his right shoulder, palm toward the shoulder, hand relaxed. As he starts forward he throws his arm forward full-length toward the object, palm up. He follows this with a similar motion with the left arm, continuing thus, first one arm and then the other, throwing once on each step. The motion of the arm is bold and strong, but the hand stays relaxed, the fingers bent naturally.

PLAYING ON THE CROWD.—Not often does our Indian dancer take notice of his audience for dancing effect, but when he does he is dramatic, sending creepy feelings up the spine, conjuring up memories of childhood story days "when the Indians were after you." The procedure is exactly as in playing on an object—the sudden stop, the long look, the sidewise dancing, with much shading of the eyes with the arm, and finally a swoop forward terminated by fear-stepping away again.

Moments of Spectacle

Reference has already been made to the tendency of the Indian to alternate periods of quiet movement with spasms of dashing vigor and brilliant action. This protects him from the exertion of long-continued extreme effort and at the same time makes his colorful flourishes seem still more spectacular by contrast to the quiet background.

In planning a dance routine the steps should be so arranged that the dance will take on ever-increasing interest, gaining force and momentum, building up to higher and higher pitches of dramatic appeal. This crescendo, however, is not constant and unremitting, but rather develops in waves, with a lull or drop down between, each wave reaching a higher level than the proceeding. The dancer accepts a basic step or movement which he carries on throughout the dance, and intermittently inserts moments of spectacle in which dramatic interest wells up to a higher level.

These moments of spectacle, for the most part, are achieved by *changes in movement*, by *changes in tempo*, and by the use of *contrasting positions*.

THE DRAMATIC EFFECT OF CHANGES IN MOVEMENT

A dance should move along in the same mood and with the same foot movement and body style until the audience is fully in the swing of it and has absorbed its aesthetic feel. Then the movement should change momentarily to a different but related one. That is the purpose of the variations of the basic steps. If the basic step is the toe-heel, for example, it is pointed up with one of its many amplifications—with the heel taps, the glides or the kick pivots, for example,—after which the original step is employed again, later to be enlivened by other variations. While these changes in movement come suddenly the transitions must be smooth and unforced, and each new movement must seem somehow to belong.

THE DRAMATIC EFFECT OF CHANGES IN TEMPO

A sudden change in tempo is always dramatically effective. A favorite device is to start the dance with slow tempo, stepping on every other beat of the drum, then suddenly and without warning, to burst into double time, stepping on every beat of the drum. This explosion of power and speed is startling and often breath-taking. But if its full dramatic value is to be brought out, there must also be a corresponding contrast in *mood*. During the slow time the dancer flows gracefully along without a semblance of concern, in disinterested mood and wholly relaxed, and then with the sudden change of tempo he abruptly bursts into strong action, aggressive, alert, dashing.

If it is a solo, the drummer sets his time to that desired by the dancer, beating very slowly on the start and changing suddenly to fast time on a prearranged signal. The booming drum voice suddenly increasing in volume and tempo, also adds to the startling effect of the contrast.

THE DRAMATIC EFFECT OF CONTRASTING POSITIONS

Second only to "power explosiveness," and usually affiliated with it, is a sudden change in body position. There are several types of these contrasts. Some typical ones follow.

FROM THE UPRIGHT POSITION TO THE CROUCH.—Dancing preferably with the double toe-heel step and fully relaxed in the upright position, the dancer drops abruptly into the full crouch with his hands reaching for the earth, shaking his whole body and jarring his heels, as described on page 46. A moment of this and he suddenly straightens to full height again, later to renew the crouch. The utter contrast between the leaping, skyward, aspiring mood of the upright style, and the downward, earthy accent of the full crouch, is arresting and has all of the qualities of elemental appeal.

WITH ONE LEG IN AIR.—In the playful mood of "powwow" dancing, the Plains Indians often bend abruptly forward and place the left hand on the ground, raise the right leg out behind and kick it backward to ring the ankle bells to the rhythm. About eight kicks is the usual number before rising to full height again.

WITH ONE KNEE ON THE GROUND.—Another popular Indian maneuver of the same type is suddenly to drop to one knee. From the upright position drop to a semi-crouch for a moment of shaking and heel jarring, then drop to the right knee, hitting it on the ground on the drumbeat and coming up immediately, taking three counts to rise, shaking the body hard on each count. Then continue to dance in the upright position.

PARALLEL TO THE GROUND.—Still more dramatic is this "prostrate" position, in which the leg is stretched far out behind, with the body as near to the ground as it can get, as shown in Figure 13. The weight is on the left leg and the left shoulder on the left knee. If on the stage turn the right side to the

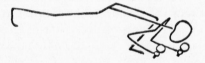

Figure 13. Parallel-to-ground Position

audience. Drop abruptly into this position, jar the left heel to the rhythm for four counts, then shake the whole body up and down for four counts with much action of arms and shoulders. Stop suddenly and turn the head to the right as if something attracted attention there, freeze and look for eight counts; then slowly rise on the left leg, taking four counts to it, scurry to the left with the fear step for a few steps, eyes still on the same spot, then break into the dance as usual.

USING THE TOE-HEEL-TAP-HEEL.—From the upright position bend far forward into a crouch and dance the toe-heel-tap-heel (page 28) with its kicking of the leg far out behind. After about six steps of it done strenuously, straighten up again. Sometimes this is terminated by dropping the knee to the ground as the leg is extended out behind.

USING THE FLAT-FOOT STI-YU.—From the upright position drop into a crouch and dance the Sti-yu in the flat-foot style (page 35), bringing the feet down emphatically with earthy accent and much pounding. A brief flash only, then straightened again.

Personalized Finales

Some Indians have an individual and distinctive way of ending a dance, a sort of personalized sign, a rhythmic signature. Knowing when the dance will end, they stop precisely on the final drumbeat, each with his own little flourish. With no song to indicate the ending, a louder beat of the drum can be used as a signal that in eight counts the drumming will stop. Each dancer then starts to write his signature in rhythm.

Typical movements are to drop to a crouch and rise suddenly on the last beat with one hand held in front of the face; to kick the right leg across in front of the left knee on the last beat and hold it there; to use a backward glide and stop with an emphatic stomp on the last beat. But since it is a personal sign, each must originate his own. The final position is always held for a moment after the drumming ceases.

Acting the Story Dances

The dancing Indian relates his story in a wholly natural and realistic manner within the limitations of his style of dancing, a forthright re-enactment of the exploit in rhythmic movement. The action of the story, its moods and its emotions are portrayed primarily by *body action*, with little if any support from facial expression. The face is animated, the eyes follow the action, sharp and alert, occasionally a startled look may come over the face momentarily, but to place reliance on the face for the portrayal of emotion, be it fear, anger or grief, is not in the Indian manner.

Much is told by changes in tempo. As mood changes the tempo of action changes, often abruptly. Discouraged, the dancer moves slowly; seeking the enemy, he creeps stealthily; full of the lust of battle, he dashes swiftly. The drumming for a solo may thus change in tempo and volume many times.

Most of the story dances have to do with fighting and hunting. The fighter on the warpath looks intently as he dances along, pushing the bushes aside with his hands, shading his eyes with his arm. Spotting the enemy he drops to the ground and freezes, then stealthily creeps up on him, rises cautiously, lifts his bow and shoots. The hunter seeking the deer studies the ground for tracks, pointing to them, pausing and studying them. Be it the buffalo he is seeking, he studies the distance, searching the plains for the herds, shading his eyes as he looks.

So goes the story dance. Here are the methods of depicting the various situations that arise:

PUSHING ASIDE THE BUSHES.—Hold the arms out in front at shoulder height, not fully extended but with a slightly bent elbow, palms of the hands turned outward. Dance forward, shoving first one hand out as if to push the bushes aside, then the other, continuing thus, alternating with one arm motion to each step. The hand moves out to the side about a foot and stops abruptly on the drumbeat.

LOOKING INTO THE DISTANCE.—Use the looking pose, with the arm over the eyes as described on page 51.

POINTING.—If moving toward the object at which you are pointing, extend the arm and point toward it, moving the hand back and forward, back and forward, pointing and pointing, emphatically. Make one forward motion of the pointing hand on each step.

If pointing toward an object that would be frightened by any movement, such as an animal or an enemy, freeze and point with the arm fully extended, holding it motionless.

FREEZING.—Drop to the ground in a full squat on the left leg, the buttocks sitting on the left heel, and extend the right leg full-length in front, pointing it toward the object that has startled you, sole of the right foot flat to the ground. Drop the left hand to the ground to steady yourself if necessary, and point the right arm full-length toward the object. The head and eyes are fixed on the object. Remain motionless in this position.

SHOOTING.—In many dances a freeze is followed by a shot. Hold the freeze just described long enough to create the dramatic effect (usually it is not held long enough), then move slowly forward, transferring the weight to the right foot, and rise cautiously to full height, placing the feet in a staunch stance. Raise the left hand with its imaginary bow, reach the right hand over the right shoulder and pull an imaginary arrow out of the quiver, place it in the bow and slowly pull the string. As you release the arrow, zip the right hand forward and clap it against the palm of the left as it passes. The shooting must be carefully timed so as to provide the necessary pauses for dramatic effect. The count is as follows, each count representing a loud and soft beat (1-&, 2-&, etc.):

4 counts—raise bow with left hand
4 counts—pull arrow from quiver
4 counts—put arrow in bowstring
8 counts—pull bowstring and aim
1 count—shoot, throwing right hand forward and clapping it against left

In shooting on the run, as in charging an enemy, dance forward with the left hand extended to hold the bow up in shooting position and keep pulling the bowstring with the right hand, shooting and shooting as rapidly as possible as you advance. On each shot the right hand is thrown forward, and clapped against the left.

CREEPING UP ON THE ENEMY.—Drop to the ground and freeze first, then creep forward on all fours in natural fashion, placing the hands on the ground for support. It is not necessary nor wise to try to jar the heel down on every beat of the drum when moving on all fours.

RETREATING.—In retreating use the fear steps described on page 39.

LOOKING FOR TRACKS.—Dance along with the eyes fixed on the ground, slowing up when the tracks get hot, now and then holding the hand out flat with the palm down to indicate caution; stop and bend forward to look, keeping the heel tapping to the drumming, and pointing to the tracks with the hand. Stop and squat down at times to study the track . . . feel of it with the fingers . . . pick up a leaf and toss it aside . . . look ahead to see where the track goes and point in the direction. Toss an imaginary leaf in the air to estimate the wind.

PART III

DANCES

Chapter III

DANCES OF THE POWWOW TYPE

As THE TERM is here used, a powwow is a dance of celebration, a festive dance of solid fun participated in for the pure joy of dancing.

It has two characteristics: first, the movements are bold, strong, vigorous; and second, each dancer is a law unto himself, dancing as he chooses and following no hampering ritual, and with no story to tell. To dance in powwow fashion is to dance vigorously, lustily, usually with the characteristic toe-heel and flat-foot movements.

This use of the term is far from universal. Many present-day Indian tribes regarded the word as foreign to them and do not use it in connection with their dancing. On the southern Plains, for example, this type of dance is called a war dance. That term, however, is not sufficiently descriptive for a generalized type of dancing such as this which was not always used in celebration of war. In the popular parlance of today, of course, any Indian dance or gathering is apt to be called a powwow. The word itself is of Algonquian origin and in its ancient meaning referred specifically to certain medicine-men ceremonies accompanied by noisy dancing. But in recent years the Woodland Indians, especially of the Great Lakes area, have referred to the type of dance here described as a powwow, and to the style of dancing employed as powwow dancing; moreover an evening of such dances is spoken of collectively as a powwow. Of the various terms that might be used in this connection, that of *powwow* has been selected as the most expressive.

Powwows are of particular interest and importance. They are among the most useful of dances in building programs for the entertainment of audiences. Dashing and noisy, they make the best of climaxes or peaks of action.

In this chapter are found not only the true powwows but other dances of the powwow type. From our standpoint, dances are best classified as to the *use* that can be made of them in dance programs. Here, therefore, are the dances that serve the powwow purpose of spectacular climaxes of color —rousing numbers all, replete with full-bodied action, loud in the ringing of bells, in which the interest centers in the dancing itself instead of in any ritual or story. In Chapter V are equally vigorous and colorful dances that serve the same purpose but which depict a story.

In the parlance of dancers these dances are often referred to as "dancing numbers," so called because they permit full, unreserved expression and the use of the vigorous steps, as contrasted to the ritualistic numbers with their routinized and restricted movements.

One and all, the dances in this chapter are masculine in movement, spirit and mood. They are better suited for men than women. In later chapters are those more appropriate for women.

The Powwow

This is the standard powwow, a dance in itself and the foundation of the other dances in this chapter. Given a group of dancers well-schooled in toe-heel or flat-foot dancing, it is the simplest of all dances to stage, and yet is unexcelled in the wild, free, primitive atmosphere it creates.

By whatever name it may be called, and with minor variations, the dance is well-nigh universal. The particular form here described is adopted from the Lake Superior Chippewas. In Chapter XIV, "The Give-Away Dance," the original setting and routine of the dance is described.

THE DANCE

The drumming is in two-time, accented *loud*-soft, counted *one*-and, *two*-and, etc. The tempo is medium-fast to fast. The steps are the toe-heel and the double toe-heel, or if preferred, the flat-foot. All of the variations, glides, kicks and pivots are in order.

At the first beat of the drum the dancers dash in and break into the dance. Each dances independently, going in any direction he chooses. They dance boldly, vigorously, employing their most brilliant style, filling the ring with leaping bodies. The drum voice booms, the bells ring loudly, brown limbs lift and fall, willowy bodies leap and weave—the place becomes filled with primitive abandon. With no song to terminate it, the ending is left to the judgment of the drummer. With a sharply accented beat he indicates that in eight counts the drumming will cease. The dancers stop on the final beat, each with his own little flourish, turn toward the exit and start walking out, shouting "Ho, ho" or "Hey, hey," loudly. The drum starts again and instantly they whirl back into the dance for a brief moment of "encore." The drum stops as before and they walk out the exit shouting.

This little "encore" on the end is an interesting flourish. As the Chippewas do it it is short, from 16 to 32 drumbeats (see Chapter XIV, "The Give-Away Dance"). When the powwow is used in a dancing entertainment two such "encores" are usually indicated, sometimes three, depending on the judgment of the director at the drum, and each continues as long as the drummer sees fit. The dancers never know if an "encore" is coming, and so start walking out with deep-voiced shouts when the drum stops, ready to whirl back should it strike up again.

The stimulation of the Powwow sometimes causes beginning dancers to become overzealous and lacking in restraint, exceeding the point of graceful movement. This may be forestalled by dividing the dancers into two groups depending upon ability, limiting those of the lesser group to specified steps and movements within their ability, while the better dancers are instructed to dance with full abandon, adding the color and spectacle that is the Powwow.

An interesting variation in line with good showmanship is to have the lesser dancers only enter at the beginning and dance for a moment or two in conservative style, occupying the spotlight all by themselves, then at a prearranged signal, to have the better dancers dash in with a whoop and join the dancing.

Spot Powwow

A glorified form of the powwow, this dance has the unique advantage of presenting all dancers together, yet featuring outstanding performers in solo.

If an Indian powwow is studied carefully with a view to determining what is going on, it will be found that two or three of the dancers are dancing brilliantly and with all spectacle, while the remainder are dancing very quietly, perhaps doing little more than marking time or jarring their heels to the drumming. Presently two or three of the latter leap forward in dashing style while the first ones join the ranks of those moving quietly. Later still others replace these. This serves two useful purposes—it gives each a chance to feature his dancing at its most colorful best, and it gives everyone a rest, protecting against the exertion of constant full-bodied dancing.

The following dance is therefore true to the Indian pattern, departing from it only in the formality with which the leading dancers are presented, a device necessary for adequately staging the dance.

These spot powwows are often called *challenge* powwows, since the dancers attempt to outdance each other.

THE DANCE

The drumming is in accented two-time, medium-fast to fast. The style of dancing is as in the Powwow.

The four best dancers are selected for the solos or "spots." These are referred to as lead dancers or spot dancers.

As the drumming starts, all dancers except the four leads enter and dance the powwow as already described. A moment of this and the drum hits four accented beats, at which the dancers fade back to the edge of the ring as indicated in Figure 14, and mark time. Instantly the drum picks up its rhythm again and in come the *four lead dancers*, prancing and strutting. They dance around the ring and take the four positions marked in Figure

14. These dancers are arranged in order of ability, Number 4 being the best, Number 3 the next best, etc.

Figure 14. Diagram for the Spot Powwow

As they pull into position the drum hits four accented beats and *Number 1* dances in *solo*, the other three leads marking time by jarring their heels to ring their bells. Number 1 circles the ring with his best dancing skill, bringing into play his fanciest steps in competition with the other three who will follow him. His circuit completed, he glides back into his position, the drum signalling as he does so, and *Number 2* leaps forth in *solo*, circling the ring. As he returns to position the drum signals again and *Numbers 1 and 2* dance in *duet*: each dances on his own side of the ring, his attention fixed on the other, looking at him, shading his eyes at times, each doing his best to outdance the other.

At the drum signal they return to position and *Number 3* dances in *solo*, then *Number 4* in *solo*. Then *Numbers 3 and 4* dance in *duet*.

As they finish, *all four* of the lead dancers unite in a brilliant display, which continues until the drummer sees fit to terminate it with four accented beats, whereupon *everyone* in the ring breaks into a vigorous finale, those standing around the edges joining with the leads, filling the ring with leaping bodies. The dance is terminated with the usual powwow "encores" and shouting as already described.

Following is a simple outline:

1. Group dancers enter in powwow and at signal withdraw to edge, marking time.
2. Four lead dancers enter, circle ring and take positions
3. No. 1 in solo
4. No. 2 in solo

5. Nos. 1 and 2 in duet
6. No. 3 in solo
7. No. 4 in solo
8. Nos. 3 and 4 in duet
9. Nos, 1, 2, 3, and 4 in powwow
10. Entire ensemble in powwow

SPOT POWWOW VARIATIONS.—An interesting variation of the Spot Powwow introduces the lead dancers in a different way: When the main group of dancers draw back to the edge of the ring, Number 1 enters and circles the ring in his solo, taking his usual position when he has finished. Then Number 2 enters in solo, then 3, and 4. After Number 4 has finished and is in place Numbers 1 and 2 dance in duet, then 3 and 4 in duet, then all four dance together, and the dance finishes as usual.

If there are *eight* lead dancers available, an excellent arrangement is to use the regular Spot Powwow as described with the four *lesser* lead dancers taking the spots. When they finish their routines of solos and duets, all four of them dance together. Then the remaining four lead dancers are brought in *one at a time* in solo, taking positions in between the first four. When all four are in position the usual *duet* routine follows, then all four of them dance together. This finished, all eight of the lead dancers dance, and then the entire group joins in the finale.

Burning Torch Powwow

The use of fire is potent elemental stagecraft. The truth of it was learned by those earliest Atlantic settlers who saw the dance "rattles" in the hands of red-brown dancers suddenly turn into flaming torches, setting the woods ablaze with a brilliance that transformed graceful dancers into leaping demons. They learned it anew when, unbelievingly, they saw the hoop in which a willowy form was dancing burst into flame and yet he danced within it still. Far across the country, desert travelers also learned the truth of it as Navajo Fire Dancers leaped in and on the fire as though no flame were there.

The Torch Powwow is still a breath-taking spectacle. The passing of the centuries since first the white man saw it among the Iroquois has not dimmed its brilliance.

PROPERTIES

Four torches are needed. These are made on green sticks 15 inches long and slightly thicker than a broomstick, from which the bark has been peeled. Around the ends wrap strips of burlap of varying widths, starting with wide strips and then using progressively narrower ones until a round ball has been created four inches in diameter. Drive a nail through the burlap into the stick so that there is no possibility of the ball coming off.

Then wrap a piece of white cloth over the ball and wire it. Do not use string—it burns. Four hours before the dance the torches should be set upright in a pan containing enough kerosene so that the ball of cloth is half-submerged. Leave in the kerosene until a half-hour before the time for the dance, then remove and set on the ground with the handles of the torches extending up. The excess kerosene will drip off so that the torches can be held in the hand without danger of kerosene running down the handle.

The torches are made to appear as much like dance rattles as possible in order that the spectators will not recognize them as torches, or will not be aware that there is any probability of their being used as such.

The dance is, of course, suitable only for the outdoor dancing ring. A bucket of water should be placed outside the exit to extinguish the torches at the end.

THE DANCE

The dance follows the routine of the Spot Powwow just described—is, indeed, the Spot Powwow with the added use of burning torches in the finale.

The main group of dancers enter in powwow and draw off to the edge of the ring, then the four lead dancers enter, each carrying his torch. They perform their routines of solos and duets as described. When the last two have completed their duet, all four dance together, each remaining near his own position. At a signal from the drum they swoop up to the fire and throw their arms holding the torches high above it in dramatic pose. This is accomplished in 12 steps after the drum signal, the dancers drawing back near the edge of the ring for 8 counts, then dashing up to the fire, reaching it and stopping on the 12th count. The drumming gains in volume throughout and stops with an explosive boom on the 12th count. They stand dramatically, chest out and head up, looking up at the torches held together at full arm's length. This position is held for the equivalent of four counts, when the drumming starts again and they break into another dance. At the next signal given in the same way, they repeat the advance to the fire but this time *hold their torches down and into the flame.*

The torches ablaze, the drum picks up in rapid tempo and *all dancers* in the ring leap forth in powwow. The torchbearers dance near the fire with torches high overhead, whirling them about in small circles. The flaming torches set the ring ablaze, the brilliance seeming more intense against the black background of the night. The dance continues in fullest vigor until the drum signals the finale, at which the torchbearers move over to the side of the ring opposite the Council Rock and form in line facing the exit, the other dancers massing behind them. They dance in place until everyone is in position, then break suddenly and prance swiftly across and exit, warwhooping as they go. Immediately after exiting the torchbearers douse their torches in the bucket of water, thus cutting off the light instantly.

In the hands of mature dancers with good judgment, an added feature of tossing the torches in the air may be used. Practice with unlighted torches will indicate that they can be thrown three or four feet up and caught with safety. The Burning Torch Powwow is replete with beauty and pleasing spectacle without the use of such stunts as this, however.

BURNING HOOP DANCE.—If a hoop dancer is available, the Burning Hoop Dance as described on page 214 will make an excellent addition to the Torch Powwow. After the four torchbearers light their torches they dance for a moment, then at a signal drop back to their original positions holding their torches overhead. At this point the hoop dancer enters, dances in his unlighted hoop for a moment, holds the hoop in the fire to light it, then dances in the blazing hoop. He then holds the blazing hoop overhead and circles the ring, whereupon the entire group break into the powwow and the dance is concluded as described.

Chippewa Pipe Dance

The Pipe Dance is a challenge dance. It is such among the far-flung tribes of both the Woodlands and the northern Plains. To confront one with a pipe during a dance is to invite him to dance—more, to *challenge* him to outdance the others.

Many are the ways in which a man can be challenged to dance: to step on his feet as he sits there watching, or to kick his leg as you dance past him is a time-honored Chippewa method of requesting him to take the floor. To grab him by the arm and pull him up is to challenge him, as will be seen presently in the Assiniboin Pipe Dance. But actually to hand him a pipestem or a pipe-tomahawk is the most emphatic of all. The first method can be disregarded if one chooses, but the last two permit no wavering or loss of courage.

COMEDY IN THE OLDEN DAYS

The cobwebs of time shut out from view those early days when first the Manitou gave the Pipe Dance to man and taught him how to do it. But through the haze one clear fact stands out: it was the happiest of dances, the most joyous of a fun-loving people. So it was when first the white man came among the Chippewas, and even to this day, the time-wrinkled old men smile in pleasant memory when the Pipe Dance is mentioned.

Only one person danced at a time. With a pipestem in one hand and a rattle in the other, he danced with body bent far forward in effort to represent the shape of the pipe bowl. Then he swooped up to another dancer and presented him the pipe and rattle. This challenge no one could refuse and the recipient danced forth and did his level best the better to represent the pipe. A supple body and much dancing skill were needed to dance well in the low crouch required to simulate the pipe, and the ungainly antics of many an awkward or overfat brave provided high comedy. To add to his difficulties the drummers repeatedly changed the rhythm and the tempo without warning, and often skipped a few beats at a time when least expected. To fail to dance in harmony with the changing rhythm and the tempo, or to ring one's bells by stepping when the drumming stopped, was high cause for ridicule. Only by sitting in the rear row could a person be sure of not receiving the pipe and to do that was proof of lack of courage.

To this day the Pipe Dance is often staged in its original form but more often the comedy angle of representing the pipe by body actions has given way to plain competition to outdance the others. The young dancing men love this sort of dancing competition. The changing rhythm and tempo still continues, providing added test of dancing ability. And it is no lack of good taste to laugh openly at those who fail to detect the change of time and thus blunder aloud with their bells when they should be silent.

THE DANCE

A pipe-tomahawk, or peace pipe, such as that shown in Figure 15 is best for the purpose. In another book, *Woodcraft,* I have described how these can be whittled out of wood so as to answer for show purposes. As a second choice a long pipestem will do, or a scout ax may be used in lieu of the pipe-tomahawk if the handle is wrapped with fur, or a feather or two and some ribbons attached to it as trailers.

Figure 15. Pipe-tomahawk or Peace Pipe

When used in a public presentation of dances the irregular drumming as done by the Indians is unwise and, indeed, may be wholly devastating in the eyes of those who do not understand its purpose. It would take highly skilled dancers of long experience to do it well, and even they would be placed at an unwarranted disadvantage. The drumming should be steady, medium-fast to fast, in two-time, accented *loud*-soft. Moreover, no effort is made to assume the low crouch in imitation of a pipe, but rather the modern version is used with the dancers free to dance in any style and with any steps they choose.

Six to eight good solo dancers should be selected for the challenge parts. As the drumming starts all other dancers enter and dance in powwow, continuing until a drum signal tells them to back off to the edge of the ring, their eyes fixed on the entrance. Onto the scene come the lead dancers, circling the ring, and taking positions around the edge, just in front of the outer circle of dancers, spaced equidistant from each other as in Figure 16. The pipe is in the hands of the head dancer who takes his position with the others and then immediately dances across the ring and without ceremony sticks it in the ground in front of one of the dancers or, if it is a pipestem, hands it to him, then returns to his position.

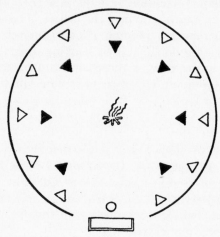

Figure 16. Diagram for the Chippewa Pipe Dance

The recipient of the tomahawk grabs it and begins dancing at his most spectacular best, circling the ring with all style, calling into play the steps best suited to him. The others merely stand and mark time. Having made the circuit he dances up to another and pretends to stick the tomahawk in the ground in front of him but darts away still holding it. He feints giving it to others in this way and finally sticks it in the ground in front of one. This dancer then takes up the dance and in turn gives the tomahawk to a third, etc., until all have danced.

When the last man has finished the tomahawk is stuck in the ground near the fire in front of the Council Rock and all of the lead dancers break into powwow. After a few moments of this the drum hits four louder beats and the outer circle of dancers join in, the entire assemblage dancing in powwow. The dance closes with the usual powwow exit.

THE USE OF CHANGING RHYTHM.—Although not recommended for use before an audience, dancing to the changing rhythm and tempo of the Pipe Dance as done by the Chippewas is excellent experience and is much loved by dancers in practice periods. It is good practice in rhythm, good training in following the drum. It has a competitive angle that is enjoyed. Often a contest is made of it, in which the dancers are eliminated when they miss the rhythm.

Assiniboin Pipe Dance

Westward on the northern Plains we find the Pipe Dance of the Assiniboins, similar in principle to that of the Chippewas, yet different enough in detail to make it useful as another dance.

Back in the 1830's George Catlin witnessed this dance and described it in the tale of his travels. The dancers gathered around the edges of the dancing area, each sitting on a buffalo robe. By the fire in the center sat the head man of the dance, his long pipe in his hand, smoking. The drumming started and one of the dancers leaped to his feet and began dancing "in the most violent manner imaginable." He went around the circle several times, brandishing his fists in the faces of the seated dancers and making passes at them, at last grabbing one by the hand and pulling him to his feet. The two danced together for a moment, then the first one left the other to dance alone and took his place beside the head man near the fire. The second dancer pulled up a third, and so on until all had danced and were standing around the fire. Then all broke into a dance together, with shouts and yells "that seemed almost to make the earth quake under our feet." *

No pipe was passed from dancer to dancer as in most Pipe Dances, but the challenge aspect was there nevertheless.

THE DANCE

The general routine is the same as for the Chippewa Pipe Dance just described.

Select six to eight of the best dancers for the solo parts. All others enter dancing in powwow and at the drum signal draw off to the edge of the ring and sit down. Then the eight solo dancers enter, circle the ring, take positions around the edge just in front of the others and sit down (Figure 16). One of them leaps to his feet and dances around the ring in solo, then prances up to another and shakes his fist in his face and feints at grabbing his arm. He makes such feints at others and finally grabs a dancer's hand and pulls him to his feet. They hook arms and dance together for a moment, then the first leaves and takes his place near the fire, facing out, standing there and marking time by jarring his heels. The second dancer then performs in solo and finally pulls the third up. This continues until all have danced.

When the last man is through, the eight men dance together in vigorous powwow and, at a drum signal, are joined by the entire assembly in finale. The exit is as in the Powwow.

* George Catlin, *The North American Indians*, Vol. I, p. 55. London: The Author, 1841.

Photograph by Paul Boris

JAMES C. STONE

JAMES C. STONE

Whip Powwow

Of all the invitations to participate in the dancing, that used by the Crow Indians is the strangest—and the most convincing! No subtle stepping on one's foot as among the Chippewas, no pulling one up by his arm, no confronting him with a pipe . . . the Crows got to the point bluntly—they *whipped* the dancers into action. And herein rests the clue to as spectacular and dashing a dance as is to be found in these pages.

AS IT USED TO BE

Important in the preparations for a dance among the Crows was the appointment of one or two whippers. When the dancers were reluctant to dance, the whippers applied the lash. To hold back long was a sign of courage, for the whippers worked with increasing vehemence. However, should a whipper become overzealous and draw blood he owed his victim a pony. Once in action, if a dancer loafed at the task the stinging bite of the whip inspired him to better effort. In some dances the dancers were required to keep on dancing until a whipper touched them with the whip, thus permitting them to sit down. Should a dancer fail to leave the ring promptly when a dance was over, the whippers took him in hand. As proof of his courage a dancer would sometimes remain dancing after the drumming had ceased and cause the whippers to make repeated efforts of increasing violence to dislodge him.

Such was the pattern of many of the Crow dances. For the whip was characteristic of most of their secular dances, regardless of their nature. It was so in social dances such as the Owl Dance, in the dances of the Hot Dancers, and of other clubs.*

The dance here described and recommended is a powwow involving the use of the whip.

THE DANCE

A slender green switch about six feet long is recommended. To its tip and at intervals of every foot throughout its length, colored ribbons should be tied with ends extending about three inches. For the role of the whipper, an animated person of striking appearance and with good dramatic judgment should be selected. The six best dancers are chosen for the leading parts.

All dancers except the six leads enter, scatter across the ring, and begin dancing as in the Powwow. A drum signal sounds, a scream is heard behind the Council Rock, and the six lead dancers dash in, looking back over their shoulders, for they are being driven by the whipper. They scurry to the far side of the ring, the whipper following them. As the

* Robert H. Lowie, *The Crow Indian*, pages 93, 174, 196, 210. New York: Farrar & Rinehart, 1935.

whipper moves across the ring the lesser dancers fade away from him and exit, leaving the scene to the six lead dancers and the whipper.

The dancers move swiftly around the ring and take positions at equal intervals near the edge, and the whipper takes position directly in front of the drummer by the Council Rock. The whipper runs up to one of the dancers with threatening motions of his whip. Trying to escape, the dancer dashes away about six feet and is stopped by the end of the whip, he darts a similar distance in the opposite direction and is met by the whip again, then he breaks into a dance and starts around the ring, the whipper encouraging him with a tap of the whip as he leaves. The whipper returns to his position and the dancer circles the ring in solo, displaying his best talent, after which he returns to his position.

The whipper then trots around looking over the dancers, feints with threatening motions at one or two, singles out the proper one and approaches him with whip in air. The dancer repeats the running away motions and then breaks into his dance. This continues until all six have danced in solo.

As the last man finishes the whipper starts around the ring clockwise, driving all the dancers to the far side of the ring, then runs back and starts around counterclockwise driving back the dancers on that side. When all are in a cluster on the far side, the whipper approaches them with sweeping swings of the whip and they break into a powwow, scattering around the ring, the whipper returning to his post. After a few minutes of this the whipper turns toward the drummer and makes threatening motions, whereupon the drummer increases his tempo and volume, and the dancers go into a frenzy of dancing.

A louder boom of the drum signals the exit whereupon the dancers gravitate to the far side of the ring, line up facing the Council Rock, prance across the ring in a spectacular finale of dash and flourish, headed for the exit. As they approach, the whipper makes wild swings with the whip in their faces and drives them back across the ring where they stand marking time, uncertain. With the whip high in the air and arm extended straight up, the whipper trots directly across the ring and through the line of dancers. Once past them he whirls and swings at them in the rear—they scream, dash across the ring, and exit, the whipper following them with menacing swings.

The dance is full of dash and spirit . . . there isn't a lull throughout. The animation is more than acting, for the whip adds incentive.

ON THE STAGE.—The drum is placed at the back of the stage midway from the sides. The whipper's position is directly in front of the drum. The dance proceeds as described and can easily be adjusted to existing stage conditions. At the exit the dancers gather at one side of the stage and the whipper stands at the other. They approach him to exit and are driven back, he crosses and passes through the line, then drives them out.

Kiowa Squat Dance

Reminiscent of the Pipe Dances with their changing rhythm is the Squat Dance of the Kiowas. But in this case, instead of dancing to the changes in rhythm, the dancers merely squat down and wait until it is back to normal again.

The general procedure is as in the Powwow. After a moment of fast drumming, the drummer abruptly changes to a slow beat, whereupon all dancers squat, place their elbows on their knees and wait motionless. When the drumming returns to the original tempo they leap up in strenuous dance again. Several such changes in rhythm take place in the course of the dance.

Good form demands that the dancers squat instantly when the drumming changes, and again that they leap up instantly when it returns to normal. To fail to detect the change and continue to dance for a step or two, or to remain squatted overlong, is cause for ridicule, just as is the missing of a rhythm in the Chippewa Pipe Dance.

This is not only an interesting dance of the powwow type but is excellent practice in rhythm.

Chippewa Bean Dance

What it means I know not, nor do I know why it should be called the Bean Dance. My Chippewa friends are silent on the matter, as if they, too, do not know, save for the fact that, like all dances, the Manito gave it to man, and since then it has been theirs to do. But that was long, long ago....

Scarcely a true powwow, yet for us it serves the powwow purpose, and is useful in its combination of solo dances and group dancing, giving all a chance to dance individually and collectively.

THE DANCE

Not more than ten to twelve dancers should be used, lest the dance become too long, selected for good solo ability. They walk in and form in two lines facing each other, as indicated by the numbers in Figure 17. They are arranged in pairs, 1 and 2 constituting a pair, 3 and 4, etc. The pairs are arranged in order of dancing ability, the two best dancers being Numbers 1 and 2, the next best 3 and 4, etc.

Only one dances at a time, the others standing and watching. As the drumming starts Number 10 dances across toward Number 9, displaying his best in a challenge to Number 9 to outdance him. He comes up in front of Number 9 with a flourish and stops, whereupon Number 9 leaps forth to take up the challenge and Number 10 steps into his position. Number 9 then dances across to Number 8 in similar fashion, Number 8 to Number 7, etc. This continues until all have crossed the ring and are on the opposite sides from their original positions. The entire group then breaks into a dance, moving about as in the Powwow but *each line remaining on its own side of the ring.*

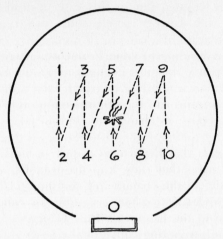

Figure 17. Diagram for the Chippewa Bean Dance

At a prearranged drum signal the two lines cross over to their original positions again and stop dancing. The entire routine of crossing over is then repeated, but this time each man dances longer, prancing up and down between the lines in brief solo before going to position in the opposite line. When all have danced the entire group breaks into a vigorous powwow, scattering around the ring.

This continues until the drummer signals the finale by a louder beat, at which all dance over to the side of the ring opposite the Council Rock where the lines form again one behind the other, both facing the exit. In this formation they dance across the ring toward the exit, heads high, strutting and swaggering, but just before reaching it they turn abruptly and dance back for a 16-count encore, in which they dance toward the fire for eight counts, then whirl, crouch, and trot out the exit with a flatfoot trot on the remaining eight counts.

Kansa Brave Man's Dance

The game of fighting carries us to the peaks of ecstasy at one moment and hurls us into the depths of heartbreak in the next. In its mingling of joy and sorrow it is like life itself. Sooner or later the shout of triumph must be followed by the heart-rending wail of grief. Both find expression in rhythmic movement, for the shout of victory terminates in dancing and the wail of heartbreak cannot end without it.

Here is the pattern of the Pipe Dance again, not in festive mood this time, but in mourning for a brave one lost in battle. But it is none the less a rousing number, combining the brilliance of solo with the zest of powwow, its interest heightened by the dramatic background of the mourners.

MEANING OF THE DANCE

For days after the death of a warrior of importance the village was filled with that most heart-rending of sounds, the wailing of Indian women. It lasted four days as a rule, longer or shorter if the relatives desired, before the Brave Man's Dance was called to end it. For the dance was the last token of love and esteem, the final gesture of honor, before village life returned to normal again.

Six were chosen by the mourners to serve as rhythm-makers. These sat on a blanket near the mourners, with drums or pans on which to beat the rhythm. Onto the scene came the dancers, fellow warriors of the departed one, bedecked in their finest regalia, the leader with a tomahawk in his hand. First the leader danced, counting his coups in honor of the departed one, dancing his heart out for his glory—and when finished, received a gift from the mourners in appreciation of his sympathy. Whereupon he gave the tomahawk to a second who danced and received his gift, and so on until all had danced.

So ended the days of mourning among the Kansa.*

PROPERTIES

Spread a blanket near the edge of the ring just to the right of the Council Rock on which the rhythm-makers sit (see Figure 18). To expedite matters these also represent the mourners and have a basket at hand containing a gift for each dancer. Appropriate Indian items should be used for gifts, such as beaded bands, feather ornaments, etc. Since the dancing is best controlled by the central drum, these rhythm-makers are given rattles instead of drums which they shake in rhythm with the drumming. A pipe-tomahawk or hatchet bedecked with fur and feathers is needed.

THE DANCE

Six to eight of the best dancers should be selected, capable of dancing in solo.

The mourners enter, walking slowly, and seat themselves on the blanket. They hang their heads with their hands to their faces, quietly weeping. The drumming starts and the mourners shake their rattles quietly to the rhythm.

Into the ring come the dancers, bold and strong, symbolizing life, on-going, eternal. With the full lust of the powwow they circle the ring,

* This dance is referred to in *Anthropological Papers of The American Museum of Natural History*, Vol. XI, part VII, p. 775. Washington: Government Printing Office.

counterclockwise, until they are directly across from the mourners, where they draw up in line and stand facing the mourners, as shown in Figure 18.

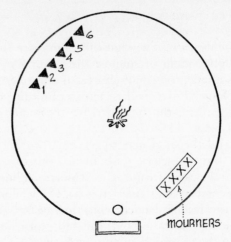

Figure 18. Diagram for the Kansa Brave Man's Dance

Once in line, the first dancer, tomahawk in hand, leaps forward in brilliant solo, honoring the departed one with his finest talent. He makes a complete circle of the ring, then swiftly dances straight across and pulls up with a flourish in front of the mourners, throwing his arm with the tomahawk overhead as he stops. The drumming crescendos as he crosses and stops with him. The leading mourner, showing deep emotion, lifts a gift from the basket and hands it to him. The dancer leaps back as he takes it and shouts, pauses for a moment, then turns and trots across to the dancers and gives the tomahawk to the next in line who repeats. This continues until all have danced.

When the last dancer returns to line the entire group breaks into a strenuous powwow which continues with increasing vigor until terminated by a drum signal, at which they dance back into their original line again, then sweep across the ring in eight counts and come up in front of the mourners with a flourish and shout, each throwing his hand overhead, the drum stopping explosively with the shout. They hold this dramatic gesture for a moment, then whirl and run out. The mourners rise and quietly walk out after them.

Medicine of the Brave

The Medicine of the Brave is a dance of the Salk and Fox Indians which, like the Kansa Brave Man's Dance, honors the spirit of a departed warrior and brings comfort to the dear ones left behind. Unlike that dance, however, the dancers give gifts to the mourning ones, rather than receive gifts from them.

MEANING OF THE DANCE

George Catlin describes it as he saw it among the Salk and Fox people in the 1830's.* When a warrior was killed in battle the returning braves would dance in front of his lodge for fifteen days in succession, an hour a day. The heart-broken widow would sit weeping in the doorway of the lodge, the departed one's medicine bag hanging over her head from a green branch attached to the top of the door. The warriors danced vigorously, recounting the exploits of the dead warrior and portraying his bravery, each throwing gifts to the weeping widow to lessen her grief.

THE DANCE

Erect a tripod at the edge of the ring to the left of the Council Rock to symbolize the doorway of the dead warrior's lodge, and on the top of it hang a medicine bag or object resembling one. Select six or eight of the best dancers for the solo parts, representing the returning warriors. Each carries a small article of Indian craft as a gift.

The widow walks in weeping and sits under the medicine bag (o in Figure 19).

Figure 19. Diagram for the Medicine of the Brave

All dancers except the six or eight warriors enter the ring and dance in powwow until a drum signal causes them to withdraw to the edge of the ring where they sit on the ground (Figure 19). In dash the warriors dancing vigorously, circle the ring in a group, then take positions equally spaced from each other just in front of the sitting dancers (Figure 19), where they stand marking time. The first warrior dances forward in solo, circling

* George Catlin, *The North American Indians*, Volume II, page 215. London: The Author, 1841.

the ring with his best performance, after which he swoops toward the weeping widow and tosses a gift to her, then pulls up in dramatic pose in front of her, throwing his arm overhead and shouting. This he holds for a moment, then dances back to position, whereupon another dancer takes up the dance and repeats. This continues until all have danced. Then all of the warriors dance together in powwow; a drum signal of four louder beats is given and the outer circle of dancers leap to their feet and join the warriors in a dashing finale. The exit is as in the Powwow, the widow rising and following the dancers out.

Striking the Post

Echoing from centuries long past, this lusty dance is mentioned again and yet again in the letters of those earliest French adventurers who braved the perils of the unexplored Great Lakes. It seems to have thrived wherever Algonquian peoples were found. Of the same type as the Discovery Dance (page 94) it adds the dramatic gesture of striking the post.

AS IT USED TO BE

Nothing did the Indian of the fighting tribes love more than to recite his exploits. The best-loved means was to dance them. In the dance arena a pole was erected, around which the men of fighting honors danced in turn, each a rhythmic re-enaction of his exploits on the battlefield. His dance ended, he dashed up and struck the pole, whereupon he received the acclaim of the assembly, or if he chose, demanded silence and added a verbal account, the better to impress his admirers. No sooner had he finished than another took his place, and so on until all had danced.

Should anyone detect that a dancer was boasting or overstating the facts, he stopped the dance and smeared the offender's face with dirt and ashes to cover up his shame. Says Charlevoix, "Thus it seems to be a received maxim amongst all nations that the surest mark of a coward is boasting. . . . The greatest Chief has no privilege above the common in this respect and must take all without murmuring." *

Thus it used to be, and could well be re-enacted today just as it was, were it not for the doubtful wisdom of presenting in succession too many story dances depicting exploits, with the sameness that unavoidably characterizes them. A better dance will result if the story feature is eliminated and the solo dancers permitted to dance as they choose, each displaying his dancing skill as best he may. Inherent in the pattern of this dance is a lusty, resounding number full of dash and zest, better achieved without the story feature. Thus it is here described among the dances of the pow-wow type rather than among the story or discovery dances.

* Charlevoix, Pierre Francois Xavier de, *Journal of a Voyage to North America.* Edited by Louise Phelps Kellogg. Volume II, page 67. Chicago: Caxton Club, 1923.

The feature of blackening the face may or may not be used, depending on circumstances. In most situations that place the emphasis on nice dancing rather than dramatics it is a doubtful contribution.

THE DANCE

Erect a pole about eight feet tall in the ring in front of the Council Rock, as near to the fire as possible. Six to eight strong dancers are needed, each carrying a sturdy club about two feet long.

The tempo is fast, the spirit dashing:

They swoop into the ring and start around counterclockwise, immediately focusing attention on the pole, looking at it, shading their eyes with their arms, etc. The circuit completed, one dashes up and hits the pole a resounding blow with his club, whereupon the others withdraw to the edge of the ring and mark time, spaced equidistant as in Figure 20.

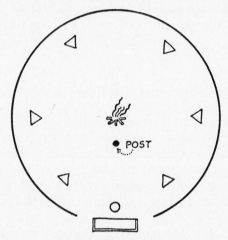

Figure 20. Diagram for Striking the Post

The ring to himself, the dancer circles it with his most brilliant and dashing solo style, then swoops up and strikes the pole again, leaping back as he does so into a dramatic pose and stands there for a moment, as if waiting for applause. The drum crescendos with the swoop and stops explosively with the strike. A moment of silence and the drumming begins again, the dancer trots to his position and the others leap into action, dancing in their positions, their sticks raised menacingly. Another dancer dashes up as if to hit the pole, turns and trots back from it with the fear step (page 39). A second repeats, swinging at the post but missing and fear-stepping away. The third hits it and takes up the solo. This continues until each have danced in solo. As in all series of solos, the dancers perform in order of ability, the better ones appearing last.

The last man having finished, the *entire group* breaks into a powwow, scattering across the ring, dancing colorfully. The powwow continues with ever-increasing vigor until the drummer, using his judgment as to time, indicates the finale with a prearranged drum signal, at which the dancers draw back near the edge of the ring for eight counts, then dash up in four counts and all strike the post together with a shout. They hit it high overhead and keep their clubs on it after striking, their heads turned upward with eyes on the clubs. For a moment of silence they stand there dramatically, then turn as the drumming starts and dance for the exit with the flat-foot trot. Eight steps and they whirl back as one man, repeat the swoop and strike the pole again, shouting as before. A long pause with arms overhead and clubs on the pole, the drum rolls and they trot out.

Plains War Dance

This rousing dance, so robust and virile in its war play, is after the manner of the Indians of the Great Plains, where its purpose was to keep aflame the zest for battle in the hearts of the young men. It is a powerful number.

The description here given follows in general the dance as described by Julian H. Salomon,* with whose permission it is used.

THE DANCE

Sixteen dancers are needed, each equipped with a war club, tomahawk, or other war weapon and, if possible, a shield. They are divided into two groups of eight, each with a leader. They walk in and line up on opposite sides of the ring, facing each other as in Figure 21, a space being left in the middle of each line as shown so as to avoid the fire.

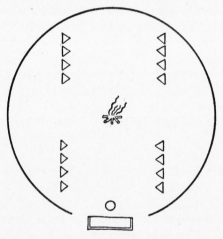

Figure 21. Diagram for the Opening of the Plains War Dance

* Julian H. Salomon, *The Book of Indian Crafts and Indian Lore*, page 351. New York: Harper and Brothers, 1928.

1. The drumming is in fast, accented two-time, the step the toe-heel and the double toe-heel. The two lines advance to meet each other in attack, following this routine:

A. 16 counts—They dance in position, eyes on opponents, shading eyes with arms, raising and lowering weapons threateningly, etc.

B. 8 counts—With weapons raised the two lines dance swiftly forward to meet.

C. 8 counts—Just before meeting they turn and retreat with the fear step (page ooo), looking back over their shoulders.

D. 16 counts—Repeat A

E. 8 counts—Repeat B

F. 8 counts—Repeat C

G. 16 counts—Repeat A

H. 8 counts—The lines dash forward and meet, stopping face to face, all throwing arms with weapons overhead and emitting a lusty shout.

I. 8 counts—They hold the pose, drum silent.

2. The drumming changes to slow two-time; the step is the toe-heel. The dancers start around the ring counterclockwise, all going in the same direction but moving irregularly, each on his own, looking for signs, following tracks, searching for the enemy, alert, stealthy, all of which movements are described on page 56. This continues for one circuit of the ring and is ended by four sharply accented drumbeats.

3. The drumming changes suddenly to fast two-time; the step is the double toe-heel. They break abruptly into strenuous dancing, depicting the charge and the battle, going in all directions, each on his own, raising weapons and charging imaginary foes, turning and retreating, crouching and rising, etc. Using his judgment as to time the drummer terminates this by four accented beats.

4. The drumming changes to medium-fast two-time; the step is the toe-heel and the double toe-heel. They dance into their original groups, each group moving to its own side of the ring and lining up as in Figure 22 with its leader in front and facing it as shown. With weapons raised each group attacks its leader, who swings his weapon at them and drives them back, then returns to his position. This is repeated three times but on the third time the leader drives them on around to the other side of the ring. Here the drummer signals a change by four accented beats.

5. The drumming changes to *very fast* two-time; the step is the double toe-heel. All break formation and scatter in a colorful powwow, each using his best performance. The fight-acting is forgotten, all concentrating on a finale of high-powered, dashing dancing. When the drummer deems wise he signals by one louder beat at which all dance back to the edge of the ring in eight counts, then on four counts dash to the center and stop with a

loud-voiced shout, their right arms with the weapons thrown high over the fire. They hold the pose for a moment, the drum rolls, they turn and trot out to exit.

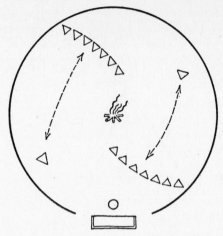

Figure 22. Diagram for the Plains War Dance

Minataree Green Corn Dance

In brilliant contrast to the sedate rituals of the corn dances of many tribes, the Green Corn Dance of the Minatarees * is a rousing drama replete with arresting dance spectacle. No hopeful prayer as seeds are planted, no hush-voiced supplication as roots begin to sprout, this is a full-lunged shout of exaltation when, at long last, the luscious ears are ripe for eating. It is a dance for seasoned men whose moccasined feet are versatile and whose athletic bodies toughened for the test. Here is dancing—strong, full-bodied dancing ... here is drama—stark stagecraft of primitive men ... here is ritual, bold and dashing. ...

From a long yesterday this dance has come. George Catlin saw it in the 1830's ere yet the last awful scourge of smallpox fell upon the Missouri River Indians in 1837 to unmake a nation and all but obliterate a culture. A brief description is given in the memorable chronicle of his travels.**

The season at hand for the ripening of the corn, a group of old women were selected by the Medicine Men to go to the fields each morning and bring in samples that the Medicine Men might inspect them. When at last it appeared that they would do, a crier was sent about the village to announce the day of the feast and dance. The Green Corn Dance accompanied the cooking of the corn. The description here given follows in the main the Indian ritual with certain departures made necessary to permit effective staging.

* Gros Ventre or Hidatsa.
** George Catlin, *The North American Indians*. Vol. I, page 189. London: The Author, 1841.

PROPERTIES

A kettle rack—four sticks arranged over the fire or in the center of the stage, as shown in Figure 23, six to seven feet high at the apex. If the sticks are forked at the top, the rack can be set up by property men just before the dance starts. From the apex a pothook is hung.

Figure 23. Kettle Rack for the Green Corn Dance

Kettle—preferably a black iron kettle, hung from the pothook, containing a little water.

Six ears of corn—preferably green corn, otherwise dry field corn.

Cornstalks—one for each dancer. If out of season the dance can be done without them.

Pottery or bark—six small bowls of Indian pottery or six pieces of bark a foot square on which to place the corn.

Fork—a two-foot stick with nails driven in the end and sharpened to serve as a fork with which to spear corn.

Rattles—six gourd dance rattles.

Prior to the dance the kettle rack is set up and the kettle put on the pothook. The fork is hung on the rack. The six bowls or pieces of bark are placed on the ground around the rack as indicated by the six small circles in Figure 24.

If on the stage the rack and kettle may be eliminated and a pile of sticks placed in the center to represent the fire. The corn is then laid in among the sticks.

THE DANCE

A medicine man is needed, for which a mature person with striking appearance and good dramatic judgment should be selected. He is not a dancer and should be dressed in dignified fashion in contrast to the breech-clothed dancers. Four to six lead dancers are needed, depending upon the number of talented solo performers at hand. The following directions assume that there are six. Six to twelve other dancers are also needed.

1. The Medicine Man walks in unaccompanied by the drum, carrying six ears of corn. He is dignified, serious, and gives careful attention to his business. He inspects the pot, places the corn in it and then walks back and takes position directly in front of the drummer. See Figure 24.

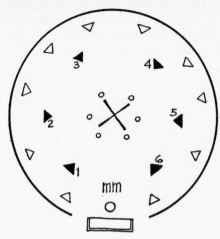

Figure 24. Diagram for the Minataree Green Corn Dance

2. The drum strikes up a fast two-time and all of the dancers except the six lead performers dance in, each carrying a cornstalk held upright in his right hand. They scatter about the ring dancing as in the Powwow, being careful to keep their cornstalks upright. A moment or two of this and the drummer strikes four louder beats whereupon the dancers fade back to the edge of the ring and stand there marking time, holding their cornstalks upright in front of them.

3. The six lead dancers swoop into the ring with a whoop, each has a rattle in his right hand and a cornstalk in his left. With all their interest centered on the pot they dance around the ring counterclockwise and take positions as indicated by the numbers in Figure 24. These dancers are not required to hold their cornstalks upright but use them as hand ornaments as an aid to dancing.

4. For 16 counts they dance back and forth in their positions with their eyes glued on the pot, shading their eyes the better to see it at times. (By a count is meant a unit of loud and soft beat.) The following routine then starts, each advance to the fire being signalled by a louder beat:

A. 8 counts—Dance forward to fire, throwing arms toward it (page 52)
B. 8 counts—Trot back to position with the flat-foot trot, looking back at pot
C. 8 counts—Dance in position, looking at pot
D. 8 counts—Repeat A

E. 8 counts—Repeat B
F. 8 counts—Repeat C
G. 8 counts—Swoop up to fire and stop on 8th count in dramatic pose, head high and chest out. The drum stops explosively on 8th count.

The picture at the top of the illustration facing page 262 shows the position of the dancers at this point.

The Medicine Man trots up, bends over the pot and inspects the corn. He looks up, his face grave, his mouth turned down, and shakes his head, indicating that the corn is not cooked. The drumming begins again, the dancers whirl back to their positions and the Medicine Man trots back to his.

5. Repeat 4.

6. Repeat 4, except that when the Medicine Man inspects the corn he finds that it is cooked. He straightens up with a yip or short, high-pitched shout. The drumming strikes up with increased tempo and volume. The six dancers whirl into a strenuous dance of celebration. They go into *full crouch* (page 45) shaking their rattles down to the ground, hard and loud. There is just a moment of this and then a drum signal sends them swooping up to the fire again in eight counts, each posed dramatically in his original position.

7. The drum is silent. The Medicine Man reaches into the kettle with his long fork, spears an ear of corn with it, straightens up holding it high in front and yips, then trots to the dancer nearest at his left and puts the corn in the bowl in front of him or lays it on the piece of bark. Immediately, this dancer leaps back, throws his right hand with his rattle high in front of him and yips, holding this pose. The Medicine Man then repeats this routine for each of the six dancers.

8. As soon as the last dancer shouts, the drum booms fast and strong. Each dancer throws his cornstalk into the fire, transfers his rattle to his left hand, picks up the ear of corn, puts it in his mouth, grasping it firmly with his teeth, and whirls into a strenuous dance in the *upright position*. After a moment or two of this a drum cue is given and they go down into the *Sti-yu* step (page 32). If the dancers cannot do this step they may repeat the low crouch as in No. 6 above. Using his judgment as to the time, the drummer signals with four louder beats whereupon the six dancers rise to the upright position and all the other dancers standing around the edges join them in powwow fashion.

9. The finale is signaled by four loud beats: The six lead dancers move to the side of the ring opposite the Council Rock and line up facing it, the corn still in their mouths. The other dancers fall in behind them and hold their cornstalks forward over the heads of the six leads. With heads high and strutting with all style the six lead performers prance across the ring and out the exit, the others following.

ON THE STAGE.—This dance is ideally suited for stage use. The routine as described can easily be adapted. The exit is accomplished by the six lead dancers lining up near the back of the stage with the others behind them, then dancing down stage to the footlights, prancing there for a moment, then turning and exiting, half to the right and half to the left.

Banda Noqai

From the pastime dance of the Shoshoni, called the Banda Noqai, comes perhaps the most spectacular and inspiring routine of the celebration type this book presents. It combines delightfully solo dances, group dancing, and spectacular routine. With good dancing talent it results in a thrilling performance. It is not recommended for beginning dancers.

Certain liberties are taken with the original Indian routine, the better to adapt the dance for use before an audience.

AS IT USED TO BE

The women prepared the Banda Noqai sticks by splitting a stick and inserting a bead or other object in the opening. These they placed before the dancers who were painted with black dots from head to foot and wore black and white painted breechcloths. The dancers danced up to the sticks, trotted away as though in fear of them, and continued thus until at last they grabbed them up. At times between their approaches to the stick they would charge the spectators and pretend to shoot them with the bows and blunt-headed arrows they carried. After they had picked up the sticks, some men standing by would sometimes approach them and throw water at them so as to get some of them wet. The dancers would then retreat a short distance where they danced and tapped their bows or sticks together overhead. As a pastime dance it was all in the spirit of fun.*

PROPERTIES

In place of the split sticks with a bead or other object in the cleft, a more ornamental stick should be made as follows: Cut green sticks a little over an inch in diameter and two feet long, removing the bark so that the white wood shows. To one end of the stick attach inch-wide ribbons so that they hang down one foot as shown in Figure 25. Contrasting colors of ribbons should be used, such as black and yellow on some sticks, red and white on others, etc. The ribbons are attached by driving a one-inch nail in the end of the stick just far enough to hold the ribbons and allowing it

* A reference to this dance may be found in *Anthropological Papers of the American Museum of Natural History*, Vol. XI, Part 7, page 818. Washington: Government Printing Office.

Photograph by Paul Boris

JAMES C. STONE

Photograph by Arthur C. Allen

LAWRENCE RATLIFF

to extend up. To this nail white fluffies are tied as illustrated. The other end of the stick should be sharpened. Ribbons are also wrapped around the stick at intervals of six inches as shown. Four to six sticks will be needed, depending upon the number of lead dancers used.

Figure 25. Banda Noqai Stick

THE DANCE

Four to six lead dancers are needed depending upon the number of sufficiently talented solo performers available. The following instructions assume that six will be used.

If two women dancers are to be had they should be used in the opening scene to put the sticks in place. If not, the opening scene can be eliminated and the sticks placed before the dance starts by a property man. The position of the sticks is indicated by the dots near the fire in Figure 26.

Figure 26. Diagram for the Banda Noqai

1. The two women enter on either side of the Council Rock, each carrying three Banda Noqai sticks laid in the crook of her left arm. They use the Women's Step described on page 40. One moves clockwise around the ring and the other counterclockwise until they pass at the far side. Then they approach the fire and stick the first two sticks in the ground as indicated (those opposite positions 2 and 5). They continue around placing the other sticks, then take positions one either side of the drummer and just in front of him as indicated by the two black dots in Figure 26.

2. All dancers except the six leading performers enter and start dancing as in the Powwow. A few moments of this and the drum hits four louder beats, at which they fade off to the edge of the ring and squat down so as not to block the view.

3. Into the ring come the six lead dancers, prancing with the double toe-heel step, their eyes fixed on the sticks. They move around the ring counterclockwise, shading their eyes with their arms at times as they look, then dance to positions as indicated by the numbers in Figure 26. The dancers are arranged in pairs, 1 and 2 constituting a pair, 3 and 4, etc. They are arranged in order of dancing ability, Numbers 1 and 2 being the poorer dancers and 5 and 6 the best.

4. They dance the following routine, each advance to the sticks being signalled by a louder beat of the drum. By a count is meant a unit of loud and soft beats.

A. 16 counts—Dance back and forth near positions, each with eyes glued on the stick in front of him and focusing attention on it
B. 8 counts—Dance forward to the sticks, throwing arms forward toward it (see page 52)
C. 8 counts—Whirl and trot back to position with the fear step (page 39)
D. 8 counts—Dance in position, eyes on stick
E. 8 counts—Repeat B
F. 8 counts—Repeat C
G. 8 counts—Repeat D
H. 8 counts—Repeat B but this time Number 1 snatches up his stick
I. 8 counts—All except Number 1 trot back to position

Having grabbed his stick, Number 1 dances in solo, while the others mark time, circling the ring with his best performance, holding up his stick at times to display it and occasionally tossing it in the air, then gliding back to his position.

The entire routine (A to I) is then repeated with Number 2 snatching his stick and dancing in solo. This is repeated until all have danced. In executing the routine those who are already holding their sticks continue to advance to the fire nevertheless.

5. Number 6 having returned to position, Numbers 1 and 2 break forth

in *duet*, dancing on their own sides of the ring, playing on each other and attempting to outdance the other. At a drum signal of a louder beat they sweep up to the fire in eight steps, stop, throw their right arms overhead and cross their sticks above the fire. It is necessary that they gauge their time and distance so that both stop in position on the eighth count. They hold this dramatic pose for eight beats of the drum, whirl and trot back to position. Immediately as they do so, Numbers 3 and 4 break into duet, to be followed in turn by 5 and 6.

6. As soon as 5 and 6 break away from the fire all six dancers begin dancing together vigorously, each staying more or less in his own territory. They dance as brilliantly as possible but in the *upright position*. At a drum cue they drop down into the *Sti-yu* step (page 32) or, if unable to do this step, each does the most spectacular step at his command, preferably in a low position such as the full crouch.

7. This continues until in the drummer's judgment it should be terminated, when he hits four louder beats and all of the dancers seated around the edge of the ring leap to their feet and the entire ensemble dances in strenuous powwow.

8. The finale is signalled by four loud beats: All dancers move to the side of the ring opposite the Council Rock, where the six lead dancers line up in a row facing the exit and the others fall in informally behind them. With heads high and Banda Noqai sticks in the air in front of them, the lead dancers prance across to the exit with the others following. Reaching the Council Rock the lead dancers turn right and left, three in one direction and three in the other, and start dancing around the ring again, while the others exit, including the two women. When the two lines meet opposite the Council Rock they form the line again and prance across the ring and out.

ON THE STAGE.—No dance is better adapted for stage use than the Banda Noqai. Some device will need to be worked out to hold the Banda Noqai sticks upright on the floor. No fire is needed—the sticks are merely set up in a circle in the center of the stage. The entire routine is followed as described, with the lesser dancers gathering across the rear of the stage. For the finale the lead dancers form a line at the back of the stage, dance down stage to the footlights, prance there for a moment, then head for the wings, three in one direction and three in the other. Reaching the wings they swing toward the back of the stage allowing the lesser dancers to exit, form the line at the rear and come down stage again and then exit.

Pueblo Comanche Dance

Once in long years past the war-like Comanches raided deep into the land of sun, silence and adobe, and attacked the peace-loving Pueblos. Makers of silver and tillers of desert soil, these quiet village folk had no special talent for war and fell easy prey. Many were taken captive and carried back to Comanche-land, where they lived as did their masters and learned to dance the Comanche way. Upon being released, they taught this way to their homefolk. Since that time the Pueblos have danced "The Comanche."

The dance is a contrast in tempo from very slow to very fast. Opening very slowly with limp, flowing motion, the tempo suddenly is quadrupled with fast, dashing movement, terminating in a frenzy of action, after which the dancers freeze motionless. The secret of its appeal is in these sudden contrasts.

THE DANCE

About eight good dancers are needed. They walk into the ring and stand informally, each by himself, awaiting the drum.

The drumming starts with a very slow, accented two-time, counted *one*-and, *two*-and, etc. By a count is meant the unit of a loud and soft beat, that is, "*one*-and" is one count. The step is the toe-heel, one step being taken to each count.

1. 24 counts—tempo very slow. Slow, graceful toe-heel movement, body limp and flowing, using body weave, arms hanging limp, every effort made to move smoothly and gracefully.

2. 24 counts—tempo quadrupled. Break into very fast toe-heel dancing, mood changing accordingly, dashing, spirited, spectacular. On the 20th count go into a flurry of motion for remaining four counts, a frenzy that contrasts with the fast time as much as does the fast time with the slow, sidestepping on toes rapidly, bending body low, hands out to the sides and fluttering, head shaking. Then freeze in position and hold motionless for equivalent of eight fast beats, drum silent.

3. Repeat 1
4. Repeat 2
5. Repeat 1
6. Repeat 2
7. 24 counts—slow time. Exit with slow motion as in 1.

Each dancer must do his own counting. The 24 counts are best counted in three units of eight. It will facilitate uniform movement if the drum accents the 20th count of the fast series by striking a little louder, indicating that the frenzy is to start.

Two departures from the authentic version may make the dance more acceptable: *First*, if the 24 slow steps are changed to 16, there will be no danger of the dance dragging. 16 slow counts as against 24 fast ones seems just the right balance. *Second*, if the slow exit is eliminated a better climax is achieved. When the dancers are freezing after the last frenzy, a roll of the drum may terminate the dance, whereupon they arise and walk out.

It takes good dancing ability to make extra slow motions pleasing to the eye. Moreover, extra fast dancing is difficult for all but experienced dancers. With average talent, it may be well to change the tempo at the start from extra slow to slow, then double it instead of quadrupling it for the fast series. This eliminates both the extra slow and the extra fast movements, but still provides enough contrast for an interesting dance. In time the two extremes will be mastered.

Oto Rabbit Dance

Always an interesting and entertaining little number, the Rabbit Dance of the Otos fills well a spot where fast dancing is desired.

THE DANCE

Eight to twelve dancers may be used. They enter the ring and stroll along in disinterested fashion awaiting the drumming. When the drumming starts they drop instantly to the right knee and shake the body up and down for 16 counts. Then they arise and dance strenuously for 32 counts.

The drumming is counted *one*-and, *two*-and, each unit of two beats being regarded as one count—that is, "*one*-and" is counted as one count.

1. 16 counts—drumming fast, soft, unaccented. Each dancer drops to his right knee and shakes up and down with much shoulder motion, once to each beat.

2. 32 counts—drumming changes to loud, accented two-time. The dancers leap to their feet and dance strenuously, using the toe-heel or the double toe-heel step, employing brilliant body action but each staying near his original spot.

3. 16 counts—repeat 1

4. 32 counts—repeat 2

5. 16 counts—repeat 1

6. Exit by arising and trotting out

The drumming is fast and the tempo remains constant throughout, although changing in accent and volume from one figure to the next. For the shaking figure it is soft and steady and unaccented, while for the dancing figure it becomes loud and accented in two-time. This indicates the change from one figure to the next, the dancers reacting immediately to the change.

Chapter IV

"I SAW" DANCES AND OTHER SOLOS

SOMETHING THAT one saw, something that he did, some experience he had, re-enacted in a dance—such is the nature of the "I Saw" dance. It is a story dance, a means of telling a tale, of relating an experience. In the old fighting days it was a favorite way of "counting coups," of retelling again the exploits that won honors. Such dances are variously called *"I Saw" dances, story dances, coup dances* and *discovery dances,* the latter name resulting from the fact that most of them are based on the themes of hunting and fighting which involved searching and final discovery.

Any event or story could be used as the basis of an "I Saw" dance, and the dancer was free to interpret it any way he desired within certain conventional limitations. This gives a flexibility to the story dances that is not found in other dances. There is no set routine which tradition demands must be followed each time, since the routine depends of necessity on the story being told. The dancer is thus afforded an opportunity for originality and creativeness in developing the dance. This was true of the dancing Indian in the old days and it is also true of the present-day interpreter of Indian dancing. With the full endorsement of Indian tradition, it permits us to use any suitable story as a basis for an "I Saw" dance, whether or not there is record of its being so used by the Indians, and to interpret it as we choose as long as we confine ourselves to authentic Indian movements and mood.

In some of the dances in this chapter the privilege of the story dancer is assumed in creating dances from Indian stories with no knowledge of their having been so used by the Indians. In other cases the dances are exact descriptions of dances done by Indians. In all cases they are true to type and in full harmony with Indian story-dance tradition.

Here are the solo dances—the group story dances are in the next chapter.

Chippewa Deer Hunter Dance

From my Chippewa friends in the Lake Superior country I learned this attractive dance. A favorite "I Saw" dance of these northern Woodland folk, I have heard it referred to by Indians from the Upper Peninsula of Michigan across to Minnesota and north into Canada.

THE STORY

Long the hunter had roamed the woods, looking, waiting, listening, but all for naught—no sign of deer could he find, no sign at all. Discouraged, tired and thirsty, he came at last to a little stream of cold, refreshing water. He stooped down to drink and as he put his face to the water he drew up in surprise—there in the sand on the bottom of the brook were tracks—deer tracks—clear and distinct, leading upstream. Quickly he drank, and followed upstream with his eyes fixed on the telltale tracks. They left the water and, as he had expected, led up to the hardwood thicket. Stealthily he followed, but only for a few yards—for there in a little opening stood the buck in plain view, his antlered head erect and stately. Long the hunter froze, then cautiously, oh so cautiously, raised his bow and shot.... With joy in his heart and the deer on his back he headed homeward, for now there would be meat in the lodge and hide for many moccasins.

THE DANCE

The drumming is in two-time, medium fast, accented *loud*-soft. The step is the toe-heel or the double toe-heel.

1st Circuit—Dancing in, the hunter starts around the ring counterclockwise. He is hunting and shows it in his actions—he shades his eyes with his arm as he looks in the distance, he fixes his gaze on the ground, he stops and studies the earth, he shoves the leaves and sticks away with his foot, he pushes the bushes aside as he advances. (For the techniques of this various business see page 55.)

2nd Circuit—Finding no signs of the deer he becomes discouraged—the drumming slows down, he stops, shakes his head and lets his shoulders droop; with head hanging and shoulders sagging he advances slowly, uninterested, with no further heart for the hunting. He continues thus until he reaches X in Figure 28. Nearing this point he spreads the bushes aside and looks ahead to discover a stream, advances to it forthwith, drops to his knees, lowers his face to the water and drinks, his hands cupped either side of his mouth. Suddenly his head and shoulders jerk up, his hands out to the sides, in surprise—there in the sandy bottom of the stream are the deer tracks! His hand points to them and his eyes turn upstream following them.

He rises and follows the edge of the stream, his eyes on the ground to his right, his hand pointing to the tracks in the stream bed. A few feet and the tracks leave the water. He follows them with increased stealth, crouching low, he tosses a leaf in the air to ascertain the wind, he stoops and feels of the tracks. Thus he completes the circuit.

3rd Circuit—The tracks get hotter and he continues with ever-increasing alertness. Reaching X he suddenly drops to the ground and freezes, for there, standing at Y, is the deer. The drumming becomes soft, steady, unaccented. For 16 counts he freezes, then with great cautiousness rises to his feet, pulls his bow and shoots. He holds for four counts, then dashes to the fallen deer at Y. (For the detail of the business of freezing and shooting, see page 56.)

Reaching the deer he stoops, examines it for a brief moment, rises and stands in exultation for a second or two, then breaks into a strong dance of celebration, using the double toe-heel step. Twice he circuits the ring in ever-increasing ecstasy and exits.

Discovery Dance

More than any other, the Discovery Dance is referred to repeatedly in the memoirs of those courageous French explorers who invaded the vast wilderness of America from 1600 to 1800. It is mentioned in anthropological writings for tribes all the way across to the Rocky Mountains, Woodland and Plains alike. And more than any other, it is described with enthusiasm growing out of happy memories of delightful entertainment.

As danced in those ancient, dramatic days when fighting was the sport of men and the theme of much of their dancing, the Discovery Dance was a long series of solos, one dancer after another leaping forward to enact his recent exploits as soon as his predecessor relinquished the floor. It is here described as a single solo, the routine developed from descriptions by men who saw it among the Woodland Indians in the 17th Century.* The stealthy entrance is added for dramatic effect.

Striking the Post, described in Chapter III, is really a form of the Discovery Dance, a series of stories told by dancing.

THE DANCE

The dancer carries a tomahawk, or hand ax bedecked with feathers or ribbons.

The Entrance—The drumming is medium-slow and very soft. On hands and feet the dancer creeps into the entrance, sticks his head into view, looks for a moment, then creeps stealthily to the center (X in Figure 27), where he pauses motionless, looking, his eyes scanning the situation. For a long moment he freezes thus, then arises and moves stealthily in crouched position a few feet to his right, where he drops and looks again.

1st Circuit—Searching for the enemy: Satisfied there is no immediate danger, he arises and begins dancing with the double toe-heel step, the drum picking up in speed and volume. Without stops he circles the ring, dancing erect, scanning the distance with his eyes, weaving from side to side at times to look from different angles. Thus he moves counterclockwise around the ring.

---

* For references to this dance and a list of these early writings, see W. B. Kinietz, *The Indians of the Western Great Lakes—1615-1760.* Ann Arbor: University of Michigan Press, 1940.

2nd Circuit—Signs of the enemy: He moves as before but with increased alertness, stopping occasionally to look, shading his eyes with his arm and keeping time by jarring his heel on the ground. Now and then his eyes drop to the ground for tracks but in the main his attention is fixed on the distance, looking in this direction and that, watching for every sound and movement. When halfway around he discovers tracks that forebode danger. He stops, bends down and points to them; he looks up to make sure the enemy is not lurking, he tosses a leaf in the air to estimate the volume and direction of the wind. Continuing, he kicks a stick aside with his foot, he pushes the bushes aside with his arms. (For details of this business see page 55.)

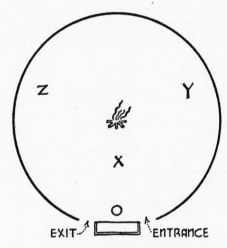

Figure 27. Diagram for the Discovery Dance

3rd Circuit—Discovering the enemy: Fresh tracks warn of immediate danger—his attitude changes, he becomes very intense, alert, ever looking and listening. The drumming becomes softer. He squats and examines the tracks, he takes a few quick, stealthy steps forward and drops again, continuing thus to Y. Here he discovers the enemy located at Z: He drops abruptly to the ground and freezes, his weight on his left foot, his buttocks resting on his left heel, his right leg extending full length toward Z, his eyes fixed on the spot. The drumming is scarcely audible. For 16 counts he holds the freeze, then stealthily shifts his weight forward and creeps up near the fire, sets himself for the leap by crouching as before, this time with his left leg in advance. He raises his tomahawk, lowers it, raises it again and lowers it, raises it a third time and simultaneously lifts his whole body, measuring the distance. He leaps forward and brings his tomahawk down on Z. Throughout the period of measuring the drum crescendos, then stops explosively as he strikes. He drops to his knees, scalps the enemy, stands erect and throws his right arm with the imaginary scalp over his head. For a brief moment he holds this pose, the drumming begins and he breaks into the finale.

Finale—From Z he makes two complete circuits of the ring, dancing with complete ecstasy and unreserved exuberation, calling upon his most spectacular style, dashing forward with leaping, full-bodied vigor, throwing his arm with the scalp up over his head at times. Near the end of his second circuit, when directly across the fire from the Council Rock, he whirls toward the fire, leaps over the top of it spectacularly and exits running.

The Lone Scout

This dance, variously known as The Lone Scout, The Lone Hunter, and The Lone Warrior is probably the most widely used of Indian solo dances because of the popularity given it by Ernest Thompson Seton who published it years ago. It is a typical "I Saw" dance and one of the best of its type. I am indebted to Mr. Seton for it and for the privilege of describing it here.*

THE STORY

Hungry for the honors of war, a young scout prepared to go forth alone to test his cunning against the enemy. With spear and shield he displayed himself in the village, proclaiming aloud his plans and boastfully prophesying great deeds for himself. Once on the warpath his loudness gave way to caution as he studied every sign and listened to every sound. Suddenly he spied one lone sentry of the enemy, quite oblivious to the presence of lurking danger. He crept up with all stealth until within striking distance. He set himself for the kill, raised his spear to leap—when suddenly a sound attracted his attention to the rear. He turned to find he had been tricked into a trap and was surrounded on all sides by the enemy. He darted about seeking a way to freedom, at last discovered an opening and darted through it. As he did so he stopped, turned back and hurled one last defiant war-whoop at the enemy, as much as to say, "Come and get me if you can."

THE DANCE

The dancer carries a spear and shield, as illustrated in Figure 32 and described on page 106.

The Entrance—To a long roll of the drum the dancer leaps into the ring, shield in left hand and spear held high in right: he dashes through the entrance and, once in the ring, makes a long leap and lands near the fire in crouched position, his weight on his right foot and his left extending out in front. As he hits the ground the roll of the drum stops with an explosive boom. There is a moment of dramatic pause—the dancer looks to

* Ernest Thompson Seton, *The Birch Bark Role of the Woodcraft League of America,* page 82. New York: Brieger Press, Inc., 1925.

the right and left, surveying the situation, then slowly rises, transfers his spear to his left hand, raises his right to his mouth and hurls forth a war-whoop. The drum starts a fast two-time, the dancer spins around by turning to his left and then starts out around the ring counterclockwise.

1st Circuit—The show-off in the village: He sweeps around the ring swiftly, head high and confident, boastful and strutting. The emphasis here is on a sweeping circuit, without pauses. The step is the double toe-heel.

2nd Circuit—Continuation of the show-off: He weaves back and forth, zigzagging from the fire to the edge of the ring. He swings the spear in the air, makes playful passes at the crowd with it. He struts and prances, and in general displays himself.

3rd Circuit—On the warpath: He has left the village now and is in the danger country. The drumming slows down to medium fast. He crouches a little and moves more cautiously, stopping now and then and shading his eyes with his shield, the better to penetrate the distance. His gaze follows the ground for tracks. He peers in this direction and that. He sticks his spear into things and picks them up for examination.

4th Circuit—Following the trail: He discovers the enemy trail—he drops suddenly to the ground pointing to it, he looks ahead to see where it goes. He picks up a leaf and tosses it in the air to discover the direction of the wind. He moves ahead with great caution and alertness. He continues thus to X in Figure 28, at which point he discovers the enemy who is located at Y. He drops to the ground and freezes, facing Y, his right leg extending full length toward Y, and his weight on his left foot.

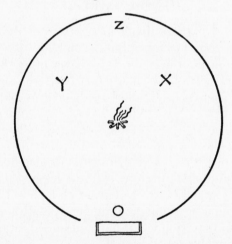

Figure 28. Diagram for The Lone Scout and The Chippewa Deer
Hunter Dances

The Charge—The drumming becomes soft, lest the enemy hear, changing from a two-time to a steady unaccented fast beat. He holds the freeze in dramatic pause for 16 beats, then very cautiously advances so as to take his weight on his right foot, and extends his left in front, thus assuming a charging position. He raises his spear as if to hurl it, lowers it, raises it again and lowers it. For the third time he raises it—the drumming increases in volume—he rises slowly and is about to leap when the drum booms explosively and grows silent. He whirls and looks behind to discover the enemy. Startled he looks in all directions, finding himself trapped in ambush. The drum beats rapidly, he scurries quickly across to Y with a short, sidestepping foot motion, then back to X, looking in all directions for an exit. He repeats the scurrying across and back twice, then suddenly spots the exit at Z, turns and darts through it. He stops in the exit, turns back into the ring, pauses and hurls a war-whoop, then whirls around and dashes out the exit.

If the council ring does not have an exit at Z, the Council Rock exit may be used.

Ish-i-buz-zhi

This powerful dance was developed from the Omaha story of Ish-i-buz-zhi as recorded by Alice C. Fletcher in 1900.* So far as I knew the story was never used by the Indians as an "I Saw" dance, but it might well have been, for it is type-perfect for such use.

As here given the story follows the original in the main but with certain minor alterations to facilitate the dance.

THE STORY

Once in the long ago there dwelt in a village of the Omaha Indians a boy named Ish-i-buz-zhi. He was a queer lad, never associating with other boys, never playing or hunting with them, never using the bow and arrow. His only friends were the old women who came to gossip with his mother. Little wonder that such as he should be ridiculed by old and young alike.

In those long winter evenings when the old men gathered by his father's fireside to relate again the tales of the long ago, telling of the heroes of bygone years, Ish-i-buz-zhi would sit back in a dark corner listening, absorbing every word. He noted that these ancient heroes never fought with bow and arrow but with clubs. Thus it happened that Ish-i-buz-zhi resolved that he, too, would learn to fight with a club. Finding a club that suited his fancy he practiced long and diligently with it. When the village boys discovered him they laughed at him and hurled biting jabs of ridicule, but Ish-i-buz-zhi kept his own counsel.

Came the day when the village was at war. Excitement and much shouting filled the air as the young men prepared for the warpath. Ish-i-buz-zhi, too, was gripped with intense desire to fight for his people, but the dis-

* Alice C. Fletcher, *Indian Story and Song from North America*, p. 14. Boston: Hale, Cushman and Flint, 1900.

heartening thought came that he could not—he did not know how—in this hour of need his club was useless to him. He threw it away, discouraged. But that night his secretive nature led him to creep up to the council of chiefs and listen to the plans for attack. Taking in every word, he resolved that even though he could only fight with a club he would fight nevertheless. He found his club again and, unbeknown to others, slipped away toward the enemy country, fortified by the reports of the scouts he had heard.

Catching sight of the enemy warriors with their famous chief to their fore, he awaited his chance and rushed upon the chief, overthrew him and killed him with his club. Just then his own war party came upon the scene and saw with amazement what he had done—how, alone and single-handed, armed only with a club, the might of his arm had killed the enemy chief and scattered the warriors.

Ish-i-buz-zhi lived to be a very old man, and he was always somewhat queer, but never again was he laughed at. Always his wisdom was sought in time of trouble.

THE DANCE

A strong, talented dancer is indicated. The properties consist of three clubs laid at different points in the dancing ring. The drumming is in two-time, the step the toe-heel or the double toe-heel.

The dance begins at the point where Ish-i-buz-zhi resolves to learn to fight with a club.

1st Circuit—Looking for a club: Ish-i-buz-zhi dances quietly into the ring and starts around counterclockwise. He seeks a club for himself and looks about the woods for it. He comes upon the first club, picks it up, weighs it and swings it, finds it not to his liking and discards it. He proceeds to the next club, finds it unsatisfactory and tosses it aside. The third club strikes his fancy—he grips it, tests it and finds it good.

2nd Circuit—Practicing with the club: He learns to use it well, swinging it vigorously in his hand to the rhythm of the dancing. He dashes to the left and swings it at an imaginary enemy, then repeats to the right. He dashes forward and hits the ground hard with it. He tosses it in the air a foot or two and catches it. He repeats these movements as fancy strikes him in making the circuit.

3rd Circuit—Ridiculed by the boys: He stops suddenly while practicing in the woods and looks back—the boys of the village have discovered him. He hides his club behind his back lest they see it, sneaks away a few feet with the fear step (page 39), stops, cringing, holding his hand over his face, palm out. Under the taunting and ridicule, he backs away farther and repeats, motioning the boys away with his hand. He changes hands, holding the club behind him with his other hand, and shoving them away again. He continues to retreat thus until halfway around the ring, at which point his tormentors leave him. He returns to the toe-heel step and dances a short distance, pauses and looks back to make sure the boys are gone, then continues practicing with his club to complete the circuit.

4th Circuit—The news of war: War breaks out and the village is seething with excitement. Ish-i-buz-zhi hears the shouting, he stops and looks back, standing erect and head high. Gripped by the excitement he throws his arm overhead, whirls about and dances strenuously; he stops again, looking across the ring, puts his hand to his mouth as if to shout the news; he throws his hand overhead as if to motion to others to come along. But his dance of excitement is short-lived—as he reaches the point marked X in Figure 29, the depressing thought comes that he cannot fight . . . he does not know how—his club is useless to him. He stops at X, his head hanging and shoulders sagging, his arms limp at his sides, the club hanging in his right hand. For eight counts he stands there, then lets the club slip from his hand to the ground and dances slowly forward in the same dejected manner. Thus he continues to Y.

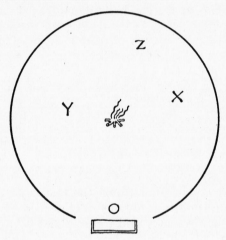

Figure 29. Diagram for Ish-i-buz-zhi

Here the idea comes to him that he can creep up to the war council of chiefs and listen to their plans. He raises his knuckle to his mouth, thinks for a moment, then turns and dances rapidly back toward Z, at which point the war council is in session. Nearing it he creeps cautiously, drops to all fours, raises his hand to his ear, and listens intently for 12 counts.* He shakes his fist emphatically, resolving that, even though he can only fight with a club, he will fight nevertheless. He retraces his steps to X, picks up his club, turns and goes counterclockwise to complete the circuit, trying out his club as he does so.

5th Circuit—Meeting the enemy: He starts on the warpath, moving cautiously, looking for tracks, pushing bushes aside, etc., continuing thus until he gets to X. From this point he sees the enemy approaching in the direc-

* By a count is meant a unit of loud and soft beat, such as "one-and."

tion of Y, their chief to the fore. He drops to the ground and freezes, his weight on his left foot and his right leg extending toward Y. For 16 counts he freezes, then slowly shifts his weight to his front leg and extends his left leg toward Y. He holds the club out behind him and gets set for the leap. Once set he holds for 12 beats, then leaps forward, dashes to Y and swings his club down hard. He drops to the ground, takes the scalp and holds it dramatically overhead for a moment, then breaks into a strong powwow to complete the circuit.

6th Circuit—The dance of celebration: Using the double toe-heel step he dances with all the power and brilliance at his command, throwing his right hand with the scalp overhead at times. The circuit completed he prepares for the dramatic finale: A loud beat of the drum gives him his cue, after which the drumming changes from two-time to four-time, counted *one*-two-three-four. The loud beat indicates that in 12 counts he must strike a dramatic pose before the fire: On 1 he drops his right hand with the scalp low and behind, then in 12 counts he prances up to the fire in front of the Council Rock, and, on 12, throws his hand with the scalp high in the air and stops, holding the pose for 8 counts. He drops his hand and makes a complete spin to the left, taking 12 counts to it, and then throws his hand up again on 12. Holding the pose for 8 counts, he drops his hand and throws it up again on 4 counts. This he repeats, and repeats again, coming up on 4 counts, rising higher on his toes each time. On the third time up the drum hits an explosive boom and becomes silent. There he stands in dramatic, triumphant pose for a moment. The drum rolls, he ducks down and darts out the exit beside the Council Rock.

The Falling Eagle

He who has seen an eagle soaring gracefully against the high blue dome of heaven, he who knows the symbolism of this fighting chief of the sky, will understand this dance. Its mood will need no description.

It is not a typical "I Saw" dance of the fighting or hunting type, nor is it based on a dance as done by the Indians, but its harmony with the Indian spirit is obvious.

THE STORY

On a lazy summer day a red-brown boy lay on a mesa top, his face turned up to the vastness of the blue above, his eyes on a slowly soaring eagle. Transfixed by the floating lightness, the effortless, soaring gracefulness, his mind drifted dreamily, far away from all reality ... his spirit was high up yonder, soaring, floating. Abruptly a shot rang out—a shot from a white man's rifle. The eagle reared, staggered for a moment, his left wing drooping. Desperately he fought with his one remaining wing, then reeled earthward ... he struck the ground with a sickening thud, quivered for a moment and then was still.

THE DANCE

Much depends upon the dancer. Only an unusually sensitive spirit, a delicately graceful body can truly portray the mood. The dancer wears eagle wings and tail, the construction of which is clearly shown in Figure 30. The drumming is soft, steady, unaccented, medium fast. The step is a light graceful toe-trot, done without jar to create a feeling of soaring and gliding.

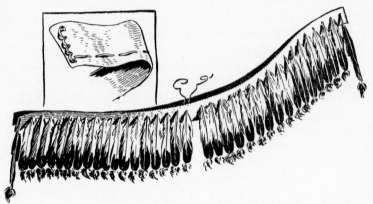

Figure 30. Wings for the Eagle

1st Circuit—The dancer sails in with wings outspread, moving counter-clockwise. He glides one-fourth of the way around the ring and then floats around in a small circle, about six feet in diameter, the floating effect being achieved by the light toe-trot and the spread wings. Completing this, he soars over to the halfway mark and repeats the circle, then to the three-quarter mark and repeats it again.

2nd Circuit—In front of the Council Rock he goes into a long figure-of-8, dipping his wings as he makes the turns and floating effortlessly. He repeats this figure-of-8 movement at each of the four winds as he makes the circuit of the ring.

3rd Circuit—He soars along as before with circles and figure-of-8's until halfway around, that is, across from the Council Rock. At this point he sees the hunter with the gun on the ground below. He stops abruptly, facing the fire, wings spread and looking downward, his eyes round and staring. The drumming becomes faster and increases in volume. For 16 counts he stands there looking. He begins trembling, rising higher and higher on his toes. He backs up two steps, raising his wings a few inches, stops and trembles for four counts, takes two more steps backward, raising his wings still higher, trembling more violently, his eyes growing larger. The drum hits with an explosive thud. He stretches to full length in the air, then his left wing collapses as his body bends forward, his right wing high in the air. For a moment he stands there staggering. The drum slows down. He takes two faltering steps to the left and stops, his right wing fighting to keep him up. He continues thus to the left, staggering and stopping, until he has made three such stops. He drops to his knees, his right wing feebly in motion, then falls prostrate. His wing flaps twice, he trembles from head to foot for a moment and then all is still. For a long moment he lies there . . . the drum rolls and he arises and quietly slips out the exit.

Chippewa Tomahawk Dance

This dance I witnessed several years ago, done by I-in-gi-ge-jig (Invisible Blue Sky), an elderly Chippewa of the Lac du Flambeau Reservation in northern Wisconsin. It is not an "I Saw" dance. It does not tell a story, although it has much of story business in it. Rather it is a solo in which the chief interest centers around the handling of a tomahawk. In capable hands it becomes a memorable number.

THE DANCE

A tomahawk is needed. A scout ax may be made to look the part if strips of fur are wound around the handle and a small feather or two, or strips of ribbon attached to it.

1st Circuit—With tomahawk in hand, the dancer enters, using the toe-heel or double toe-heel step, and starts around the ring counterclockwise. He dances erect and proud but holds the tomahawk close into his side and makes no effort to display it. He continues thus until he reaches the point marked X in Figure 31, where he bends down and unobtrusively sticks the tomahawk in the ground. He does not stop to do this, merely stooping as he dances along; he does not look down at the spot nor look back at the tomahawk after placing it—there is no flourish about it at all, no effort to attract attention to the movement, and once placed, the tomahawk is forgotten and the dancer goes on his way.

2nd Circuit—He dances along, displaying himself with pleasing style until he reaches Y, from which point he sees the tomahawk at X and begins playing upon it: He stops abruptly as if startled, looks at the tomahawk for eight counts, then bends down and looks for four counts, rises and looks again from another angle. He raises his arm to shade his eyes, the better to see it. Then he starts dancing back and forth, going to the left for four steps, to the right for four steps, raising one hand and the other to shade his eyes. After four such sidewise trips he advances swiftly to the tomahawk, throwing his arms toward it as described on page ooo. Reaching it he turns and runs away from it with the fear step (page 39), looking back over his shoulder. He repeats the whole affair with sidewise movements, approaching, and retreating. He repeats again but this time he advances with much greater speed, swoops down and quickly grabs the tomahawk.

3rd Circuit—Once the tomahawk is in his hands he becomes a different person—his dancing becomes more animated and spectacular. His whole interest is centered on the tomahawk and his whole purpose is to display it. He holds it high overhead and looks at it. He holds it in front at face level for a few steps, steady and without jerks so that it can be seen distinctly, then he reverses it, that is, twirls it in his hand so that the blade points in the other direction. He alternates such quick motions and steady pauses, the quick twirls attracting attention to the tomahawk and the pauses enabling the audience to see it clearly. He passes it from one hand to the other. He holds it high, low, and at all angles, all the time dancing with animation. Thus he makes the one full circuit.

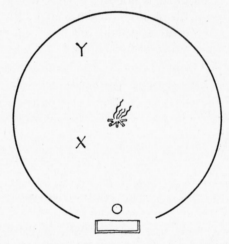

Figure 31. Diagram for the Tomahawk Dance

4th Circuit—He begins tossing the tomahawk in the air and catching it. He throws it across from one hand to the other, tosses it straight up a foot or two and catches it as it falls. After each toss he holds it steady for a moment so that it can be seen. Nearing the end of the circuit he tosses it higher and higher.

Finale—The circuit completed, he prances in front of the Council Rock for a moment in brilliant flourish before exiting. Back and forth he goes, looking at the crowd, shading his eyes with his tomahawk hand, holding the hatchet up and looking at it, shading his eyes again, bringing into play all the animation, body style and showmanship at his command. He turns as if to exit, whirls back and repeats, then darts off the scene.

Should the tomahawk be dropped in tossing it, the dancer must not admit the accident but make it appear to be part of the dance. As soon as he misses it he turns and trots away from the spot without looking at it, whirls toward it, stops and looks, then repeats the business of approaching and running away before picking it up.

Rattle Dance

To the dancing Redman, rattles are ever-popular, carried whenever permissible. They add sound and emphasis to the already vigorous, virile movements of the dance. They spur the dancer to increased effort, their clean, sharp clicking producing clean, sharp movement. They intoxicate him with the will to dance. The same dance somehow looks different once the dancer has rattles in his hands.

This is not a story dance, rather a solo in which the unique feature and focus of interest is the handling of rattles.

Two Indian rattles are needed, preferably gourd rattles. These can be made easily, or purchased inexpensively from Indian craft shops (see Chapter XVIII).

THE DANCE

1st Circuit—With a rattle in each hand and using the toe-heel and the double toe-heel steps, the dancer prances in and goes counterclockwise around the ring. From the start he dances strongly, in typical powwow style, but always in upright position, shaking the rattles with each beat of the drum but holding them close into the body and making no effort to display them. In this circuit the emphasis is on the dancing movements and not on the rattles.

2nd Circuit—The rattles come into play in pronounced fashion. The dancer becomes more vigorous, using more spectacular movements, but still remains upright. He shakes the rattles, flourishing them in all directions, to the sides, in front, high, low, always with graceful but emphatic motion, making them speak loudly. To the staccato click of the rattles the arms and body react with sharp, emphatic motions. With a kick-turn (page 28) he spins around, holding his outside arm high in the air as he pivots and *whirring* the rattle rapidly; he follows the pivot with a backward glide (page 27) in which the rattles are held in front at waist level and shaken. These motions are mingled at will in circling the ring.

3rd Circuit—From the upright position he drops abruptly into a semi-crouch, holding the rattles down toward the ground and shaking them vigorously. He shoves both rattles between his legs and out to the side behind him, he holds one arm overhead and looks up at it while keeping the other down, he reverses his hands and repeats. No progress is made while this is going on but the heels are jarred up and down to the drumming. A moment of this and he rises upright, prances forward a few feet, then drops to a semi-crouch and repeats. Four stops of this type are made in circling the ring.

4th Circuit—He goes into a *full crouch* (page 45), reaching way down to the ground with the rattles and shaking them hard at the ground as if to beat it. He jars his heels strenuously, ringing his bells loudly. All the emphasis is down, down, down onto the ground. A moment of this and he rises full height and, with his rattles shaking at chest height, prances forward a few feet, then suddenly drops to the full crouch again and repeats. Four such crouches are used in making the circuit.

The circuit completed, he goes into a full crouch in front of the exit, in a finale of frenzy with the rattles. Coming out of it, he throws himself erect with his right arm high overhead and in front, strikes a dramatic pose and stops. During this final rally the drumming increases steadily in volume and as he stops it booms explosively and goes quiet. For a moment he stands there in dramatic pose, the drum rolls, and he whirls and darts out.

Spear and Shield Dance

An age-old dancing theme, this—and for good reason! Is anything more deserving of respect than the spear, loved of old as symbol of the glad game of fighting? And is anything more colorful in the hands of a dancer? Of all things Indian, nothing that could be carried is so decorative, so ornamental, so potent in eye appeal. And nothing lends itself so exquisitely to picturesque handling, its plumes and feathers waving to augment its graceful flow. Little wonder that its popularity ranged from southwest Pueblo to northern Plains.

Not a story dance in the sense of telling a specific yarn, it is nevertheless made of the same sort of stuff, based as it is on the warrior's handling of his spear.

PROPERTIES

The spear and shield are illustrated in Figure 32. The shaft of the spear is six-and-one-half feet long, made of white cedar or other soft wood in order that it may be as light as possible to facilitate unstrained and graceful handling. A spear heavily feathered as indicated in the drawing is the type best suited for dancing. The shield may be made of canvas over a barrel hoop. The war shields of the Indians made of heavy rawhide were not used for dancing purposes but were replaced by a light ceremonial shield of similar appearance, made of buckskin over a slender hoop. In another book, *Woodcraft*, I have described the making of these items in detail.*

A small tripod of poles is built to stand five feet high and is placed at the edge of the council ring at the point marked Y in Figure 34. The shield is hung and the spear leaned against it as shown in Figure 33.

* Bernard S. Mason, *Woodcraft*, page 408. New York: A. S. Barnes & Company, 1939.

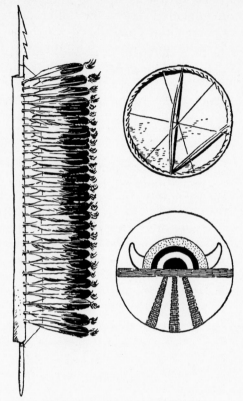

Figure 32. Spear and Shield

Figure 33. Tripod Support for Spear and Shield

THE DANCE

The Entrance—The dancer dances in at the right of the Council Rock and starts counterclockwise, but no sooner does he reach X (Figure 34) that he spots the spear on the tripod. He stops and freezes for eight counts, shades his eyes with his arm and looks for four more counts, then starts playing upon it: He dances back and forth sidewise to the spear, four steps in each direction, and after four such trips advances to the spear throwing his arms toward it (for details see page 51). Reaching it, he turns and runs back with the fear step (page 39) looking back over his shoulder. He repeats this twice, and on the third trip grabs the spear and shield, putting the shield on his left arm and holding the spear in his right at the middle of the shaft so that it is balanced.

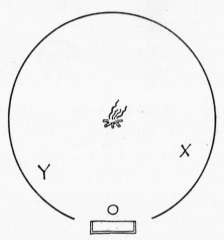

Figure 34. Diagram for the Spear and Shield Dance

1st Circuit—He places his right hand on his hip so that the spear is approximately parallel with the ground but with the pointed end slightly upward. This position of the spear contributes to a proud, prancing style. Erect and with head high, he prances around the ring with the double toe-heel step, following a grapevine course that weaves into the fire and out to the edge of the ring.

2nd Circuit—Taking his hand from his hip he holds the spear naturally, dancing with the body weave (page 47) allowing the spear to sway naturally as more or less incidental to the body motion. As yet the spear play is conservative, there being no conspicuous flourishing of it, the emphasis remaining on the dancing with the spear as incidental.

3rd Circuit—He brings the spear into full play, waving it in figure-of-8 motion in front of him as in Figure 35, turning his wrist so that the point of the spear is always leading. He continues thus halfway around the ring, then goes into still larger figure-of-8 motions with the spear carried far back to his sides, making the circular motions at his side rather than in front, crossing it over in front of him from one side to the other. The motion of the spear must be a graceful and sweeping one, unstrained and in full harmony with the dancing motions of the body.

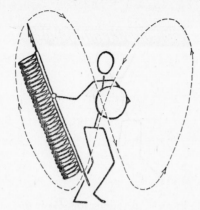

Figure 35. Figure-of-8 Motion with Spear

4th Circuit—Varying these motions he goes into occasional glides (page 27). With spear held straight up and down in front of him and close to his body, he glides backward shaking the spear sidewise with his hand with each step so as to flap the feathers. Again, he holds it parallel to the ground as he glides back, his hand close in to his stomach. He repeats this with the spear at an angle of 45 degrees to the ground, gliding back with it thus for a few steps, and then reverses the angle for a few more steps. Combining his figure-of-8 weave and the glides he completes the circuit.

5th Circuit—Here he starts making playful charges at the crowd, always with the same graceful, flowing motion. With spear overhead in charging position (Figure 36) he prances up to the edge of the ring as though charging the people sitting there, turns with a graceful sway of the spear in the air and trots back toward the fire. He repeats this about four times in making the circuit, swinging the spear in figure-of-8 fashion between times.

6th Circuit—With the spear in charging position he sweeps swiftly around the ring to the halfway mark (directly opposite the Council Rock) where he stops suddenly and looks across at the exit as if something startled him there. He holds his freeze for 16 counts, then moves back and forth in a figure-of-8 course, sidewise to the exit, always with his eyes glued on it, shading his eyes first with the shield, then with the spear. He makes four such figure-of-8's, gaining momentum all the time, then raises the spear overhead in charging position, dashes across the ring, leaps the fire and exits.

When the audience is seated around the edges of the ring, great care must be taken not to approach too close with the spear. Concerned only with his dance, the dancer often unconsciously approaches so close as to cause the spectators concern less the spear hit them. This creates the situation in which it is impossible to enjoy the beauty of the dance.

If the dance proves too long for the endurance of the dancer, Circuit 2 may be eliminated.

Figure 36. Charging Position

ON THE STAGE.—When done on the stage each circuit of the ring as described should be regarded as a unit of the dance. Rather than circling the stage the dancer moves about at random, blending one unit after another into the dance. The dance concluded with the charging motions of Circuit 5, after which the spear is placed on the hip for a strutting exit.

Pueblo Spear and Shield Dance

This is the picturesque Spear and Shield Dance of the Laguna Pueblo Indians from whom it was learned, presented with minor adaptations. Involving two spear-aimed warriors it is out of place in this chapter of solo dances, but is here included because of its close relationship to the Spear and Shield solo just described. It has long been a favorite because of the beauty of plume-bedecked spears gracefully waving in the air.

Two spears and two shields are needed made as illustrated in Figure 32. The spears should be well-plumed as shown. Should a plain unfeathered lance be used the dance would lose one of its chief appeals.

THE DANCE

The step is an ordinary skip as in the skipping of children, done lightly and gracefully. The drumming is in medium tempo, accented in two-time. The dancers enter from opposite sides of the ring if there are two entrances, otherwise one enters and is followed shortly by the other.

Holding the spear at arm's length and waving it gracefully across in front of the body in a figure-of-8 motion, the dancers circle the ring and

maneuver until they are on opposite sides from each other as indicated by
1 and 2 in Figure 37. Here they discover each other and begin the war play
on each other.

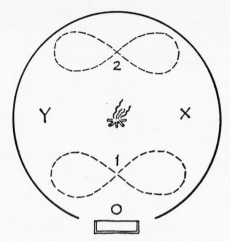

Figure 37. Diagram for the Spear and Shield Duet

1. With spear held at shoulder height in charging position (Figure 36)
they skip along a figure-of-8 course as indicated by the lines in Figure 37,
both going in the same direction and moving parallel to each other. Then
they charge each other by sweeping up to X, with the spears in charging
position overhead, but just before coming together they whirl and retreat,
allowing the spear to flow gracefully through the air at arm's length on the
turn.

2. They follow the figure-of-8 course again, then charge each other at
Y in the same way.

3. They follow the figure-of-8 course and charge at X, this time dodg-
ing to one side and passing each other, changing sides of the ring.

4. Repeat 1

5. Repeat 2

6. Repeat 3, returning to their original sides of the ring again.

7. They follow the figure-of-8 course and charge each other at X, this
time Number 2 whirling and retreating and Number 1 following, his spear
overhead and thrusting it downward at him on each step. When Number 2
reaches his own side he whirls back as if to attack and Number 1 turns and
dances back.

8. They follow the figure-of-8 course and charge at Y, repeating 7
with Number 1 retreating and Number 2 pursuing.

9. They follow the figure-of-8 course and charge each other at X,
Number 2 turning and retreating and Number 1 pursuing with his spear
at hip level and prodding at his rear, chasing him all the way around to Y,
at which point Number 2 reverses his direction and chases Number 1 in

the same manner all the way back to his own side, where Number 1 whirls around and Number 2 retreats to his own side.

10. They follow the figure-of-8 and charge at X, Number 2 turning and retreating and Number 1 following, chasing him all around to Y. Here Number 2 turns around and starts back, Number 1 dodges him, turns and pursues. With Number 1 right behind him and his spear menacing him, Number 2 follows his figure-of-8 course on his own side twice with ever-increasing speed, then throws both arms overhead, dashes toward the fire, leaps over it and exits, Number 1 following with his spear overhead in charging position.

It is the rule in spear dances that one must never turn his face away from his enemy's spear. In retreating the head should be turned so as to face the spear constantly.

Chapter V

DRAMATIC STORY DANCES

THESE DRAMATIC story dances differ from the "I Saw" dances of the last chapter in that they are group dances rather than solos. They are of the same type and kind, however, and grant the same privileges of freedom of interpretation that is characteristic of all story dances.

These are all vigorous, rousing numbers, calling for toe-heel dancing of the powwow type, and, like the powwows, are useful as climaxes of sound, motion and color.

Chippewa Brave Man's Dance

The Brave Man's Dance carries us back in spirit on the trail of the long ago to those wild romantic days of freedom and fighting. At the Lac du Flambeau reservation in northern Wisconsin I first saw it, danced by old Aniwabi (Sits Farther Along), and in later years by his son I-in-gi-ge-jig (Invisible Blue Sky). I have seen it in various places among the Wisconsin Chippewas.

True to story-dance tradition, the routine varied in detail from time to time, and place to place, depending on the whims of the dancers, but always it was the same story, and told in essentially the same way. The years have routinized this story dance to a greater degree than is typical.

The Brave Man's Dance has been unusually popular among our present-day dancers in the Redman's way. It is an extremely useful dance, for two reasons: first, its dramatic story is simple and easy to enact because it calls for *walking* and not dancing, and second, this story is preliminary to a vigorous powwow—is, in fact, a dramatic means of introducing a powwow. The dance thus combines the dramatic appeal of the story dance and the dashing spectacle of the powwow.

The version here given is as learned from I-in-gi-ge-jig. The directions follow exactly the dance as it was done.

THE STORY

Two warriors, acting as scouts in advance of a war party, cautiously move along in the danger country. They pick up the trail and follow it

113

stealthily until they discover a lone enemy warrior. Creeping up, they send the arrow that ends his days. The war party, arriving in time to see the kill, dash forward to celebrate the triumph.

THE DANCE

Stick a tomahawk in the ground directly opposite the Council Rock entrance to the dancing ring (see Figure 38). This symbolizes the enemy warrior. There is no drumming at the start of the dance.

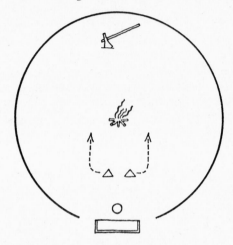

Figure 38. Diagram for the Chippewa Brave Man's Dance

Two dancers enter walking and start around the ring counterclockwise. Relaxed and at ease they move along leisurely but with their eyes on the ground in search of tracks and signs, pausing to push the leaves aside with their feet now and then. Passing the tomahawk without seeing it, they suddenly discover tracks—they stoop and examine the earth, look inquiringly at each other and then down to the tracks again. With frequent pauses to study the telltale signs they move along with increasing caution, their steps stealthy, their eyes ever-seeing, their ears ever-hearing. When directly in front of the Council Rock, they suddenly drop to the ground as one man and freeze, their eyes fixed on the tomahawk (Figure 38).

For six to eight seconds they hold the freeze. The leader of the two then raises his right hand very cautiously and motions his partner to the right. He himself creeps a little to the left, far enough so that he can see past the fire to the tomahawk, and his partner moves a corresponding distance to the right. Then both creep forward with all stealth until near the fire, where the leader rises slowly to his feet, his partner remaining crouched. The leader raises his imaginary bow with his left hand, pulls the string with his right, aims for five seconds in dramatic pause, then shoots (see page 56 for method). Simultaneously the drummer strikes the drum with an explosive boom, the partner emits a war-whoop, leaps forward and grabs the tomahawk.

No sooner does the war-whoop ring out than a chorus of whoops sound behind the Council Rock and into the ring dash a dozen or more warriors. The drum strikes up in fast tempo and a strong dance of celebration is on, which follows the full course of the Powwow (page 62) and ends in the usual manner.

VARIATION.—Although usually done as described, the opening episode may be danced instead of walked. Using the toe-heel step the two dancers move through the routine with the same sort of interpretation used in the "I Saw" dances.

ON THE STAGE.—If the dance is on the stage instead of in the council ring, the tomahawk is placed near the front right. Two warriors enter from the left, circle the stage, and spot the enemy from the back left. They creep to the center to shoot. The main body of warriors then enter from the left.

Chippewa Scalp Dance

Of true ancient vintage, this magnificent dance portrays again, and with unsurpassed brilliance, the oft-told tale of the hunting down of the enemy and the kill.

Boastful of their exploits, with the flush of victory still in their cheeks, the returning Chippewas danced lustily before their village folk, a rhythmic re-enactment of the high daring that brought the shout of victory.

In the Lake Superior country "dancing the scalp" involved three phases or episodes which together constituted the dance: *

1. The pre-fight ceremony: with the warrior-dancers sitting in a circle, their chief smoked the pipe and offering it in usual fashion to the Four Winds, and then to each dancer for one puff, after which he addressed the war party, invoking the aid of the One Above, and calling upon his men for courage. Then followed the Chippewa War Dance (page 136).

2. The re-enactment of the fight, with the warriors dancing out the story of what happened.

3. Competition for the scalp, a sort of dancing game in which the scalp is placed upon a short stick in the ground, with the warriors dancing in a circle around it; when the drum stopped they made a dash for it, each trying to secure it.

In the old days of fighting the story part of the dance (section 2) was always different, depending on what happened in the fight that was being celebrated and re-enacted. But with the passing of those colorful days, it became more or less standardized and continued as a spectacle, although,

* As learned from I-in-gi-ge-jig.

as in all story dances, liberties were given the imagination and ingenuity of the dancers in telling the story. It became the story of an historic fight, always the same in its major routine, but with the details left to the whim of the dancers.

Although the ceremony may be done in its entirety, it is the story part (section 2) that is most often seen—it is lifted out and done as a dance by itself. That is the dance described here. The competition for the scalp is often used as another dance and is described in this book on page 219 in Chapter XIII.

THE DANCE

The splendor of the spectacle that is the Scalp Dance emanates largely from the fact that it is a group dance in which all dancers make precisely the same motions at the same time. It goes without saying that gifted dancers can lift it to a higher level of dramatic appeal than lesser ones. Its full beauty blooms when a group of accomplished performers develop a teamwork that enables them to move as one man. The following description varies from the authentic version in its uniformity of motion and in certain details of arrangements to facilitate such movement without undue rehearsal.

Eight dancers give the best results, arranged in the form of an arrowhead:

<pre>
            1

        2   5
       3   6
      4   8   7
</pre>

The leader who sets the style is in the Number 1 position and the others are in a compact group behind, so close they almost touch each other. The arrowhead arrangement is important because it enables everyone to see the leader, who gives certain cues and whose motions are copied by the others in follow-the-leader fashion. This permits uniform movement without the endless rehearsal that otherwise would be needed. A group with good teamwork can follow its leader's motions with such instantaneous precision that all motions seems to be simultaneous.

The group moves around the area counterclockwise. The step is the toe-heel or the double toe-heel. The drumming is moderately fast to fast, depending upon the capacity of the dancers, accented *loud*-soft.

The dance consists of five circuits of the dancing ring:

1st Circuit—Enter to right of the Council Rock (Figure 39). Dance with body upright, head high and shoulders back, looking into distance—proud and full of self-assurance. Make the circuit of the ring until opposite the entrance again.

2nd Circuit—Go into the body weave (page 47) looking ahead all the time. The leader sets the weave and the others follow in unison. Make the full circuit in this way.

3rd Circuit—The searching for the enemy starts: Raise the hand and shade the eyes for four steps, then repeat with the other hand. Point at the ground with the right hand for four steps, then straighten and point in the distance. Hold the right hand forward, palm of hand flat to ground and look at the ground. Repeat any and all of these movements in making the circuit. Each motion is instigated by the leader and copied instantly.

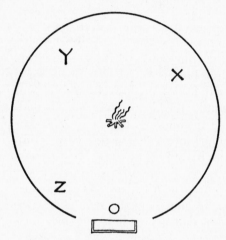

Figure 39. Diagram for the Chippewa Scalp Dance

4th Circuit—Repeat 3 until the point marked X in Figure 39 is reached. Eight steps before reaching this point the leader turns both right and left hands out a little in an inconspicuous signal to indicate that in eight steps a dramatic stop is to be made by all in unison. Stop suddenly by whirling toward the fire and stand in dramatic pose, right foot in advance, head high and shoulders back, looking across the fire into the distance as though something attracted attention there. Keep right heel tapping to drumming and hold pose for 16 taps, then swing into usual formation and complete circuit as in 3.

5th Circuit—Continue as in 3 with increased alertness until point Y is reached. It is here that the enemy is sighted, located at point Z. Eight steps before Y the cue is given as before. Suddenly all dancers drop to the ground in unison as follows: Squat with buttocks resting on right heel, shoving left leg full-length in front, pointing it toward Z, knee straight; drop right hand to the ground behind for support, and extend the left arm full-length in front pointing at Z. Freeze in this position.

As dancers drop the drumming changes from an accented *loud*-soft to a steady fast beat, accented on every *eighth* beat. In this cautious moment the drumming is soft lest the enemy hear.

16 Counts—Hold freeze
  8 counts—Shift weight to front or left foot by moving body slowly
         forward and pulling right foot up beside left, still remaining
         crouched
  8 counts—Rise slowly to erect standing position
  8 counts—Hold motionless, looking at enemy
  8 counts—Raise left hand with imaginary bow
  8 counts—Raise right hand slowly and grip bow string
  8 counts—Pull bow string back slowly
  8 counts—Aim
  1 count —Shoot (see page 56 for method)

The slowness of the rising and shooting provides the pause necessary for
dramatic effect. As the bow is raised and aimed, the drumming crescendos
and, as the shot is fired, booms explosively and becomes silent. The dancers
pause for three seconds, the drum rolls and they dash to the imaginary
enemy. The leader scalps him in a flash and the drum picks up a fast two-
time. The dancers whirl into a strong powwow, scattering across the ring,
each dancing by himself, and lustily. The usual powwow encore follows.

ON THE STAGE.—If on the stage the dancers enter from the back left, circling
the stage in the same fashion as in the ring. The enemy is stationed at the
front right corner. The dancers see him and freeze at the back right corner.

COSTUMING.—Best effect is produced if all dancers are dressed alike, with
feather warbonnets on their heads, large bustles in the middle of their backs
and smaller bustles on the arms between elbow and shoulder. If bustles
are scarce, each dancer may wear one arm bustle only, on his outside arm,
leaving the concealed inside arm bare.

The Other Buffalo

There is importance in a man's name. That which is given him at birth
is but a childhood name, to be discarded once his manhood has been established. One's name is earned by performing some deed. It serves to recall
the deed and in a sense throws light on the kind of a person he is. More
often than not it is complimentary, but then again it may not be.

So it is, or rather was, among the Redmen of the Plains. And the earning
of a name is the basis of this delightful dance.

From Ernest Thompson Seton came the story, oft told by him in his
inimitable way. The hearing of the story inspired the dance, which in due
course of time, was created as here recorded and used with brilliant success.

I have no knowledge that this story was danced by the Indians although
it might well have been, for the function of the story dance is to re-enact

important happenings. Its lack of historic background needs no apology, for any event may be used as the basis for a story dance.

THE STORY

The gist of it is this, based in the main upon the tale as told by Seton: Among the Crows who live up Montana way there was a boy overboastful of his power, overzealous to prove his manhood. At long last consent was given for him to accompany the buffalo hunters. When the party neared the herd the Chief told the boy to point out the buffalo he would kill. This he promptly did. He shot—and the buffalo fell. Racing forward to claim his prize, he was confronted by another Indian who claimed it was he who killed the buffalo. In the argument that followed the intruder told the boy to examine the arrow in the buffalo. He was amazed to discover that it was not his arrow . . . whereupon laughter and ridicule emanated from those in the hunting party. Then the Chief pointed to another buffalo dead upon the plains a short distance away, telling the boy that it was the buffalo he had killed. Full of unbelief, the boy nevertheless went to the other buffalo —and lo, his arrow was in it! *He had aimed at one buffalo and killed another buffalo.* Hence the name he carried ever after—"The Other Buffalo."

THE DANCE

It may be done as a solo although it lends itself better to a group dance with eight participating. The formation and general procedure is as in the Chippewa Scalp Dance just described. All motions are made in unison, the leader at the apex of the arrow formation starting the motions and the dancers picking them up instantly. The boy hunter is in position No. 3 (page 116).

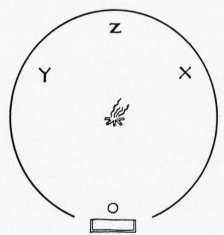

Figure 40. Diagram for The Other Buffalo

It consists of four circuits:

1st Circuit—Starting on the buffalo hunt: Enter at the right of the Council Rock (Figure 40), moving counterclockwise around the ring, with the toe-heel or double toe-heel step. Proud and full of confidence, dance with body erect and head high, using the strutting arm swing (page 43), lifting the arms high in front at each step and swaggering the shoulders correspondingly, all arms moving in unison.

2nd Circuit—Looking for the buffalo herd: Continuing in the upright position, shade the eyes with the right arm for four steps (see page 51 for method), then repeat with other arm. Push bushes and tall grass aside with the hands (page 55). Repeat this business at will throughout the circuit. The buffalo will be seen in the distance—there is no looking for tracks on the ground.

3rd Circuit—Continue as in 2. Stop occasionally and look in the distance, tapping one heel to the drumming and holding the pause for 12 taps. Near the end of the circuit the buffalo are sighted—stop and look, then point with right hand emphatically and repeatedly (page 56). Dance forward continuing the pointing for a few steps.

4th Circuit—Continue as in 3 until reaching the point marked X in Figure 40. On a prearranged arm signal by the leader, stop abruptly, whirl and face Y, with right foot in advance, striking a dramatic pose.

The leader steps forward two or three steps, points to the buffalo at Y, then points to the boy, and again at the buffalo. The boy steps out of the group of dancers and walks up beside the Chief. He studies the herd and dramatically points out the buffalo he will shoot. He raises his bow and shoots (see page 56 for method), then rushes forward to the buffalo at Y.

While this action is going on another Indian entered the scene: As the boy walks up beside the Chief to shoot, the intruder enters to the left of the Council Rock and stands there unnoticed. As the boy shoots he also shoots, and when the boy runs to the buffalo he also walks up to it.

The intruder points to the buffalo and then to himself, as if to say it is his. The boy then claims the buffalo by pointing at it and then to himself. This business is repeated with increasing anger upon the part of the boy. The intruder then points to the buffalo and looks at the boy, as if telling him to examine the arrow. The boy stoops, pulls the arrow and examines it—his arms drop to his sides, his head droops and his shoulders sag, portraying disappointment and broken spirit. At this point the group of hunters, still standing at X, burst into laughter: They open their mouths wide as in laughing, shake their bodies from head to foot, ringing their ankle bells loudly by jarring their heels; they lean way back, then way forward, then up again, and down in unison.

The Chief then points to Z and looks at the boy, as if to tell him that the buffalo he killed is over there. The boy looks down at the buffalo at Y, then at Z, and shakes his head. The Chief again points to Z and the boy walks slowly over to Z. He stoops, pulls the arrow, and his face brightens with surprise and pride. Laughter again breaks forth from the dancers as before.

The tempo of the drumming increases: the boy leaps forward and dances around the ring in a solo of exultation and celebration, going counterclockwise. When he comes up to the group of dancers they all break into a vigorous powwow, scattering across the ring.

When the drummer feels the powwow has continued long enough he so indicates by a louder beat of the drum, at which the boy dances over to Z and the dancers gather around him, still dancing in powwow. With the boy leading the entire group prances across the ring and exits.

Zon-zi-mon-de

The Omaha story of Zon-zi-mon-de recorded by Alice C. Fletcher is the basis of this dramatic dance. Reeking with blood and battle, yet its major theme is one of tenderness, of respect for the aged, of honor for the ancient ones. There is truth in its portrayal, for among the Redmen the lusty life and high-pulsed hope of fighting men are less worthy of esteem than are the wrinkles of many years.

The story is quoted from Alice C. Fletcher.* The dance adaptation is original. There is no record that the participants re-enacted the exploit in story dance, but well they might have, and probably did, for such was the custom following battle, although more often as a solo than as a group dance.

THE STORY

"Years ago the Omaha tribe and the Sioux met while searching for a buffalo herd; and, as was usual, a battle ensued, for each tribe was determined to drive the other from the region of the game. Although the Sioux outnumbered the Omaha, the latter remained victors of the field.

"An old Omaha, interested to observe how some of the tribe would conduct themselves in their first battle, made his way toward the scene of conflict. It chanced that just as a Sioux warrior had fallen, pierced by an arrow, and the Omaha men were rushing forward to secure their war honours, this old man was discovered coming up the hill, aided by his bow, which he used as a staff. One of the young warriors called to his companions: —

" 'Hold! Yonder comes Zon-zi-mon-de, let us give him the honours.'

"Then, out of courtesy to the veteran, each young warrior paused and stepped aside, while the old man, all out of breath, hastened to the fallen foe. There he turned and thanked the young men for permitting him, whom age had brought to the edge of the grave, to count yet one more honour as a warrior."

* Alice C. Fletcher, *Indian Story and Song from North America*, p. 45. Boston: Hale, Cushman and Flint, Inc., 1900.

THE DANCE

The character of Zon-zi-mon-de calls for a non-dancing man made up to represent old age. He carries a bow. Eight to twelve dancers are needed, one of whom is designated as Chief.

The step is the toe-heel or double toe-heel. The drumming is medium-fast to fast, accented in two-time.

1. The dancers enter from the Council Rock and start around the ring counterclockwise. Behind them as they enter comes old Zon-zi-mon-de leaning on his bow as a walking stick. He stops just inside the ring (at X in Figure 41), and remains there watching the young warriors to whom he has taught the arts of battle.

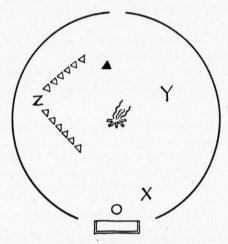

Figure 41. Diagram for Zon-zi-mon-de

2. Staying in a compact group with their Chief slightly in advance, the warriors dance erect with heads high and shoulders back, alert and looking for the enemy. Halfway around the ring, that is, when opposite the Council Rock, they discover the foe and begin shooting arrows (see page 56 for shooting technique). The shooting is done in unison, each pulling his bow at the same time, following the lead set by the Chief. It is done to a count of four steps (&-1, &-2, &-3, &-4), the bow pulled for three counts and the arrow shot on the fourth. The shooting is kept up constantly, dancing forward all the while, and is continued for a full circuit, that is, until opposite the Council Rock again.

3. This skirmish won, the dancers cease shooting and dance on, looking ahead for the enemy, shading their eyes with their hands at times (page 51), continuing thus until they reach the point marked Y in Figure 41, from which point they spot a lone enemy located at Z. Eight steps before reaching Y the Chief indicates by a prearranged *arm signal* that in eight steps a stop will be made—all stop in unison on the eighth step by whirling

to the left, their eyes fixed on Z. For 12 counts they hold the freeze, then the Chief steps forward a step or two, raises his bow and shoots (see page 56 for method).

4. Immediately as the arrow is shot, old Zon-zi-mon-de, still standing unnoticed at X, lets out a war-whoop. The warriors dash for the enemy's body at Z, but just before reaching it the Chief shouts "Ho" and points toward Zon-zi-mon-de. All stop, lining up in a "V" formation radiating from the fallen enemy at Z, as shown in Figure 41. The Chief points to the enemy and looks at Zon-zi-mon-de who hobbles forward, going to the right of the fire past Y and over to the Chief. The Chief points to him and then to the enemy. Old Zon-zi-mon-de nods his head, hobbles to Z and takes the scalp. He raises it high overhead and all break into a strong pow-wow dancing around him, Zon-zi-mon-de joining in as best his feeble legs will let him.

5. A moment of this and Zon-zi-mon-de sensing danger, stops dancing, war-whoops and points his bow toward the exit opposite the Council Rock (Figure 41). Startled, the dancers back away toward the Council Rock where they line up and start fighting their way toward the exit, shooting all the while as before. Almost reaching the exit they are driven back by the imaginary enemy; they approach again and retreat, but the third time force their way through and exit.

6. All the time the shooting is going on Zon-zi-mon-de stands behind his warriors, feebly motioning them forward. As the last successful attack is made he hobbles over to the Council Rock where he stops, looks across the ring and out the exit through which his fighting boys have gone, nods his head in satisfaction, and then hobbles out the exit.

Should there be only one exit in the ring, the directions can be altered accordingly.

If desired the dance may stop, as does the story, with Zon-zi-mon-de taking the scalp and the dance of celebration that follows, eliminating the final charge.

Apache Devil Dance

Those gorgeously ornamented Devil Dancers of the Apaches, so much photographed and publicized, are quite impossible of imitation without great effort, their huge intricate head-rigs of wood and fabric defying all efforts at quick construction.

Using the Devil Dance of the Apaches as a springboard, however, Julia M. Buttree has conceived a routine that has proved a powerful and compelling number, long used with certain alterations by our troupe of dancers.* The following is a description of that dance.

* Julia M. Buttree, *Rhythm of the Redman*, page 130. New York: A. S. Barnes & Co., 1930.

THE STORY

A strong dancer commands the scene. A Black Spirit enters, filling the ring with a sinister power, evil and malign. The dancer weakens under the deadly spell, struggles futilely to shake it off, and finally falls to the ground, the victim of the Evil One. In the exotic manner of his kind, the Black Spirit dances his devilish delight over the triumph. A Medicine Man enters with a holy wand. The Evil One's step falters under a spell he cannot explain. He turns to see the wand of the Medicine Man, cringes back in fear . . . then gradually his anger wells up and he charges the Holy One. In the play that follows between the conflicting powers of good and evil, the Black One gradually gains ascendancy. The retreating Medicine Man motions in three other Medicine Men, each with a holy wand. The combined power of four wands overcome the Evil One and he runs off screaming loudly. The dancer rises and dances again with all his original power and glory.

COSTUMING AND PROPERTIES

The black tights for the Devil are made from a suit of long underwear dyed black. While a breechcloth is not necessary, if two skunk skins are to be had they lend themselves admirably for the purpose, placed front and back. Strips of skunk skin wrapped around the wrists and ankles also add, but are not essential.

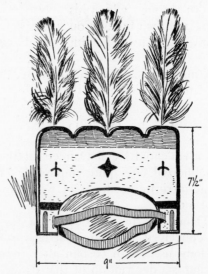

Figure 42. Medicine Man's Headdress

For his face a mask is needed made of papier-mâché. It should be made large to give a massive appearance, 8 by 12 inches in size, painted black

with white and red lines to bring out the features. It should take the form
of the human face, but distorted with passion, its mouth open and de-
formed. To the top of the head long hair from a horse's tail is attached to
hang down over one shoulder in front. Black cloth is attached to the back
to cover the head. If no mask can be had the Devil's face can be painted
black with white eyebrows and expression lines, with a black skull cap
worn on his head.

The devil carries a double gourd rattle.

The four Medicine Men are most appropriate wearing Indian wigs over
which the easily made head-rig shown in Figure 42 is placed. These are
made from very heavy packing-box cardboard painted white and decorated with red and blue lines. They are held on by elastic bands as shown
in the illustration. In the top of the Medicine Man's Headdress three fluffies
are stuck.

Four wands are also needed, illustrated in Figure 43, made from thin
wood strips about one inch wide and painted white. The upright piece is
16 inches long, the crosspieces 11 inches.

Figure 43. Medicine Man's Wand for the Apache Devil Dance

THE DEVIL'S STEP

When he enters he uses the flat-heel step. The following movements
apply to his dance of triumph.

He crouches with knees widespread, assuming the position shown at 1
in Figure 44. At times he hops forward on both feet and again he follows
the routine shown in Figure 44, as follows:

1   Jump on both feet
&   Jump on left foot raising right
2   Jump on both feet
&   Jump on right foot raising left

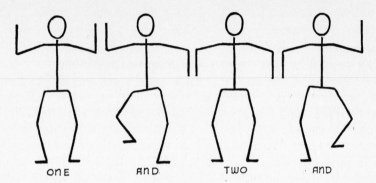

ONE   AND   TWO   AND

Figure 44.

These are his basic movements. Near the end of his dance he performs a movement shown in Figure 45, with one leg extended far out and twisted around so that the sole of the foot is up. He does this in the following routine:

1   Jump on both feet
&   Jump on left extending right out
2   Jump on both feet
&   Jump on right foot extending left out

Figure 45.

For his finale he extends the leg out *on every count*, first right, then left, continuing for four such movements only. This last maneuver is difficult and may be eliminated if it cannot be done.

Throughout all of his performance he holds his arms in the angular positions shown in Figure 44. It should not be assumed that the arms must take the positions shown on each step—the drawing merely shows various characteristic arm positions. He assumes one of these arm positions and holds it for three or four steps.

THE DANCE

1. To medium fast two-time, the dancer enters and circles the ring counterclockwise in nice performance, strong and self-reliant.

2. As he passes the entrance in completing the circuit the Devil enters, crouched and slinking. He looks the dancer over and starts trailing him, using the flat-heel step. The dancer weaves and circles so as not to gain ground on the cumbersome Devil. The drumming slows down as the dancer begins to falter under the spell—he stops dancing for a moment and raises his hand to his face, shakes his head to free himself, continues a step or two, and falls to his knees at X (Figure 46). With the Devil prancing over him he gradually settles down on his face and lies prostrate. As the dancer falls lower and lower the Devil rises to greater and greater heights.

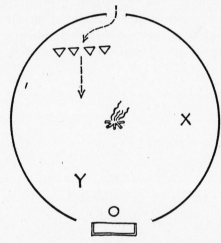

Figure 46. Diagram for the Apache Devil Dance

3. The Devil moves between the fallen dancer at X and the edge of the ring, thus facing the fire. He looks the dancer over, rises to full height and leaps over him toward the fire. Then using the basic step as described, he dances counterclockwise a quarter of the way around the ring, stops directly across from the Council Rock, faces the fire and dances in position, finishing by doing the side-kick step about four times. He advances a quarter of the ring, stops and repeats, then continues on.

4. Into the entrance opposite the Council Rock comes the Medicine Man (Figure 46) holding his wand in front, using the flat-foot step and shoving the wand forward on each step. He is calm and composed, his face expressionless. He stops just inside the ring as shown, marking time. The Devil continues around with faltering step, pauses as he nears the Council Rock and shakes his head to rid himself of the spell. He looks around and sees the Medicine Man, runs quickly back to Y and crouches there facing the Medicine Man. He takes his long hair in both fists as it hangs in front

of his chest and begins to twist it in his anger—he pants audibly with a hissing sound. A moment of this and he dashes toward the Medicine Man, his feet skidding as he puts on the brakes, his hands pawing the air overhead as he falls backward at the feet of the Medicine Man. As the Devil approaches the Medicine Man backs up a step or two. The Devil scrambles to his feet and scurries backward to Y, his anger increasing. The Medicine Man looks over his shoulder to the exit and motions with his left arm.

5. Three other Medicine Men enter and the four line up abreast as shown, calm and serene. The Devil repeats his charge and retreats again to Y. The Medicine Men advance very slowly, with the flat-foot step. Twice more the Devil charges but each time the Medicine Men keep coming. As they come abreast of the fire the left-hand Medicine Man cuts over to the other side of it and the Devil charges him there, but retreats again. At last the Medicine Men surround him in front of the Council Rock. He throws his arms overhead, spins around in a circle screaming, and dashes out. The Medicine Men about-face, calmly dance across the ring and exit.

6. As the Medicine Men gain control of the situation the dancer comes out of his trance and looks up. He rises higher and higher as the Devil's power declines and comes to his feet as the Devil dashes out. He stands there quietly until the Medicine Men leave.

7. The drumming increases in tempo and he breaks in a solo, more powerful and brilliant than ever, circling the ring three times and exits.

Pueblo Dog Dance

Water-color artists of Pueblo-land who find in it a favorite theme have done much to give prominence to the Dog Dance. The gorgeously adorned "dogs" painted black from head to foot, wearing a dark feather headdress that trails to the ground behind and carrying a feathered stick in the hand, held on leash by women in exquisite colorful attire, are familiar enough to all who find delight in Pueblo paintings. Such gorgeous ornamentation is scarcely within the scope of easy imitation but happily, a delightful little dance can be achieved without it.

Two men representing the dogs advance and retreat from each other with combative but graceful gestures and in the end drop to their knees and fight over a loaf of bread. Evans and Evans describe the dance as seen at San Ildefonso and say that, oddly enough, it symbolizes *peace*, depicting a conflict in the ancient days when war was sometimes settled by single combat between the opposing chiefs.*

Among the Sioux far to the northward is found a Dog Feast Dance that is similar in routine to the Pueblo dance. And the Dog Societies of other Plains tribes have dances with elements so similar that all seem to have stemmed from the same source.

* Bessie and May G. Evans, *American Indian Dance Steps*, page 93. New York: A. S. Barnes and Company, 1931.

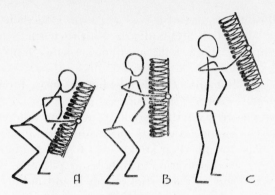

Figure 47. Dog Dance Positions

The following dance is based on the Pueblo version but of necessity takes certain liberties to adapt it to average conditions today.

The dance is effective enough in ordinary dancing costume but the two feathered sticks are necessary. These are about five feet long and made as shown in Figure 47. They are carried in the right hand and a rattle in the left.

THE DANCE

The step is an ordinary trot done on the ball of the foot, light and graceful, with knees and ankles soft so as to take up jar. The stick is held at its middle as in Figure 47.

In the possession of the drummer is half a loaf of stale bread, of such consistency that it can be picked up by the teeth and held in the mouth.

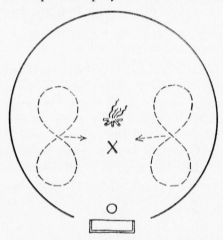

Figure 48. Diagram for the Pueblo Dog Dance

The dancers enter either side of the Council Rock and begin dancing around in a figure-of-8 course, each on his own side of the ring, as indicated in Figure 48. Their eyes are fixed on each other.

1. They follow the figure-of-8 course 4 times and then dance forward to meet at X, crouch low and stop with their sticks crossed, held as in A, Figure 47. They hold motionless for 4 counts then turn and dance back.
2. They repeat 1 but cross their sticks high as in C, Figure 47.
3. They repeat 1, crossing their sticks as in B.
4. They repeat 1, crossing their sticks as in A and holding for 4 counts, then changing the position to B and holding for 4 counts.
5. They repeat, crossing their sticks as in C and holding for 4 counts, then changing to the position in B, holding 4 counts.
6. They repeat, crossing their sticks as in B and holding for 4 counts, then change to the position in C for 4 counts, then change to the position in A for 4 counts.
7. They dance the figure-of-8 routine 4 times, after which the drummer tosses the loaf of bread down at X. The dancers dart forward, drop to their knees and fight to secure possession of the bread with their mouths. They grab for it with their teeth, feint and withdraw, eye each other, growl and snarl, and otherwise simulate fighting dogs. At last one gets hold of it solidly with his teeth, rises and trots swiftly around the ring and exits with the other following close on his heels.

Winnebago War Dance

With the kind permission of Julia M. Buttree, this dance is taken from her *Rhythm of the Redman*,* altered in detail, as is the right of the story dancer, so as to describe it as our dancers have developed it.

The dance possesses much of comedy, resulting from the riding of the stick "horses."

THE STORY

The Winnebagos were close on the trail of the Pawnees. Knowing that they were being followed the Pawnees had succeeded in slipping away each time a battle seemed imminent. At last the Winnebagos caught up with them and the two parties prepared for the fight, each dancing its war dance. The Winnebagos charged the Pawnees, and the Pawnees, apparently eager for the fray, sallied forth to meet them, when suddenly they whirled as one man and fled, scattering in all directions. The Winnebagos stopped in surprise, looked at each other in disgust, but accepted the affair as victory, as proof that the Pawnees were the cowards they had always held them to be.

PROPERTIES

A "horse" is needed for each dancer in the Winnebago group. This consists of a stick four feet long, of the thickness of a broomstick. At the head

* Julia M. Buttree, *Rhythm of the Redman*, page 136. New York: A. S. Barnes & Company, 1930.

end a leather thong or light rope is attached, so arranged as to represent the horse's reins.

THE DANCE

Two groups are needed, the Pawnees and the Winnebagos, six to eight dancers in each.

1. The Pawnees enter with the toe-heel step, looking back at the entrance as though fearful of being followed. They dance a few steps, stop and shade their eyes (see page 51 for method), then continue around the ring, always looking back over their shoulders. When halfway around they stop and look again, but seeing no danger break into a reserved pow-wow on that side of the ring.

2. Suddenly they become alarmed and sneak back, using the fear step (page 39), stop and crouch with their bodies turned away from the entrance.

3. A war-whoop sounds behind the Council Rock and in come the Winnebagos, each riding a "horse" (astride a stick) using the flat-foot trot (page 37). They are alert and looking for the Pawnees. They dance counterclockwise one-fourth of the way around the ring, stop, shade their eyes and look. They turn and dance back toward the entrance and go one-fourth of the way around the ring in the opposite direction where they stop again as before. They spot the hiding Pawnees. They point at them and back up to the Council Rock.

4. The Pawnees, seeing themselves detected, arise and prepare for battle. They form a semicircle on their side of the ring, facing the Winnebagos, and the Winnebagos form a similar semicircle on their side in front of the Council Rock. Both parties dance the war dance (for convenience use the Chippewa War Dance on page 136).

5. This ended, both parties move to battle using the toe-heel step; the Winnebagos raise their war-clubs and go counterclockwise a quarter of the circuit, and the Pawnees do likewise, also going counterclockwise. The Winnebagos then whirl toward the Pawnees and start advancing directly across the ring toward them, their war-clubs menacing. The Pawnees advance a few feet to meet them, then suddenly break and scatter, all running for the nearest exit.

6. The Winnebagos lower their clubs in surprise, then put their hands on their hips and look at each other in disgust. They hold this for a moment and then burst into a powwow of victory.

7. The drum signals with a loud beat and they dance over to the far side of the ring, opposite the Council Rock, line up and prance across the ring on their "horses," and exit.

Throughout the whole dance the Winnebagos are riding their "horses."

It is from the handling of the "horses" that the dance achieves its unique character and its comedy. The dancers straddle the stick and hold it with both hands in front. As they dance they jerk the stick up and down in imitation of the movements of a horse. In the final vigorous powwow of victory the horses become animated, with the dancers leaping in the air at times and shaking the stick vigorously.

The Passing of White Dog

The Indian sings his way through life. He sings to the sunrise in the morning and to the sunset at night, when he plants the seeds and when he reaps the harvest, when the little one is born and when the dear one is taken from him. He writes his own death song, putting into it all the beauty at his command, hoping that when his time comes to cross the Great Divide he may do so standing on his two feet and singing.

This is the story of the last singing of White Dog's death song. It is not a dance in the Indian sense, it is not a reproduction of a dance as done by the Indians. Rather it is a brief pageant, a moment of history depicting the going yonder of the spirit of White Dog, Medicine Man of the Blackfeet. But it is a lofty moment, replete with true Indian values—respect for the aged, glorification of all events by song, death as the great experience of life, the meeting of it standing on one's feet and singing.

It is a perfect moment with which to close the program, perfect in its sadness and its beauty . . . after the climax of brilliance and vigor, the finale of sadness and death seems best to portray the Indian theme.

A brief reference to the story that inspired the dance can be found in *Long Lance* by Buffalo Child Long Lance.*

THE STORY

Asleep was the village of the Blood Blackfeet, deep in sleep, for it was past the midnight hour. There came a noise, a weird sound . . . a tepee became astir, then another, and another as ever-restless warriors shook free from the spell of slumber. It was a strange sound—and yet a familiar one . . . a song . . . a *death* song. Something was happening—something terrible. Louder came the chanting, its familiar voice recognized—it was White Dog, Medicine Man of the Blackfeet! What awful hour was this that White Dog should be singing his death song? Moccasined feet of men were coming from all directions—gravitating to White Dog's lodge, forming in a semicircle at respectful distance. There could be no mistaking it—White Dog's face was painted to meet his fathers, his lips were chanting the telltale words. Once, twice, he sang it through—*his* death song. The third time he started it, but no mortal ears heard its end, for it was finished on the other side. The old man's legs crumbled beneath him and he joined his fathers as all men hope to join them, standing on his two feet and singing. Thus passed White Dog, Medicine Man of the Blackfeet.

* Buffalo Child Long Lance, *Long Lance*. New York: Farrar and Rinehart, 1928.

The Last Song

Let— it be beau—ti—ful when I sing the last song!

Let it be day! I would stand up—on my

two feet sing—ing, I would look up-ward with o—pen eyes

sing ing! I would have the winds to en—vel—ope my

bod—y, I would have the sun to shine up—on my

bod—y, the whole World I would have to make mu—sic with me!

Let— it be beau—ti—ful when thou would slay me, O Shin—ing

One— Let it be day—— when I sing the last song!

From Hartley Alexander, *Manito Masks*, page 27. By permission of E. P. Dutton and Company, Inc., publishers.

THE DANCE

The central role is that of White Dog, to be played by a person with a good singing voice and an excellent dramatic sense. In addition thirteen to fifteen dancers are needed. All bells are removed. There is no drumming at the start but the drummer is standing at his drum.

For the death song, "The Last Song" by Hartley Alexander is used, words and music recorded in his *Manito Masks*.

The dancers enter quietly and sit down on the far side of the council ring opposite the Council Rock, as indicated by the numbers in Figure 49. The leading dancer sits in Number 1 position. Numbers 2 and 3, either side of him, are performers with good dramatic judgment each with a coup stick or feathered spear such as that shown in Figure 32. The other dancers are paired up as to size and ability, Numbers 4 and 5 being a pair, 6 and 7, etc., the larger ones near the center and fanning down to the smallest at the ends.

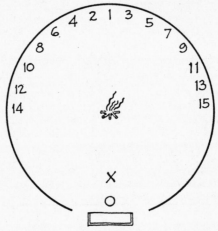

Figure 49. Diagram for The Passing of White Dog

When seated the dancers lie down and pretend to sleep. There is a long moment of silence, then behind the Council Rock comes the voice of White Dog singing his death song, softly as if far away. It increases in volume and comes nearer. Number 5 of the sleeping Indians awakens and sits up, startled. He awakens those on either side of him, who in turn wake those next to them, and so on. All sit up startled and, with reserved action, portray on their faces the death meaning of the scene. Numbers 2 and 3 come up to their knees, and Number 1 arises to his knee and one foot so as to elevate him above the others. Although the rest remain seated they are alert, intense, awestruck....

As the last words of his song die away behind the scenes, White Dog enters, walking slowly but with firm tread, to point X in Figure 49. Here

Photograph by Ralph Haburton

ROBERT RAYMOND

Photograph by Ralph Haburton   ROBERT RAYMOND AND JOHN LANDIS HOLDEN

Finger Movement in the Ant Dance

he stands for a moment, erect and stately, his eyes fixed on the distance, then begins singing his song again, his voice full of emotion, wavering and faltering a little near the end. He staggers a step or two, catches himself, sings the first line again—his legs crumble and he falls to the ground, lying face up, parallel to the Council Rock at X in Figure 49.

A long moment of silence and the drum begins beating very softly. Very quietly and with utmost reverence, without the slightest jar or sudden motion, Number 2 arises and, with the flat-heel step, moves slowly and with dignity across the ring and sticks his spear in the ground so that it stands erect at White Dog's head. He then takes off his warbonnet and spreads it over White Dog's face, and exits quietly. Then Number 3 repeats, placing his spear at White Dog's feet and his headdress on his chest. Next Numbers 14 and 15 arise together, move across and spread their warbonnets on the body, then 12 and 13, and so on until only Number 1 is left. He then arises, moves across the ring, leans his shield against the spear at the dead man's head, places his headdress on the body, and exits. The ring is empty—the dead one is left to sleep.

The dancers so place their warbonnets that the body is completely covered and no part of it can be seen. As it lies there completely enshrouded in gorgeous eagle feathers it looks strangely like a grave.

In the presence of death, all movements, dancing and otherwise, are reserved, subdued, quiet, reverent. The body remains on the ground until the closing ceremony of the council fire is reverently completed and the audience begins to leave, or if on the stage, until the curtain is slowly lowered.

The medicine of this dance is powerful and it pulls heavily at the heartstrings.

COSTUMING.—White Dog is an old man and must be dressed accordingly. His face is made up to show age. He wears clothes in contrast to the breechclothed dancers—leggings, shirt or vest, perhaps blanket. On his head is a medicine-man's headdress or a warbonnet.

Chapter VI

GROUP DANCES OF THE CHIPPEWAS

UNDER NORTHLAND pines the booming dance-drum changes mood anon and yet again. Full of manly vigor, it shouts for virile powwows. Flush with success afield, it clamors for boastful story dances. Eager for the zest of battle, it demands restless war dances. Again, in friendly mood, it suggests pleasant, homey social dances.

Its noisy powwows and showy story dances have been described. And now the fancy changes, first to the war dance for a moment, then to the delightful pastime dances—chorus dances all.

In no respect difficult, demanding no intricate or overstrenuous movements, these are within the reach of all, however inexperienced. The movements are wholly natural, simple and conservative.

Scarcely in the brilliant category, these dances are nevertheless welcomed numbers always, especially sought after as lead-ups and breathers, before and in between the more rousing, spirited dances.

Chippewa War Dance

So simple is this dance, so easily mastered that a group of beginners can often learn it well enough to present in public in a half-hour of practice. Differing in type from any other dance in this volume, it nevertheless has a peculiar fascination, a charm all its own, an atmosphere unmistakably primitive, especially when done with the shifting shadows of the campfire as its background.

This is a true war dance—a preparation for the battle, not an aftermath of celebration for victories won. No idle pastime this, no mere showoff— it was the producer of fighting men. The rhythm of it, danced over and over, on and on, had a marked psychological effect, filling the warrior with ecstasy, with increased importance, causing him to feel himself stronger and more powerful than he was, more certain of success. The intoxication of the rhythm with everyone doing it together developed a solidarity, a oneness of purpose, a harmony, each with all. For these reasons war dances were widespread, if not universal, not only among the Indian tribes but among all primitive folk.

With the passing of the glad fighting days the original usefulness of the war dance of the Chippewas was no more. But it has continued on to the present to brighten up a drab today with memories of an exciting and glorious yesterday, and to unite the village the better to solve the problems of peace.

DRUM RHYTHM

The rhythm of the War Dance differs from that of any other dance here recorded and, for best results, must receive careful attention by the drummer. Instead of the usual two-time, the accented beat is held—

The held beat is the loud beat. Characteristic rhythm and sound is achieved by leaving the beater on the drum after the loud beat is struck until necessary to remove it for the next beat. This, of course, differs from most drumming in which the beater is allowed to rebound from its impact with the drum. It is allowed to rebound from the soft or fast beat but is held on the drum for the loud beat. It is possible to do the War Dance to a regular two-time rhythm but the dancers will swing into the characteristic movement better if correct drumming is used. A little practice on the part of the drummer will perfect it. The tempo is medium-fast to fast.

The drum best suited is a hoop-drum, or hand-drum, such as is illustrated in Figure 109. Among the Chippewas this is called a *war-drum* or *chief's drum* because its size and lightness permitted it to be taken along on war parties by the Chief for use in war dances. A hard beater should be used (see page 248).

BODY MOVEMENT

There is no movement of the feet but rather an up-and-down motion of the body with the feet stationary. Stand with the feet side by side, normal distance apart. Flex the knees to lower the body on the loud beat and raise it on the soft beat, as indicated in Figure 50. It is not an *even* up-and-down motion but rather conforms to the accent of the drumming. The emphasis is downward, which is natural since the downward motion is on the accented beat of the drum. The body remains down longer, going up only long enough to come down again. The body is held down for the full length of the held beat and goes up only for the length of the short one. In other words, the dancer does not stand erect and go down and up, but rather takes the down position as shown in B, and goes up and down from it. The downward motion is quick and emphatic—the muscles of the legs are relaxed and the body dropped to be caught as the loud beat hits. The legs are raised to their full height on the up beat, however, the knees being jerked back straight on the count.

The body is bent slightly forward at the hips, the head is erect and the elbows out to the side at an angle as shown, the eyes are full and large, the face alert and pleasant.

Once the movement is mastered the feet may be moved slightly when doing it strenuously. They are jerked back an inch or so on the up movement and forward a similar distance on the down movement. This should not be encouraged too much, however, lest the dance lose its atmosphere of reserved motion. It will come naturally enough when the situation is right for it.

Figure 50. Chippewa War Dance Movement

THE DANCE

Any number of dancers can participate. They stand in a slightly curved line conforming to the edge of the dancing ring, arranged according to height with the tallest in the middle. To the drumming they go up and down, up and down, as described, all moving in unison. With alert face and large eyes they are constantly looking, eyes darting here and there.

The drumming starts softly and increases gradually in volume for 24 counts (&-1, &-2, etc. to 24), the 24th count being hit strongly, after which the drumming becomes soft again beginning the next count of 24. As the drumming increases in volume the dancers dance harder. As the drum booms loudly on the 24th beat they drop lower, bending the body forward at the hips, raise the right hand over their eyes as in C and, remaining down, look for four counts. On the first of these four counts all look to the left, on the second to the front, on the third to the right, on the fourth they drop their hands, jerk their heads to look back to the left and straighten up in the usual dance position.

The dance continues for *four of these sequences of 24 counts*. As the dancers come up from the crouch at the end of the last sequence the drum hits four steady beats and stops. The dancers raise their right hands to their mouths and war-whoop to terminate the dance.

If done in the council ring with the crowd sitting all around the edges, it is well to line up the dancers in front of the Council Rock for the dance, then after the war-whoop, have them walk directly across the ring and form the line on the other side, facing the Council Rock, where the full dance is repeated.

An excellent and characteristic finale for the War Dance is to have the dancers break formation and go into the Powwow (page 62).

Acorn Dance

The Acorn is one of those joyous social dances that are done in couples, sometimes mixed couples of men and women, sometimes all men, or all women. It has the very appealing virtue of being easy for beginners to learn since it does not call for toe-heel dancing—any average group unfamiliar with Indian dancing can develop it in a half-hour and have a good time doing it.

It is a chorus dance in which the couples move around in a column, with all movements done in unison. Such quiet chorus numbers are effective, particularly early in a program. They provide contrast for the more brilliant powwow numbers, making them appear even more spectacular by comparison.

The Acorn was learned while among the Chippewas of northern Wisconsin.

It calls for a special step that does not appear in other dances.

THE STEP

To make it clear, let us suppose a line is drawn on the floor. Stand with both feet on this line as if to walk it, the left foot directly in front of the right, the left heel about four inches in front of the right toe. The right foot remains at this same distance behind the left throughout—in other words the left foot always leads. The right foot steps on the line on every step whereas the left steps first to one side of the line and then the other:

1. Step left toe at right of line
2. Step right toe back on line
3. Step left toe at left of line
4. Step right toe back on line

Practice it on the spot without making progress until the movements are familiar. It is a prancing motion with the left leg, the right merely following along. Both feet spring up from the floor, the right rising only an inch or two while the left comes up about six inches so as to lift the knee in prancing style. The left knee is kept flexible and bends slightly as it is raised. The step is done with animation but progress forward is made slowly, advancing no more than six inches to a step. The body is held upright.

Old folks do the step in a quiet, walking sort of way, but young bloods snap up the action reminding one of spirited colts in trotting harness.

The drumming is in accented two-time, medium fast.

THE DANCE

The dancers should be paired up as to size and type, experimenting until couples are found that move nicely together. If the couples are made up of men and women, the man's position is to the left with the woman at his right. They put their arms around each other's waist, and allow their outside arms to hang naturally at the side. The couples should be arranged in a compact column according to height, with the larger couples leading, except that one larger and experienced couple should be placed at the end of the line to bring up the rear.

The column forms outside the entrance and marks time off stage until all are moving in unison. It moves clockwise around the ring or stage.

1. 24 counts—Move forward with the Acorn step as described, the drumming gradually increasing in volume until the 24th beat
2. 8 counts—Each couple turns on the spot, using the same step, turning to the left, completing the turn in eight steps and facing in the original direction again. The drumming is soft throughout
3. 24 counts—Repeat 1
4. 8 counts—Repeat 2

Repeat thus through the dance.

In making the turn the left-hand dancer of each couple, playing the man's role, takes the initiative and leads. He holds his partner firmly with his arm so that the two move as one man.

The cue for the turn is the loud beat of the drum on the 24th count, after which it becomes soft for the eight counts of the turn, then gradually gains in volume the next 24 counts.

The dancers should stand erect with heads up and should be cautioned not to look at their feet.

The dance continues until the drummer feels it should be terminated, whereupon he skips a beat for four counts, that is, hits the loud beat only and skips the soft beat. Hearing this, the dancers break formation and walk out. One circuit of the ring, or a circuit and a half at the most, or two circuits of the stage, should be sufficient.

A dance of this type is often used as an introduction to another dance. For example, when the dancers break their formation they might line up at once in the War Dance (page 136), after which they might go into the Powwow (page 62), thus making a unit of three Chippewa dances without leaving the stage.

Forty-nine

The story has it that fifty Indians from a Wisconsin reservation went to the first World War and forty-nine returned home afterward. So happy were the people at the return of these forty-nine that they created a dance in their honor and called it the Forty-nine. The dance is thus strictly a modern one, the most recent of all Chippewa dances.

The Forty-nine is a social dance very similar to the Acorn, the only difference being in the step used. It is done in the same formation and follows the same routine, but presents a different appearance and one that is, if anything, more attractive. The movement is very easy to learn, the only difficulty arising in all doing it together with good chorus effect.

THE STEP

1. Step on left toe, raising right
2. Hop on left toe and kick right out in front
3. Step on right toe, raising left
4. Hop on right toe and kick left out in front

The kick is done with the lower leg. As the left foot steps the right foot is raised as in walking, then as the left foot hops in place, the right is kicked forward at the knee so that the leg straightens in the air with a jerk on the count. The leg is thus kicked out straight. The toe is not pointed on the kick but the foot remains turned up at the natural angle. The drumming is in medium tempo but progress forward is made slowly, the emphasis being on the forward kick of the legs and not on covering the ground.

THE DANCE

The dance follows the exact routine of the Acorn except for the step. The couples are arranged in a column as in that dance and the entrance is made in the same way.

1. 24 counts—Dance forward with the Forty-nine step, the drumming gradually increasing in volume until the 24th count
2. 8 counts—Each couple turns on the spot, using the same step, turning to the left, completing the turn in eight steps and facing in the original direction again

Repeat throughout the dance.
All instructions given for the Acorn apply.

Waboos (Rabbit) Dance

Most popular of all social dances among the Minnesota Chippewas is the Waboos . . . most useful, too, from our standpoint, easier to learn and more dependable than either the Acorn or the Forty-nine. As done by these Minnesota people it is identical with the Rabbit Dance of their neighbors to the westward, the Sioux. It is described in Chapter VII, "Group Dances of the Plains."

Chippewa Deer Dance

The eternal drama of two bucks fighting for a doe is the theme of this delightful little dance, as clever a little number as is to be found in these pages. Yet, it takes no special dancing talent to do it, the old hands having no advantage over beginners. Boys love it much because of its simplicity, its imitative aspect, and the fight with which it ends.

In mood it is typical of the jovial, woods-loving Chippewas of the northern Wisconsin lake country from whom it was learned.

THE STEP

The step is a natural trot. The weight is taken on the ball of the foot as in ordinary trotting, but the steps are short, keeping the feet under the body. The knees are soft and flexible, the arms hang naturally at the sides and the whole body is relaxed. It is done to medium-fast drumming and the feet are snapped up with zest.

The drumming is in eight-time, accented on one.

THE DANCE

Three dancers are required—two bucks and a doe. It can be done with several such groups of three arranged in a column, but one is more satisfactory and is the usual arrangement. The two bucks should pair up nicely as to size and type—two boys small in stature, well-built and athletic, quick of movement and with good co-ordination. The boy playing the doe's role should be more slender by comparison.

The two bucks stand side by side about three feet apart, with the doe between and slightly in front of them, as indicated in Figure 51. The bucks stand erect with heads high, proud and showy.

1. 8 counts—Trot forward
2. 8 counts—The bucks whirl abruptly toward each other, crouch a little and cross over behind the doe, nudging their heads toward each other as they pass, then trot up beside the doe, each on the opposite side from which they started, as indicated in Figure 51. After they pass the doe slows down so that she is slightly behind the bucks
3. 8 counts—Trot forward
4. 8 counts—The bucks whirl toward each other as before but pass *in front* of the doe, the doe speeding up after they have

passed so that she is slightly in front of them in the same
position as at the start.

Repeat throughout dance until fight starts.

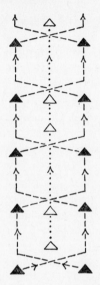

Figure 51. Diagram for the Chippewa Deer Dance

It thus appears that the bucks pass first behind and then in front of the
doe. They take eight counts to pass, then continue forward for eight
counts before crossing again. The bucks advance at the same rate of progress all the time—it is the doe's business to change her speed of progress to
permit the bucks to cross first in front of her and then behind her.

This part of the dance forbodes the fight that is coming. Each time they
pass the bucks threaten each other—they whirl abruptly to pass, crouch a
little and bend forward, turning their horns toward each other but do not
touch. Once passed they straighten up to full height and prance forward,
paying no attention to each other until they whirl abruptly for the next
pass. This continues for one circuit and a half of the council ring, or two
circuits of the stage. The drum booms loudly heralding the fight, increasing
in tempo; the doe trots about ten feet forward and stands with her back to
the bucks. With graceful dancing movement and still trotting in rhythm
they fight as follows:

A.   4 counts—Crouch and charge, barely touching
B.   4 counts—Retreat and straighten up
C.   4 counts—Repeat A
D.   4 counts—Repeat B
E.   4 counts—Repeat A
F.   4 counts—Repeat B

G.   4 counts—Repeat A, locking right shoulders and pushing
H. 12 counts—Spin around together three times, 4 counts to each spin, pushing hard
I.   4 counts—One falls and the other trots back and straightens

The triumphant buck trots up beside the doe and the two trot around the ring or stage with heads high and exit. In the meantime the defeated buck comes slowly to his feet and, as the drum slows down, limps along on one foot, his head and shoulders drooping and exits.

COSTUMES.—No effort is made to imitate the deer in costuming the dancers. They use the usual dancing costume with breechcloth, headdress, bustles, etc.

Chippewa Chicken Dance

Two cocks fighting for the possession of a hen—such is the plot of the Chippewa Chicken Dance. In theme it duplicates exactly the Deer Dance just described, but chickens move in nowise like deer, and so there is no similarity in the pictures created. Good judgment would scarcely schedule both on the same program, however.

Like the Deer Dance it is simple, easy to learn, and is much loved by youngsters.

It was learned from the northern Wisconsin Chippewas.

THE STEP

Stand on the balls of the feet with the knees slightly bent and extend the arms out to the sides to resemble chicken wings, the fingers extended stiffly. Trot forward with *very rapid*, tiny steps. *The knees are hard*, the feet are barely lifted from the floor and advance but five or six inches with each step. The drumming is very fast and the feet seem to flutter forward. At the same time the hands flutter up and down a little to the rhythm.

THE DANCE

For the cocks select a well-matched pair, small in stature and quick of movement. They stand side by side about four feet apart, with the hen between and about a foot in advance of them. They bend forward at the waist as need be to facilitate the movement but hold their heads high, the two cocks turning their heads very slightly toward each other and keeping eyes focused on each other.

To very fast unaccented drumming, they flutter forward in this formation, circling the ring or stage one-and-one-half times. The drum booms and the two cocks whirl toward each other, the hen moving a few feet away and standing, her wings trembling slightly. They fight with the following routine:

A. 8 counts—Bend forward and swoop together, barely touching
B. 8 counts—Flutter back and straighten up
C. 8 counts—Repeat A
D. 8 counts—Repeat B
E. 8 counts—Repeat A
F. 8 counts—Repeat B
G. 8 counts—Repeat A, bringing right shoulders together and push
H. 24 counts—Spin around together three times, 8 counts to each spin, fluttering outstretched wings hard
I. 8 counts—One falls, other flutters back.

The winning cock flutters up beside the hen and the two dance around the ring or stage and exit. The defeated one rises and limps out on one leg, stepping on every other beat, his wings drooping.

COSTUMING.—The dance is done in the usual dancing costume with no effort made to simulate the appearance of chickens.

Chapter VII

GROUP DANCES FROM THE PLAINS

THE PATTERN of dancing is strikingly similar among the Chippewas of the Great Lakes region and the Sioux to the westward. If we were to remain in the sphere of powwow dancing there would indeed be little worth recording to differentiate the two peoples, and even in some of the ceremonial dances there are similarities so obvious that they must have stemmed from the same roots or have been learned one from the other. An example is found in the Rabbit Dance which I first learned from the Sioux and later saw danced in identical fashion among the Chippewas.

But as the mode of life changes as we go from the woods to the Plains new elements appear which are, as would be expected, reflected in the ceremonial dances. Notable is the presence of the buffalo that dominated the life of the Red Horsemen of the prairies and found prominent representation in the Buffalo Dances. Another is the Messianism that swept the Plains in the form of the Ghost Dance, engulfing the northern Plains but losing its momentum before invading the woodlands.

Like all chorus dances the routines in this chapter are well suited for beginners.

Sioux Rabbit Dance

Perhaps it is unfair to label it a Sioux Rabbit Dance, for I have also danced it with the Chippewas of Minnesota who regard it as their own, and indeed, their most popular social dance, although the Chippewas farther eastward in Wisconsin do not dance it. And even as I write, I learn a Rabbit Dance of the Kiowas far to the southward of the Sioux which uses the same basic movement.

The Rabbit Dance is reminiscent of the Acorn and the Forty-nine of Chapter VI which it resembles. It is, if anything, a more satisfying dance than either of these.

THE STEP

1. Jump forward on left foot
2. Step back on right foot
3. Step back on left foot
4. Step forward on right foot

The drumming is in four-time, accented on one.

This is what is known as a *recoil step*. The jump with the left foot on 1 is longer than the other steps, the foot picked up higher. As the weight is taken on it the body recoils for two shorter steps on 2 and 3 and then comes back to a stable position with a short step forward on 4. The longer step on 1 permits making progress forward.

The outline above is to facilitate learning. Once the movement is learned it should be snapped up, using a trotting motion on 2, 3, and 4 rather than a stepping one. The weight is always taken on the ball of the foot. The left knee is raised with a prancing effect on 1, the body springing forward, and from this impact it recoils with the next three little trots. The knees are soft, taking up the jar.

This is a *rabbit* dance and should be done with all the lightness and spring the name implies. Only the older folk do it in walking fashion.

THE DANCE

Arrange the dancers in pairs according to size and type. They place their arms around each other's waists, each grasping his partner firmly, allowing the other arm to hang naturally at the side. The couples should be arranged in a compact column, according to height with the larger ones in front and tapering back, except that one larger couple is placed on the end to bring up the rear.

The columns mark time off stage until everyone is moving in unison and enters dancing, moving around the ring clockwise.

1. 36 counts—Move forward with the rabbit step as described, the drum increasing gradually in volume until the 36th count.
2. 4 counts—Crouch and trot forward for 4 steps. The drumming is soft.
3. 36 counts—Repeat 1
4. 4 counts—Repeat 2

Repeat thus throughout the dance.

The cue for the four-count trot is the loud beat of the drum on the 36th count, after which it becomes soft for the four counts of the trot.

To do the four-count trot, each couple crouches down a little, trots forward with four long gliding steps bringing the feet down flat. Having made the four steps they rise erect and proceed as before. The dancers should be cautioned to stand erect and keep their eyes off their feet.

The dance is terminated by the drummer, using his own judgment as to time. It is ended by four accented beats, whereupon the dancers break their formation and walk out. One circuit of the ring or a circuit and a half at the most, or two circuits of the stage, is the usual length.

As in the Acorn and the Forty-nine this dance is often used as an introduction to another dance. As the dancers break their formation from the Rabbit Dance they go into formation for the next dance without leaving the stage or arena.

Sioux Buffalo Dance

Closest of all things to the life of the people, source of food, shelter, clothing, of most of life's needs, was the buffalo—teacher of the Medicine Men in the healing of wounds, symbol of long life and plenty, loved and revered as the most gentle and generous of creatures. It was good to have a buffalo skull near one in the lodge always, good to have his horns on the heads of the chiefs for it labeled them as the highest of the high, good to dance often in his honor that his favor might be courted, that he might dwell long and abundantly in the homeland of the sweeping prairies.

Typical of the Siouan peoples, this Buffalo Dance contrasts interestingly with that of the adobe-dwelling Pueblos described on page ooo, and again with that of the Cheyennes which follows. It may well follow those dances on the same program. In its general pattern the description here given follows that provided by Julian H. Salomon in his *The Book of Indian Crafts and Indian Lore.**

THE DANCE

About 16 dancers are needed, all good toe-heel performers. They carry war clubs, tomahawks, or spears, and if possible, shields. If these instruments are not at hand their absence will not detract materially.

The dancers must bear in mind that they are imitating buffalo in their movements:

1. The drumming is in slow accented two-time. The dancers enter in an informal group and start around counterclockwise, using the flat-heel step. They step heavily on the loud beat with a stamping motion and bring the heel down again on the half-beat, moving gracefully to stimulate the slowly undulating buffalo herd, swaying from side to side with shoulders and head in buffalo style on each step. When halfway around the ring they begin to form a circle close around the fire, one stopping to start the circle and the others continuing on around and falling in until the full circle is formed, facing the fire and dancing in place.

2. The slow drumming continues. At a drum signal they all kneel facing the fire, continuing the dancing motion with their bodies, swaying from side to side and shaking heads in rhythm. The drummer uses his judgment as to the time to end this movement and start the next.

3. A sharp beat of the drum and one dancer arises and begins dancing the toe-heel drag step (page 23) in place, swaying his body, shaking his head and snorting loudly, buffalo-like. The signal is repeated and another arises, and so on until all are standing and dancing in a circle. The interval between each rising signal is eight counts.

4. Following a signal of four accented beats the drumming suddenly changes to very fast two-time. The dancers whirl from the circle into a

* Julian H. Salomon, *The Book of Indian Crafts and Indian Lore,* page 338. New York: Harper and Brothers, 1928.

wild powwow, using the toe-heel and the double toe-heel steps, scattering around the ring. Four of the better dancers are instructed to charge the audience with their weapons, another four to attack each other with their horns, while the remainder continue in vigorous powwow, bringing the dance up to a climax of noise and action.

5. Using his judgment as to time the drummer gradually slows down the drumming until the original slow tempo is established again. The dancers move with less and less vigor as the drumming slows until they are doing the original slow stamping with the flat-heel step. With this they move to the edge and exit.

Cheyenne Buffalo Dance

The pattern changes as we leave the Sioux Buffalo Dance and go farther southward on the Plains to the Cheyenne country. But the same reverence for the life-giving buffalo is found, the same gentleness of feeling.

This is a quiet dance but a picturesque one.

THE DANCE

Four good dancers are needed for the buffalo hunters, and eight or ten others for the buffalo. Each of the hunters must have a spear, either feathered throughout it's length as shown in Figure 32, or with occasional clusters of feathers attached here and there.

The step is the flat-heel.

1. The buffalo enter to medium-slow two-time drumming, bending forward with arms hanging down to resemble legs, and moving in imitation of buffalo. Staying together as a herd they move around the ring counter-clockwise.

2. When the buffalo reach Y the four hunters enter and start around in the same direction after them. The hunters are in file, one behind the other, each gripping his spear at its middle and holding it overhead in charging position (Figure 36), all four spears at the same level. They move at the same rate of speed as the buffalo so that they remain directly across the ring from them at all times. Their eyes are fixed on the buffalo constantly. They continue following for one full circuit, until the buffalo are back at Y and the hunters at X.

3. The drum rolls, the hunters break formation and dash across the ring, using a long stride and skip, and all unite to spear the same buffalo. The stricken buffalo falls and the other buffalo scatter and run out the nearest exit.

4. The drumming returns to the original moderate two-time. The hunters pick up the fallen buffalo and dance across to X where they gently lay him down, parallel to the Council Rock. They then take positions around the buffalo as shown by the numbers in Figure 52, six to eight feet

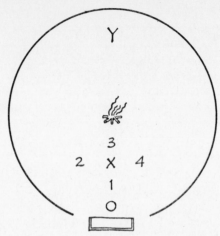

Figure 52. Diagram for the Cheyenne Buffalo Dance

from him as space permits and facing him. With spears raised above in charging position and with eyes on the buffalo they dance the following routine:

A. 16 counts—Sidestep one-fourth of the way around the circle with the flat-heel step (until No. 1 is in No. 2's position, No. 2 in No. 3's, etc.)
B. 8 counts—Dance up to the buffalo
C. 8 counts—Turning the palm of the spear hand upward so that the shaft of the spear rests on it, lower the point of the spear and very gently touch the buffalo with it
D. 4 counts—Raise spear again
E. 8 counts—Dance backward to position

Repeat A to E three times. Exit walking.

Careful attention should be given to the gesture of the spear and the touching of the buffalo with it. The turning of the palm of the hand upward so that the shaft of the spear rests on it is important—it relieves all harshness, all impression of death-dealing thrust, and makes of it a gesture of gentleness and grace, of feeling for the buffalo. The body is touched very softly.

In the authentic version the hunters sidestep all the way around the buffalo each time before each spear gesture but in order to shorten the routine to reasonable length it is recommended they move only one-fourth of the way around as described.

Ghost Dance

In this heart-rending dance the drama of the last stand of the Indian of the Plains is depicted, and that last stand was not a fighting stand!

JAMES C. STONE

Photograph by Arthur C. Allen

ROBERT MEEKER

All else had failed. Out of the east pale-faced men had come in never-ceasing thousands. There seemed no end to their coming. Valiantly the men had fought them, but in vain. They could not match their weapons nor their numbers. The buffalo were gone—the children were starving. In that dark hour they turned to religion, for only the gods could save them now —they danced the dances, sang the songs, more faithfully, and fervently than ever in the past. But death continued as the ruler of every day . . . and still the white ones came. Even their gods had failed them. . . .

Then out of the west there came a magic word, the Ghost Dance, spoken by Wovoka, prophet of the Piutes,—a new religion that promised life anew for the Red children, promised the passing of the white man and the return of the old way of life—if only they would lay down their arms and love their neighbors. It swept the Plains like wildfire and at last reached the Sioux. Men danced it everywhere—oh, how they danced it—their last pathetic prayer for life itself. The Ghost Dance was the last stand of the Plains Indian . . . that last stand was a *praying* stand.

They were dancing it on Wounded Knee in 1890, praying in this spirit of brotherly love when the white army shot them down, lest their savage "war dance" lead to an uprising! Thus ended a culture.

The Ghost Dance has been much discussed and described in written word. Its full record is set forth by Mooney.* To re-enact it in its entirety would be quite impossible and indeed, an unrewarding effort if it could be done. All that is here attempted is a fragment, using the basic movements augmented so as to create the mood and convey the message. In building the routine, evidence and suggestions from many sources have been utilized, combined with experience in presenting it in public countless times.

This impressive dance which tugs so heavily at the heartstrings is one of the simplest to produce, for anyone who can walk can dance it at first effort. Yet, no dance appeals so powerfully to the emotions.

COSTUMING

The costume worn by the Ghost Dancers consisted of a white shirt of cotton cloth painted with symbols. The use of such shirts is not at all necessary to achieve the effect of the dance. It is recommended that the dancers appear in ordinary dancing costume as in any other number, with the exception that *all bells must be removed*.

THE STEP

Stand erect and relaxed, with forearms held forward as in Figure 53, fists clenched. The drumming is in four-time, medium slow.

* James Mooney, *The Ghost-Dance Religion*, 14th Annual Report, Bureau of American Ethnology. Washington: Government Printing Office, 1896.

1. Step forward on left foot
2. Step back on right foot
3. Step back on left foot
4. Step forward on right foot

It is done in place. It is a sort of rocking motion, back and forth, back and forth, on and on monotonously. It is done without bells and without jar, silent and smooth. The right foot is brought down on the same spot each time, the left foot stepping a normal walking distance in front and in rear. The feet are brought down flat, avoiding the tendency to bring the heel down first as in walking. If the toes are curled up against the top of the moccasin or shoe it becomes easier to do it correctly. The knees are slightly bent and are flexible so as to take up the jar. The body is fully erect, head high, eyes fixed in the distance, face immobile and expressionless. In the routine of the dance, the dancers move to the left very gradually and almost imperceptibly.

Figure 53. Ghost Dancers in Team Arrangement

The dance also involves a movement into the fire and back, accompanied by an arm gesture illustrated in Figure 54. This very simple maneuver is done as follows:

1. 4 counts—Crouch and lean forward with left arm extended, palm of hand up, as shown in A, Figure 54. Take 4 long steps forward, the advancing leg fully extended and the foot brought down flat.
2. 4 counts—Raise left hand overhead, palm of hand facing back, rising to full height and looking up, as in B, Figure 54, marking time the while.
3. 4 counts—Raise right hand up overhead by carrying it up behind in a semi-circular course as indicated in C, Figure 54, at the same time lowering left hand, marking time the while. The palm of the right hand should face backward when it is overhead.

4. 4 counts—Bend forward into original crouch with right arm still extended as in D, marking time.
5. 4 counts—Take 4 steps backward into original position, retaining the crouch as in D throughout.
6. 4 counts—Mark time, still crouched
7. 4 counts—Repeat 1. The right arm is extended this time.
8. 4 counts—Repeat 2, raising right arm
9. 4 counts—Repeat 3, raising left arm and lowering right
10. 4 counts—Repeat 4, lowering left arm
11. 4 counts—Repeat 5
12. 4 counts—Mark time, rising into erect position

The whole movement is done tensely, fervently. The minute the crouch is assumed the dancers eyes are fixed forward, the hand held out with palm up and fingers extended, pointing forward, in which position the hand *is trembled up and down to portray emotion.* When the dancers take the 4 steps forward their feet lead far forward, toes pointing, as though some force pulls them on. When the arm is raised overhead it goes up *with the hand shaking* and when lowered it is brought down *tensely with hard shaking of the hand* as though to pull down some power that is in the heavens. Much of the effect of the dance rests in the serious, tense, fervent way these movements are made.

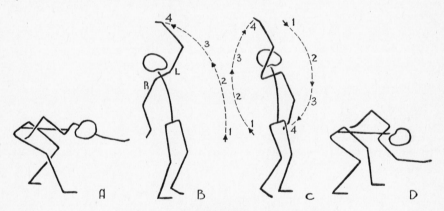

Figure 54. Ghost Dance Movement

THE DANCE

The mood of the dance is more important than the movements. *It is silent*—all bells are removed and the drumming is very soft, just loud enough to be audible to the dancers, done with a soft beater to muffle and soften the sound. *It is serious*—expressing the last hope, depicting the last stand of men after all else has failed. *It is religious*—a beseeching of the One Above for that which mortal effort can no longer bring.

As they dance the dancers must be fully sensitive that they are praying
... praying for food, clothing, shelter, for life itself, for themselves and
those they love. And the audience should be informed in preliminary statement of the tragic purpose behind the drama.

It is not necessary that the dancers have special dancing skill, since little
dancing is expected of them, but a Medicine Man with talent is required,
gifted in dramatic ability and judgment, and with good speaking voice. He
is the only one who need know the routine thoroughly, the dancers taking
their cues from him.

The Medicine Man carries a long feather or a feathered wand which he
holds up in front just above head level and manipulates by raising it to
arm's length overhead and lowering it, shaking it sidewise at the same time
to make it tremble.

As to numbers 20, 24, or 28 dancers may be used, 24 being recommended.
They are arranged in four balanced groups of six each. Each has a leader—
an old head, mature and experienced. The groups arrange themselves in lines
as indicated in Figure 55, with the leader of each group stationed near the
middle of the line, and all lock arms as in Figure 53, holding forearms forward with fists clenched. With arms thus locked it is possible for the leader
to control his dancers and prevent mismoves.

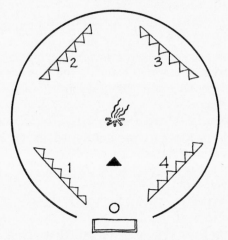

Figure 55. Diagram for the Ghost Dance

The dancers walk in and take positions. The Medicine Man takes his
position in front of the drum as indicated in Figure 55. For a long moment
they stand there motionless. The Medicine Man begins dancing the Ghost
Dance step as described. After he has taken four steps to set the rhythm the
drumming begins very softly and all start dancing. The count is medium-
slow, the rhythm never changing. From the start all eyes are fixed in the
distance, over the heads of all assembled, as though oblivious to all surroundings.

1. 32 counts—Dance with Ghost Dance step without alteration of expression
2. 16 counts—The Medicine Man silently signals that an approach to the central fire is to be made. This he does by holding his feather out at full arm's length horizontally and dramatically swinging it around in a circle as though pointing to everyone, looking at each team as he does so, the feather being caused to tremble and to flutter by shaking the hand. This wave is repeated twice as follows:

    A. 4 counts—Wave around in a circle with feather trembling
    B. 4 counts—Raise arm full length overhead and lower, feather trembling
    C. 4 counts—Repeat A
    D. 4 counts—Repeat B

3. 48 counts—On 1 the Medicine Man throws his hand with the feather toward the fire and instantly all unlock arms, crouch, advance to the fire and execute the arm gesture described on page 153 (Figure 54)
4. 32 counts—Lock arms and repeat 1
5. 16 counts—The Medicine Man signals to Groups 1 and 3 to advance to the fire using the same routine as in 2 but pointing to the two teams instead of swinging his arm in a circle
6. 48 counts—Repeat 3, with Groups 1 and 3 advancing to the fire and Groups 2 and 4 continuing to dance in position
7. 32 counts—Repeat 1
8. 16 counts—Repeat 5, pointing to Groups 2 and 4
9. 48 counts—Repeat 3, Groups 2 and 4 advancing and 1 and 3 dancing in position
10. 32 counts—Repeat 1
11. 16 counts—Repeat 2
12. 48 counts—Repeat 3, all advancing to the fire. Here the hypnotic effect of the dance begins to take effect. As they back up from the fire the second time one member of Group 1 falters and staggers for a moment. The Medicine Man flutters his feather in his face and he falls forward on his face, his arm still extended toward the fire, and remains motionless.
13. 32 counts—Repeat 1
14. 16 counts—Repeat 5, Medicine Man pointing to Groups 1 and 3
15. 48 counts—Repeat 3, Groups 1 and 3 going to the fire; as they back up to position a member of Group 3 falls to the ground
16. 32 counts—Repeat 1
17. 16 counts—Repeat 5, pointing to Groups 2 and 4

18. 48 counts—Repeat 3, Groups 2 and 4 advancing to the fire; as they
        advance a member of Group 2 falls, and as they back
        up a member of Group 4 falls
19. 32 counts—Repeat 1
20. 16 counts—Repeat 2
21. 48 counts—Repeat 3, all advancing to the fire more intensely and
        fervently than ever. As they back up, one dancer from
        Group 2 and one from Group 3 fall. *There are now six
        dancers lying prostrate on the ground.*
22. The ranks still standing continue dancing as before, all eyes wide
     and staring, more tense than ever in this final dramatic moment.
     The Medicine Man moves to directly in front of the Council Rock
     and the groups square off from him as in Figure 55, continuing the
     dance but not moving from position.
     The Medicine Man looks upward to the heavens, raising and lower-
     ing his feather on each 4 counts, fluttering it frantically. He stag-
     gers at times and misses rhythm as he catches himself. He pants
     audibly a time or two, then in a high-pitched wavery voice, he be-
     seeches the Great One:
          "Even to the East Wind (*pause 4 steps, panting*)
            From whence cometh the sun
          Even to the South Wind (pause 4 steps, panting)
            From whence cometh the warmth
          Even to the West Wind (pause 4 steps, panting)
            From whence cometh the rain
          Even to the North Wind (pause 4 faltering steps)
            From whence cometh the snow
          (*Looking downward and waving feather toward the earth*)
          Even to Maka Ina, Mother Earth (pause falteringly)
            From whence cometh our food.
          (*Looking heavenward, voice increasing in volume and rising
          in pitch*)
          Even to the Gitche Manito, the One Great Spirit
            From whence cometh all things
          Wakonda, *Wakonda*, WAKON...."
     The Medicine Man and all the dancers fall prostrate on their faces
     and lie motionless.
     For a long moment they lie thus, then the Medicine Man very
     slowly arises, and with hushed voice conducts the closing solemn
     ritual of the Grand Council. The dancers remain prostrate until the
     audience begins to leave.

Points to watch:
  1. *Eyes and facial expression*—keep eyes stary and focused on distance as
though transfixed.

2. *Tempo of step*—it will increase slightly in spite of all effort to prevent, but it must be kept as constant as possible, never hurried.

3. *Tenseness of hands in making the fire gesture*—they must shake conspicuously when raised and lowered, pulling down the Spirit Power from above.

4. *Movement to left*—it is *very* gradual, the groups moving no more than halfway around the ring in the course of the entire dance.

5. *Movement of Medicine Man*—he moves to left faster than the dancers, moving one-fourth of the way around the ring after each gesture sending the dancers into the fire. When the dancers are in the center doing the hand gestures he pleads desperately, waving his plume heavenward with increased vigor, up and down, fluttering it from side to side.

6. *Falling to ground*—this is done by placing the hands beside the chest to catch the weight. Instantly upon hitting the ground the hands are withdrawn and one arm extended toward the fire, after which there is no motion.

7. *Length of dance*—if the dance proves too long it may be shortened by cutting down the period between each advance to the fire. The routine as stated calls for 32 counts. This can be shortened to 16 if necessary. The 32 counts is merely suggestive, the exact length depending on the judgment of the Medicine Man.

Chapter VIII

GROUP DANCES OF THE CHEROKEES

As DELIGHTFUL and as useful a set of dances as is to be found in this volume are these Cherokee routines from the Great Smoky Mountains. Their charm rests in part in their utter simplicity, their naturalness. The war theme so rampant in the dancing of the northern Woodlands and Plains is conspicuously absent, so too the hunting theme, replaced by a delightful imitation of the world of nature. There is a lightness of touch, a cleverness, a playful quality about many of these dances. They possess a certain pleasantness that makes them enjoyed by spectators and participants. Quite lacking in brilliance and showy splendor, their appeal is nevertheless basic. Although unsuited as major numbers on a dance program, they are the best of introductory or build-up dances for the more dashing and elaborate spectacles.

One and all these dances call for "stomp dancing." This simple step in itself has a peculiar charm. When many do it together a unified up-and-down motion results that is unmistakably primitive and elemental. Dances that use it, spoken of as Stomp Dances, are common among all the tribes of the South, and appear across to Oklahoma and northward onto the Plains. It is thought by some that in ancient times this stomp style was Seminole and that it diffused from them westward and northward. Curtis describes the Stomp Dance of the Comanches in Oklahoma and relates that the old men refused to dance it, saying "It is not ours." *

These are the best of dances for beginners, entirely within their capacity because they demand no toe-heel dancing, no individual performance with intricate movements. Anyone who can walk can quickly learn to do them well.

Snake Dance

Simplest of all the Cherokee dances, the Snake Dance is the one with which to introduce this style of dancing. For in itself it is appealing and, once learned, provides the basis for the quick mastering of any Cherokee routine.

* Edward S. Curtis, *The North American Indian*. Volume XIX, page 214. Published by the author, 1930.

THE DANCE

Twenty dancers is the recommended number, a few more or less making little difference. They are arranged in one long file with the leader at the head. They stand close together, one behind the other, and must keep their distance throughout, never allowing the line to straggle out.

Figure 56. Snake Dance Spiral

The step is the stomp step described on page 37. In the later stages the double stomp is employed. This is a follow-the-leader dance. The drumming starts in medium tempo, unaccented.

1. 64 counts—With the stomp step done lightly, dance forward and then go into a spiral as indicated in Figure 56, making the spiral tighter and tighter until a compact group of dancers is formed.
2. 64 counts—The leader calls "Yo-o ho ho ho-o-o," raises his left arm overhead and points backward, turns to his right and starts in the opposite direction, unwinding the spiral and leading out into a straight line again. As the drum stops on the 64th count all stop with a quick, staccato shout, "Ho." They stand there naturally for a moment awaiting the drum.

3. Repeat 1 and 2. The tempo of the drumming is faster. The step changes to a more distinct stomp.
4. Repeat 1 and 2. The drumming increases in tempo and volume. The step changes to the *double stomp* and is done more strenuously. At the end they walk off the scene.

There is no need for the dancers to count their steps—that is done by the drummer who indicates by a louder beat that the direction is to be reversed and the spiral unwound. Indeed, the 64 counts is but indicative of the proper length and is not a hard and fast rule. The drummer uses his judgment as to the time to unwind the spiral. At the end he signals the finish by a louder beat at which the dancers stop and shout. As danced by the Cherokees the accompanying song determines the time for the unwinding and the finish; the 64 counts is taken from the song, but when songs are not used the length should be flexible, depending upon the drummer's judgment.

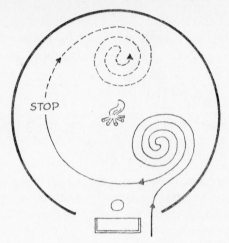

Figure 57. Diagram for the Snake Dance

The leader should begin the spiral very shortly after the dance starts, taking no more than 12 steps before so doing. The most appealing moments of the dance come when the line is tightly spiralled so as to form a solid mass of dancers moving up and down in unison in the characteristic movement of the stomp step. This being true the mass formation should be quickly developed and continued long enough to bring out its full effectiveness.

As done by the Cherokees the dance is repeated six times instead of three, gaining gradually in tempo and momentum throughout. For average use, however, three times is sufficient.

COMANCHE STOMP DANCE.—The Stomp Dance of the Comanches in Oklahoma is strikingly like the Cherokee Snake Dance. It opens with the line merely dancing around the area without spiralling. In the second unit the line spirals as in the Snake Dance except that the dancers join hands and unwind the line more vigorously as in the children's game of "crack the whip." In the third unit the spiral is repeated but with increasing tempo and more vigorous movement.

Ant Dance

He who has seen two friendly ants greet each other will know the truth of this dance in imitation of the Ant People. Long they pause with heads close together and flick their antennae in each other's faces. Such is the motif of this dance, the dance of a people who live close to the earth and are one with all its people, big and small.

Thoroughly typical of the Cherokee dance mood, it is one of the cleverest and best-loved of their dances.

THE DANCE

Sixteen dancers is the ideal number, arranged in two groups of eight, each with a mature and dependable leader. Arrange each group in a file with its leader at the head. Group 2 falls in behind Group 1 to form one long file.

It is a follow-the-leader dance and only the leaders need to know the routine in detail. The step is the usual stomp step described on page 37. The drumming is in medium tempo, unaccented.

1. The column trots in with the stomp step done lightly and goes counterclockwise around the ring or stage as indicated by the line in Figure 58, continuing thus until halfway around.

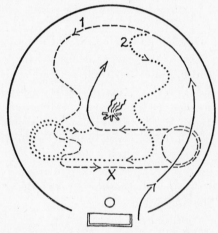

Figure 58. Diagram for the Ant Dance

2. Here the leader of Group 2 leads his dancers out of the line, as indicated in the diagram, while Group 1 continues on. Each group weaves along following the curving course shown in Figure 57 until they pass each other at the point marked X.

3. As the two leaders come abreast in passing at X they stop, turn their faces toward each other, look each other squarely in the eyes, hold the ends of their two index fingers directly in front of their eyes, and flick the fingers down and up four times in rhythm, marking time with their feet the while (see page 135). The other dancers mark time while this is going on. The two leaders then pass on to the next

two dancers and repeat, continuing thus until each dancer in each line has flicked his fingers at each dancer in the other.

4. The two lines continue on in opposite direction and each goes into a small circle as shown in Figure 58. They go around the circle one-and-one-half times.

5. The leaders lead their dancers out of the circle, Group 1 moving across toward Group 2, and Group 2 joining on the end of Group 1, as indicated by the lines in Figure 58, thus forming one long line and moving clockwise. As soon as the line straightens out the drumming stops, all stop dancing, and shout a quick staccato "Ho."

6. *Repeat the entire dance.* The drumming is faster and the step is a more emphatic stomp, the dance moving with greater animation. The line is moving clockwise this time.

7. *Repeat the entire dance again.* The step changes to the *double stomp* and is done with still greater zest.

The unique feature that gives color and interest to the dance is the ant-like flicking of the fingers, a cute bit of business when well-done. The dancer should turn his head to one side, look the other squarely in the eyes, and smile. The fingertips should be directly in front of his eyes from which position the fingers are moved down and up. Plenty of time should be allowed for this, the dancers should be cautioned not to rush it. The photograph facing page 135 shows the proper head and finger positions.

Much depends on the judgment of the two leaders in timing the various maneuvers. When the dance is repeated the second time the leaders maneuver so as to bring the two lines past each other at a different point in the ring or on the stage. A still different location is chosen the third time. This is important to permit the spectators to see the finger flicking from different angles.

The diagram in Figure 58 shows the course to be followed in the first dance. In the second the line is moving around the ring or stage in the opposite direction. The judgment of the leaders must be relied upon to approximate the same routine each time.

Careful attention should be given to the description of the stomp step on page 37.

Pigeon Dance

Timid, frail, defenseless, the pigeons live in mortal fear of the eagle. Tremblingly the flock stops and scans the sky less the frightful one be coming. When at last he swoops upon them they cringe helplessly and huddle together. The eagle selects a young and tender one and carries him away. Deep in despair, with feathers drooping, the pigeons depart.

Such is the Pigeon Dance, typically Cherokee in mood and pattern.

THE DANCE

Sixteen to twenty dancers are needed, divided into two equal groups, each with a leader. Each group is arranged in a file according to height with the leader at the head. Another dancer is needed to represent the eagle.

The step is the flat-foot trot done in a gentle and pigeon-like manner, without stomping. The dancers hold their arms out to the sides to represent wings. The drumming is in medium tempo, unaccented.

The diagram for the stage is shown in Figure 59 and for the council ring in Figure 10. The following description applies to the council ring—if on the stage the directions can easily be applied to Figure 59.

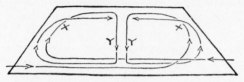

Figure 59. Diagram for the Pigeon Dance on the Stage

1. The two lines enter one either side of the Council Rock as shown in Figure 60, and start in opposite directions around the ring. With wings outspread and bodies bent slightly forward at the hips, the pigeons dance timidly along, their heads turned up toward the sky, ever-fearful of the eagle. They continue until they reach the point marked X. Here the drum hits a louder beat indicating that after four steps a stop is to be made.

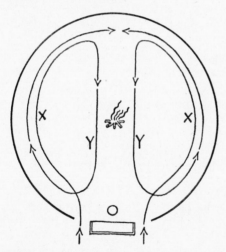

Figure 60. Diagram for the First Part of the Pigeon Dance

2. All stop and scan the sky for the eagle—they crouch a little, their heads turned upward, looking from side to side across the sky, their eyes

large and fearful in expression, their hands trembling. For *eight counts* they stand, moving up and down by flexing their knees to the drumming.

3. They continue around until the two lines meet, then turn toward the fire in a double column, two abreast, passing either side of the fire as shown. They continue to the point marked Y where the drum signals to indicate a stop as before.
4. They stop and repeat 2.
5. They continue across the ring and start around again as shown until they reach X where another stop is made as before.
6. They repeat 2, pausing for the *eight counts*, after which they hop backward on both feet for *four hops*, then pause and repeat 2 again.
7. They continue around until the two lines meet as shown. At this point the eagle enters from the Council Rock. The pigeons squat to the ground, cringing and trembling, stark fear on their faces.
8. Using a light toe-trot and with wings outspread, the eagle swoops into the ring and soars back and forth in a figure-of-8 course between the Council Rock and the fire, looking over the pigeons. He moves closer to them, his eyes centering on the one marked by the arrow in Figure 61.

Figure 61. Diagram for the Last Part of the Pigeon Dance

9. The doomed pigeon flutters over to the open space where the two lines meet, following the course of the dotted line. The pigeons near him move in front of him to protect him.
10. The eagle soars closer and the pigeons draw away from the doomed one, cringing to the ground and leaving him to his fate. The eagle swoops upon him, grabs him by the arm, crosses the ring and exits, pulling him along behind.

11. The depressed pigeons arise and form their lines again. With feathers drooping and heads hanging they trot slowly across the ring in a double column, two abreast, passing either side of the fire, and exit.

This is one of those rare dances where facial expression plays a large part. The timidity and anxiety of the pigeons must be shown on their faces from the start and their fear of the eagle when he enters must be evident. They must remember they are pigeons.

If eagle wings such as shown in Figure 30 are available they should be used on the eagle's arms, otherwise he may merely hold out his arms to represent wings and proceed unornamented.

Beaver Dance

Here is comedy—here is actual competition instead of make-believe— here is unrehearsed action—all of which combines to make of the Beaver Dance the most popular in this chapter of popular dances. Here the characteristic mood of the Cherokees is at its best.

Of all the animals, the beaver is the most industrious, the most human in his planning for the days ahead. He harms no one and was harmed by no one unnecessarily—until the white man came. Alas, the white man killed him by the thousands and the hundreds of thousands—it seemed that the white man loved to kill! But happily, the white man's aim is not always good!

The "beaver" is a bundle of fur on a rope attached to a pulley. By pulling the rope back and forth the Beaver Handler can make him jump about in life-like fashion. Each armed with a three-foot stick the dancers in turn attempt to hit the beaver but, agile as he is, their aim is usually not good enough. The dance is a contest to hit the beaver and much comedy results from the failures, which are always more numerous than the successes.

As done by the Cherokees, both men and women participate in couples, and the serious but futile antics of the squaws to contact the beaver provide a high point of interest.

PROPERTIES

Sixteen three-foot sticks are needed, of about the thickness of a broomstick. The bark should be peeled off to reveal the white wood.

The "beaver" can be made from any piece of old fur or from a piece of canvas, wrapped over a padding of burlap, and attached to a rope. Figure 62 shows one made from a ground-hog skin and indicates the shape. There is no particular need to make it look like an animal. It should measure about 18 inches long and 4 inches in thickness. Secure 25 to 40 feet of cotton clothesline, the length depending upon the space. Build the "beaver" around the rope so that the rope goes right through it, thus giving it strength. Wrap strips of burlap or old cloth around the rope for padding until the "beaver" takes on the proper shape. Around this sew the fur or canvas. If white canvas is used the rope should be dyed black for contrast so that the "beaver" can be easily seen.

Figure 62. "The Beaver"

Drive an 18-inch pole in the ground at the edge of the council ring, at P in Figure 65. Run the rope through a small pulley and wire the pulley to the pole. The Beaver Handler is at H holding the rope so that he can pull the "beaver" back and forth. The "beaver" itself is located at B.

On the stage, the pulley can be attached to a wing near the front of the stage, with the Beaver Handler near the wings at the other side. If the "beaver" cannot be seen from all points of the house as it lies on the stage floor, the handler can raise it by stretching the rope tight and manipulate it in the air.

THE DANCE

Sixteen dancers are needed, arranged in pairs. Each has one of the sticks. The dance is in two parts:

I

With the sticks on their shoulders the dancers walk in in one long file and form a circle around the fire as shown in Figure 63. 1 and 2 constitute

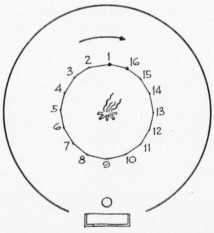

Figure 63. Diagram for the Opening of the Beaver Dance

Photograph by Paul Boris

JAMES C. STONE

Photograph by Homer Jensen

Laborers in Darkness

a pair, 3 and 4, etc., but they stand one behind the other as shown, all facing in the direction of the arrow. When the circle is formed each swings his stick down from his right shoulder and holds it in front at hip level so that the man in front of him can grasp the end of it in his right hand. Each man thus holds two sticks in his right hand, the end of his own and the end of the man's behind him. A complete circle of sticks is thus formed.

1. 64 counts—The drumming is medium-slow, unaccented. The drummer hits one preliminary beat and all shout "Yo-o ho ho ho-o-o" and the dance begins. With the stomp done lightly they dance around the circle clockwise as shown by the arrow. At the end all stop and shout a short, staccato "Ho."

2. 64 counts—Repeat 1. The drumming is faster; the stomp step is done more emphatically.

3. 64 counts—Repeat 1. The drumming is still faster, the step the *double stomp*.

II

Each dancer releases the stick of the man in back of him and raises his own stick over his shoulder as in "shoulder arms". The couples form, No. 2 walking up beside No. 1, No. 4 beside No. 3, etc. They close up to form a column, two abreast.

1. The drumming is medium fast, the step is the stomp step done lightly. The column turns to the left and moves in the direction of the arrow in Figure 64, the first couple leading and the rest following. They continue on and go into a circular formation as shown in Figure 65, still dancing two abreast, moving around in the direction of the arrow.

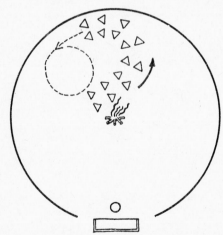

Figure 64. Diagram for the Beaver Dance

2. The leading couple shouts "Yo-o ho ho ho-o-o," turns out of the group and starts around it in the opposite direction, as indicated by the dotted line in Figure 65, the rest of the group dancing on as usual. The couple continues around to X where No. 2 remains and No. 1 continues on to the beaver. Nearing the beaver he takes his stick from his shoulder and prepares for action. The Beaver Handler jerks the beaver, making it jump and hop. The dancer moves back and forth,

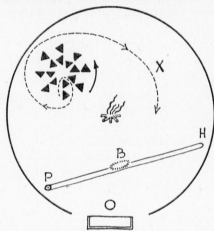

Figure 65. Diagram for the Beaver Dance

his eyes glued on the beaver, making passes at it with his stick. It is a forthright contest, the dancer attempting to hit the beaver and the Beaver Handler attempting to make him miss. Seeing his chance, the dancer swings his stick down hard. If he misses he throws his stick hard on the ground in front of the drum and exits. If he hits it he trots out, dropping his stick down in front of the drum as he passes. Then his partner, No. 2, dances up and repeats.

3. Repeat until each couple has had its try at the beaver.

Of course, the unique feature of the dance is the effort to hit the beaver and the interest of the spectators centers there. Good dancers augment this interest by preliminary business and, by so doing, also increase their chances of making a hit. Merely to dance up and swing at the beaver is poor showmanship, and poor competitive technique—it provides little spectacle and little chance of scoring. As the Beaver Handler jerks the beaver and feints with it, the dancer feints with his stick, dancing up and back and from side to side, trying to outsmart the Handler. When he does swing to hit, good sportsmanship demands that he make a full-arm swing and not hold his stick a foot or so above the beaver and tap at it.

A dramatic touch is added if the drummer shouts to indicate whether or not a hit is scored. In case of a hit he shouts, "Ho ho-o-o." In case of a failure, "Wah, wah."

Social Dance

Happiest of all dances is the Social Dance, most enjoyed by the dancers themselves. It is in the lightest of moods, playful always. It is a follow-the-leader dance wherein each repeats precisely what the head man does—indeed, in the later stages the leader deliberately tries to confuse the dancers into error by feinting with false moves. If this fact is announced before the dance starts the mistakes will prove amusing and serve as a contribution rather than a detriment.

Chief among its many charms, however, is the use of calls made by the leader in sing-song fashion and echoed by the dancers in unison. Each call has an accompanying gesture which is made by the leader and imitated by the others.

The more gifted the leader and the better his showmanship, the more chance will the dance have to provide good entertainment.

In the following description the Indian words are spelled as they sound, rather than with their authentic spelling. Indeed many of the authentic words are distorted by the Indians in the dance in much the same way that English words are corrupted by the Square Dance caller.

THE DANCE

Any number of dancers may be used, 16 being desirable. They stand in one long file behind the leader. The step is the stomp step. The dance is done by the Cherokees without drumming but the use of the drum is strongly recommended as a means to keeping the dancers moving in unison. The dance is controlled by the leader, however, and not by the drummer, the latter taking his cues from the calls.

The dance is in a series of units, at the end of each the dancers stopping and standing for a moment until the start of the next.

They walk in in line and wait for the start.

1. The leader calls "Yo-o ho ho ho-o-o" and the drumming starts. They dance forward with the stomp step. The leader calls "Ho-he" and all answer in unison "Ho-he." As the leader calls, he raises his right hand and points to someone in the crowd. All dancers then raise their hands and point in the same direction. The calling and the pointing are done in rhythm, the leader calling the first syllable "Ho" as he steps with his left foot and the second syllable "he" as he steps with his right. As he says "Ho" he raises his right hand and when he says "he" he points with it. On the next two steps the dancers call and point, then the leader repeats, etc. There is thus a call on every step. In count it goes as follows:

(1) Leader calls "Ho" raising hand
(2) Leader calls "He" pointing
(3) Dancers call "Ho" raising hands

(4) Dancers call "He" pointing

(5) Leader calls "Ho" raising hand, etc.

This continues halfway around the ring when the leader yips loudly and stops, all doing likewise.

2. Repeat 1. *The call*—"Hō-yā."

The motion—(1) raise both hands in front of chest, (2) throw them out to left side, palms up, as if handing something to someone. The arms are not fully extended, the elbows remaining at the sides

3. Repeat 1. *The call*—"Hō'ho-yā'."

The motion—raise both hands slightly above head level on the first syllable and drop them to the level of the ears on the second.

4. Repeat 1. *The call*—"Gē-stew" (rabbit) The "ge" is pronounced as in geese.

The motion—(1) hold both hands out to left side, (2) grab as if to grab the rabbit.

5. Repeat 1. *The call*—"Ush-kon" (rabbit's head). The last syllable is nasal.

The motion—(1) hold hands out to left side, fists closed, right above left, (2) twist the rabbit's head off.

6. Repeat 1. *The call*—"Te-yō'hä-lā'" (lizard).

The answer—"Yä'-yä-ho'."

The motion—(a) (1) Point to left and upward (to the mountain where the lizards were seen), (2) pull hand back. Repeat 3 times.

(b) (1) Hold hands up and make circles with the thumb and middle finger of each hand (he had big eyes), (2) drop hands. Repeat 3 times.

(c) Hold right hand out flat, palm down, fingers together and wiggle fingers up and down (his tail went like this). Repeat 3 times.

7. Repeat 1. *The call*—"Wä'-wä-hoo'" (owl).

The answer—"Yä'-yä-hō'."

The motion—(1) reach hands overhead and grab as if to grab the owl, (2) lower hands.

8. The leader calls "Yo-o ho ho ho-o-o" and about-faces. All odd-numbered men in the line about-face (Nos. 1, 3, 5, etc.) and each joins hands with the man behind, right hands together and left hands together, as in A, Figure 66. The arms are thus crossed. The right hands should be under-

neath the left hands. The following directions apply to the odd men (Nos. 1, 3, 5, etc.), their partners making the necessary corresponding movements:

   a. 4 counts—Dance backward
   b. 4 counts—Go to the left and step behind partner, both now facing in same direction, raising left arm over his head in passing and placing arms on his shoulders, hands still clasped, as in B, Figure 66.
   c. 4 counts—Dance forward
   d. 4 counts—Go to right and step in front of partner, facing him as before, lifting left arm over his head in passing.

Repeat throughout.

The call and the answer is "Hō'-hē'."

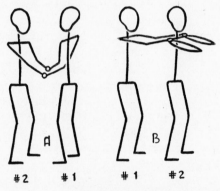

Figure 66.

9. Here the leader attempts to confuse the dancers who are expected to follow his every move. He calls "Yo-o ho ho ho-o-o" as usual and starts forward. The call and the answer is "Hō'-yā'." The following are typical movements—these and similar ones can be used in any order to suit the fancy of the leader:

   a. Turn around and dance in opposite direction 4 steps, then turn front again.
   b. Turn part way around, then suddenly turn front again
   c. Turn all the way around, then turn to the rear and start dancing in the opposite direction; continue 4 steps and then start backing up.
   d. Spin all the way around quickly in 2 counts—repeat several times if desired
   e. Turn toward the fire and dance toward it 4 steps then dance backward into line.
   f. Dance in a Figure-of-8 course, toward the fire and out, 4 steps in each direction.

The leader often feints with these movements, making a motion as though to start one and changing to something else. The unit ends with the usual yip.

10. The leader calls "Yo-o ho ho ho-o-o" and the line starts forward. The leader calls "Sti-yu" (dance hard), whereupon they all go into the Sti-yu step (page 32), if they can do it, otherwise the double stomp. The call is not repeated throughout but is merely called once by the leader, after which the drumming increases in tempo and the more strenuous dancing begins. The leader yips to finish and they walk out to exit.

Corn-meal Dance

A group that knows several of the Cherokee dances will like this Corn-meal Dance. It is not recommended as the first Cherokee routine to be learned.

As the dance opens the women are symbolizing the pounding of the corn meal as they dance the stomp step. The men come in from the fields to eat, carrying their hoes (sticks) on their shoulders. The handling of the sticks in the dance represents the use of the hoe in the field.

THE DANCE

Twelve to sixteen dancers are needed, divided into two groups, one representing the women and the other the men. Each is arranged in a file behind its leader. The more experienced and dependable dancers should be used for the men. Each man carries a stick three feet long and about as thick as a broomstick. The step is the stomp step. The drumming is in medium tempo, unaccented.

The dance is in a series of units, at the end of each the dancers stopping and standing for a moment until the drum starts for the next unit. The dancers go around and around the ring in counterclockwise direction:

1. 64 counts—The women enter and dance forward with the stomp step. After 32 counts the men enter with the stomp step done lightly, the sticks on their right shoulders as in "shoulder arms." They dance directly across and join on behind the women, making one long line. The drumming stops, all shout "Ho" and stop dancing.

2. 32 counts—They dance forward for eight steps, then the leader of the men leads his group out of the line, the women proceeding as usual. The men dance up beside the women and fall in between them, the women spreading to provide space. The men take positions 1, 3, 5, etc., in the line. The drumming stops and all shout "Ho."

3. 32 counts—They dance forward with the stomp step. The men swing their sticks down from their shoulders, take them in both

hands and make a pass at the ground as though to dig it up and then place them back on their shoulders. As they shove at the ground all yip. This is done in one quick flourish, completed in four drumbeats. They dance forward four counts with sticks on shoulders, flourish them forward on the next four counts, keep them on shoulders for the next four, etc. The drum stops and all shout.

4. 32 counts—Repeat 3. The drum is faster, the stomp step done more emphatically.

5. 32 counts—Repeat 3. The drum is louder, the step is the *double stomp*.

6. 48 counts—The step changes to the original quiet stomp step. The men pair up together and the women together: the man in No. 3 position dances up beside No. 1, the woman in No. 4 position beside No. 2, etc. Thus there are pairs of men and pairs of women alternating throughout the line. The men take their sticks from their shoulders and hold them lightly in both hands crosswise in front of their chests. They move the sticks up and down as they dance, up as they step with the left foot and down on the right, the sticks being moved only a few inches by turning the wrists up and down. The drumming stops, all yip and stop dancing.

7. 48 counts—Repeat 6. The drumming is faster, the stomp step more emphatic, the sticks held higher, in front of the face, and moved up and farther on each step.

8. 48 counts—Repeat 7. The *double stomp* step is done vigorously, the sticks held at the level of the top of the head.

They break formation and walk out to exit.

Quail Dance

Reflecting again the inclination of the Cherokees to take their motifs from the world of nature, this dance is in imitation of the movements of a covey of quail.

THE DANCE

Twelve to sixteen dancers are needed, divided into two groups, each arranged in a file behind its leader. Group 2 falls in behind Group 1 to make one long line. The step is the stomp step described on page 37. The drumming is in medium tempo, unaccented.

1. Dancing the stomp step lightly the column enters and goes counter-clockwise until halfway around the ring, where Group 2 turns out of line and the two groups form a double column as indicated in

Figure 67, and go directly across the ring. When the leaders reach the edge of the ring all stop suddenly.

2. They hold four counts, then make four long hops backward on both feet, hold four counts, and trot forward three steps and hop on the fourth, to stop suddenly with both feet together.

3. Repeat 2

4. Repeat 2

5. The lines face each other. Group 2 marks time with the stomp step, Group 1 dances backward to the edge of the ring with the double stomp step for 16 counts, then advances for 16 counts to the original position. This is repeated twice more, three times in all, with increasing vigor each time. Both groups turn toward the drum and stop suddenly.

6. Repeat 2, three times

7. Repeat 5, with Group 2 doing the dancing and Group 1 marking time.

8. Repeat 2, three times

9. The leader of Group 1 leads his line out toward the edge of the ring and Group 2 join on behind to form one long line. They go into a circle around the fire and dance the double stomp step vigorously.

10. The drum indicates the finale by four skipped beats and stops. They break formation, all whirl toward the exit, crouch, spread their arms as wings, and with a very fast toe-trot, flutter out like a covey of quail suddenly frightened. No drumming accompanies the exit.

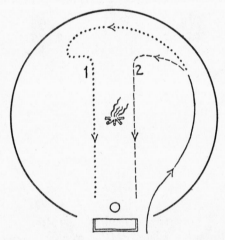

Figure 67. Diagram for the Quail Dance

The main difficulty encountered is in causing all dancers to stop together for routine 2. A drum signal will facilitate this. As the dancers come up to the edge of the ring at the end of routine 1, the drum indicates by a louder beat that in 4 steps the stop is to be made. If all stop together the dancers will have no difficulty in hopping and stopping in unison throughout routine 2.

Eagle Dance

This beautiful dance is unique among the Cherokee dances—indeed, among all of the dances in this book regardless of tribe. While reserved, as are all Cherokee routines, it involves a spectacular waving of feather fans in chorus fashion of a type seldom seen in Indian dancing, and a kind of showmanship unusual among the Cherokees. For stage use it is unexcelled. Its second part is built on the war motif and features a touch of toe-heel dancing, again departing from the Great Smoky Mountain type.

Here are really two dances in one, two distinct and unrelated units, either one of which could be used as a separate dance. In fact these are but two of many episodes or separate units of the Eagle Dance, selected as the most appealing and useful, the others being laid aside only because of lack of space.

PROPERTIES

Eight fans are needed, illustrated in Figure 68, the authentic Cherokee fan at A, and a homemade but very satisfactory substitute at B. In the authentic fan the white-and-black-tipped eagle feathers are held in a wooden frame. For a quickly made substitute, secure heavy cardboard from a corrugated box and cut into curved pieces as shown, 8 inches long

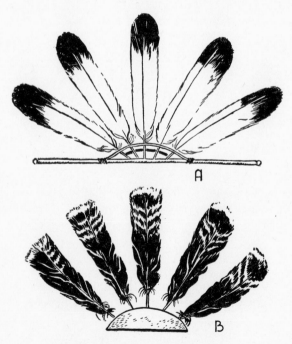

Figure 68. Eagle Dance Fans

and 2½ inches wide at the middle. Run an ice pick into the edge to make a hole and then insert the quills of the feathers. In this way the whole eight fans can be made in a half-hour. Dark turkey feathers are excellent if eagle feathers cannot be had, the white bands across the tips creating delightful effects as the fans are waved.

THE STEP

Hold the fan overhead with both hands as shown in A, Figure 69, the fingers placed on the back and the thumb in front. Standing fully erect dance forward with the flat-foot trot:
1. 4 counts—Dip deeply to the left as shown in B, Figure 69
2. 4 counts—Repeat to the right

The fan is thus waved from side to side, four steps to each sideward dip. The body bends from the hips and the whole movement is done with a smooth and graceful sway.

Figure 69. Position of Fans in Part I of the Eagle Dance

THE DANCE

Eight dancers are needed for the chorus. The dance is in two distinct units which are really separate dances. In the second, a good toe-heel dancer is needed in addition to the chorus.

I

The dancers walk in and arrange themselves in two lines as shown in Figure 70, the dancers spaced four feet apart. They hold their fans overhead as described.
1. 16 counts—Dance forward waving fans in unison on every 4 counts, first to the left and then to the right, as described

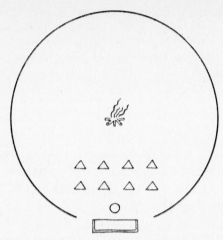

Figure 70. Diagram for Part I of the Eagle Dance

2. 16 counts—Dance backward to the original position, waving fans as before

3. 16 counts—Repeat 1

4. 16 counts—Repeat 2

5. 16 counts—The front line repeats 1, the back line marks time but waves the fans as usual

6. 4 counts—The front line about-faces without stopping the fan wave, the back line marking time

7. 16 counts—The two lines dance up and meet on 8 counts and dance backward on 8 counts—the fans in the two lines are now moving in opposite directions

8. 16 counts—Repeat 7

9. 16 counts—The lines dance toward each other and pass on through, changing positions

10. 4 counts—Each line about-faces, facing each other, without breaking the fan sway

11. 16 counts—Repeat 7

12. 16 counts—Repeat 7

13. 16 counts—Repeat 9

14. 4 counts—The back line about-faces, front line marking time— both lines are now facing in the same direction with fans waving in the same direction

15. 16 counts—Front line dances backward to the position held at the beginning of the dance

16. 16 counts—Both lines dance forward and stop, holding fans overhead for a moment to finish, then lower fans and walk to position for the second part of the dance

II

The dancers walk from the formation at the end of Part I into the formation shown in Figure 71. Each holds his fan in front of him in the position shown in Figure 72. The drumming changes to a medium fast, accented two-time. The chorus is to dance around the ring with the flat-foot trot *stepping on the loud beat only* and taking very short steps so as to advance slowly. *On each step they snap the fans up and down by an emphatic bending the wrist.*

The toe-heel dancer called the Scalp Boy enters, stands in front of the chorus as shown in Figure 71. He is to dance in front of the chorus portraying his war exploit in three episodes, and after each, stops and explains his story to the group in pantomime.

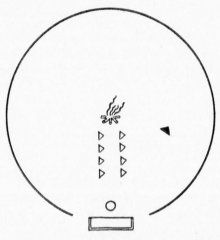

Figure 71. Diagram for Part II of the Eagle Dance

1. The chorus dances around the ring quietly as described, the Scalp Boy moving in advance and displaying himself with toe-heel dancing. He is ever-alert for the enemy, looking into the distance, shading his eyes, pushing bushes aside, etc., all of which movements are described on page 55. He looks at the ground, discovers tracks, stoops and examines them, then straightens up and whirls toward the group. The drumming ceases and all stop.

Facing the chorus the Scalp Boy further explains by gestures what happened on the exploit he is re-enacting: He points to the tracks, bends down and indicates their position, looks ahead in the direction the tracks go, points in the distance as if to say, "I found his tracks here and they went that way. I figured I'd find him over there." After each movement he looks at the chorus as though explaining to them.

2. The drumming starts and they proceed as before. The Scalp Boy follows the tracks rapidly to gain distance ahead of the chorus, then stops

and looks at them, dances a few steps farther, drops to the ground and freezes for a moment. He arises, faces the chorus, and all stop.

The Scalp Boy explains the situation—he points ahead cautiously, nods his head to the chorus, holds up one finger to indicate one enemy, as if to say, "I discovered one enemy over there."

Figure 72. Position of Fans in Part II of the Eagle Dance

3. The dance starts again. The Scalp Boy creeps forward rapidly, holds a moment, creeps farther and then drops to the ground and freezes. He raises his tomahawk twice in measuring the distance, then slowly comes to his feet and leaps on the enemy, bringing the tomahawk down hard. He drops to the ground, takes the scalp, rises and holds it overhead, looking at the chorus.

4. The drumming increases in tempo and the chorus breaks into a pow-wow, scattering across the ring, the Scalp Boy joining them. They hold their fans in their right hands overhead, waving and waving them back and forth. All dance in the upright position, moving gracefully and placing the emphasis on the waving of the fans. A delightful picture results. The dance ends in the Powwow (page 62).

Chapter IX

GROUP DANCES FROM THE SOUTHWEST

OUT OF THE astounding galaxy of chorus dances, the brilliance and artistry of which have brought well-deserved fame to the Southwest tribes, four have been selected which are of sufficient simplicity as to offer hope of easy presentation. All are of the quiet, reserved type characteristic of those gentle, gracious, gifted artists of the sunlit mesa country.

Aleo

It is in the corral that the Aleo is danced. It has been so for long years. Beyond that I confess to know nothing. Queries bring only the answer, "It is in the corral that the Aleo is danced."

From the Jemez Pueblo it comes where fluid bodies lend to it a grace and charm found only in Adobe Land. A superb quiet number, indicated for a spot early in the program.

THE STEP

The drumming is slow, of about the tempo used in very slow walking. It is in two-time, accented *loud*-soft.

The step is danced in place without making progress:

1. Jump on left foot and at the same time tap right toe in front
& Raise left heel and at the same time lift right foot, then drop left heel down on the count and simultaneously tap right toe beside left foot.
2. Jump on right foot and at the same time tap left toe in front
& Raise right heel and at the same time lift left foot, then bring right heel down on the count and simultaneously tap left toe beside right foot.

It is a limp flowing motion without the slightest jerk or jar. This is accomplished by the handling of the feet. To make it clear, let us discuss it step by step:

1. When you jump on the left foot the weight is taken on the ball of the foot, after which the heel is immediately dropped softly. The foot thus

serves as a spring to relieve the jar, and the knee which is soft, also serves in this capacity. At the same time that the left foot jumps the right toe is tapped gently in front at normal walking distance forward.

&. The left heel is raised slowly and lowered again on the count, thus raising and lowering the whole body. As this is done the right foot is raised from its position in front to a height of about six inches and is drawn back in a semi-circular course, the toe placed gently beside the left foot.

On the next count the movements are reversed as the right foot jumps.

The body is held erect and is thoroughly relaxed throughout, with the arms hanging in languid fashion at the sides. Once learned the step is very simple, the only difficulty being one of keeping balance to the slow drumming in raising and lowering.

THE DANCE

Four dancers are needed, arranged in the following formation:

4

I   2

3

Numbers 1 and 2 face each other, and 3 and 4 do likewise. The distance between 1 and 2, and between 3 and 4 is twelve feet. They walk in and take their positions before the drumming starts. The drumming is in two-time, accented on one, counted 1-&, 2-&, etc. Each unit of loud and soft beat is considered one count.

1. 24 counts—Dance in position using the Aleo step.
2. 4 counts—1 and 2 trot across to change positions, using a slow flat-foot trot, stepping on each drumbeat. 3 and 4 continue dancing in position.
3. 4 counts—3 and 4 trot across to change positions, using a slow flat-foot trot, stepping on each drumbeat. 1 and 2 continue dancing in position.
4. 24 counts—Repeat 1
5. 4 counts—Repeat 2
6. 4 counts—Repeat 3
7. 24 counts—Repeat 1
8. 4 counts—Repeat 2
9. 4 counts—Repeat 3
10. 24 counts—Repeat 1
11. 4 counts—Repeat 2
12. 4 counts—Repeat 3
13. 24 counts—Repeat 1
14. 16 counts—1 and 2 trot to center and meet, 1 turns toward exit and 2 follows him, 3 falls in behind 2 and 4 brings up the end—in file they trot off and exit.

When the dancers trot across to change positions they use a relaxed flat-foot trot in which the ball of the foot touches the ground a fraction of a second before the heel is brought down in order to relieve the jar. The knee is very soft and flexes with each step. As the dancers start across they crouch just a little, dropping the head and shoulders for two steps, then coming up straight again as they pass each other. They cross in six steps and turn around into position on the 7th and 8th steps.

The secret of this dance rests in a completely relaxed, fluid body.

Jemez Buffalo Dance

Buffalo dances there are, and many, among the Western tribes, and each one differs from the others, yet when well danced, each could be unmistakably recognized as a buffalo dance even though its name were not known. The dance of each tribe reflects the temperament of the tribe, yet each imitates the characteristic movements of those big, gentle cattle of the prairies. It is not surprising that the buffalo dance of the quiet Pueblo artists should stand out in contrast to that of the dashing, fighting Sioux of the northern Plains, described on page 148, but both are unmistakably buffalo dances. So different are they in mood that an interesting study in contrast results if the two are staged one after the other, first the Jemez Buffalo, and then the Sioux Buffalo.

One who has witnessed the Buffalo Dance in the Southwest with all its gorgeous costuming including the buffalo headpiece, may question the dance as possible without all these adornments. Needless to say it would be more dramatic with them, not to say authentic, yet there is no gainsaying that a delightful dance results when the routine is followed in ordinary dancing costume without special makeup.

The routine here given follows the original as closely as is practical to attempt without the use of the songs.

THE STEP

There are two special movements or steps involved:

The first represents the slowly undulating motion of the buffalo as the herd is grazing. The drumming is in slow accented two-time. The step is done in place, without making progress.

1. Step on the left foot and bend the knee slowly, thus lowering the body
&. Straighten the left leg slowly thus raising the body
2. Step on right foot and bend the knee slowly, thus lowering the body
&. Straighten the right leg slowly, thus raising the body

The result is a lowering and raising of the body accomplished entirely by knee action. It is a smooth, even, up-and-down motion. As the weight

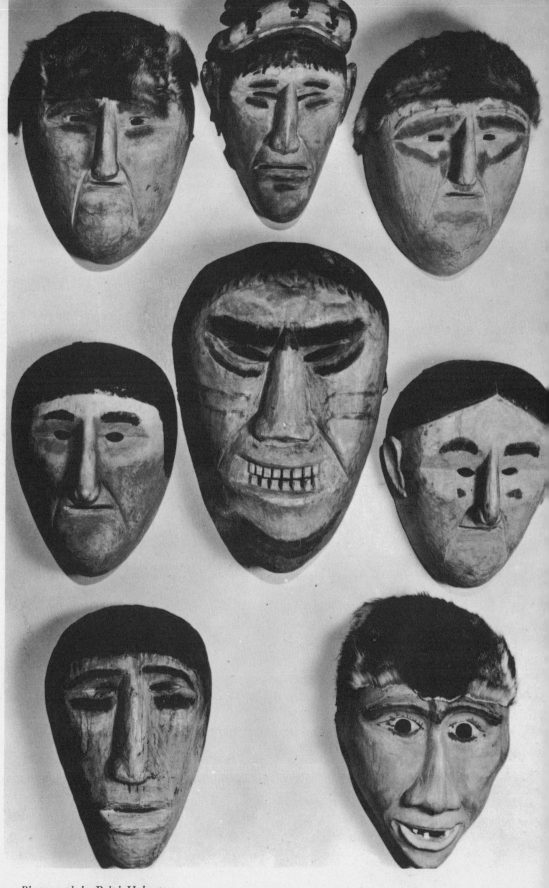

Masks of the Smoky Mountain Cherokees

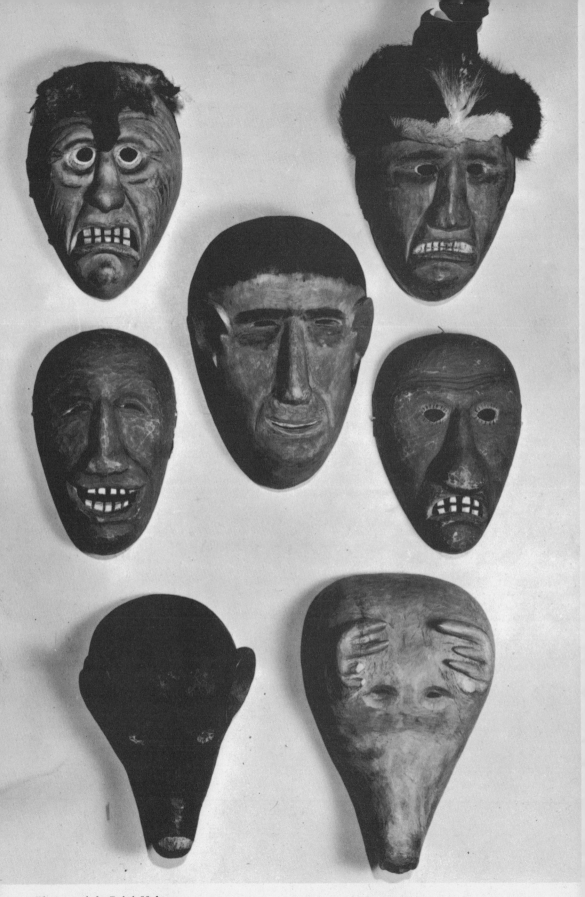

Masks of the Smoky Mountain Cherokees

is taken on one foot and that knee bends slowly, the other foot is raised with corresponding motion to a height of four or five inches. The body remains bent slightly forward at the hips throughout, and the arms hang naturally at the sides, the elbows slightly akimbo. The head turns slowly from side to side as the weight is taken on one foot and then on the other. All motions must harmonize and blend together to create the slowly undulating buffalo-like movement. The dancers should remind themselves constantly that they are representing these ponderous slow-moving cattle.

The second motion represents the pawing of the ground as all hoofed animals are wont to do. The drumming doubles in time, fast and unaccented.

1. Hop on left foot, raising right
2. Hop on left foot, kicking right down on ground
3. Hop on left foot, raising right
4. Hop on left foot, kicking right down on ground

It is done without making progress. In making the kick the right foot is raised to the position shown in Figure 73. The hop with the left foot is low, placing the emphasis on kick with the right.

Figure 73.

THE DANCE

Four dancers are needed, arranged as follows:

3

4   2

1

Numbers 1 and 3 face each other, and 2 and 4 do likewise. The distance across is about 12 feet. They walk in and take their positions. The drumming is in very slow, accented two-time, counted 1-&, 2-&, each unit of a loud and soft beat being regarded as one count.

1. 15 counts—Dance in position with the slow buffalo step as described (movement 1)
2. 1 count —Stop and stand on both feet
3. 15 counts—Repeat 1
4. 1 count —Repeat 2
5. 15 counts—Repeat 1
6. 1 count —Repeat 2
7. 48 counts—Drumming medium-slow. Using toe-heel step in relaxed manner, dance around near position, turning informally
8. 16 counts—Tempo of drumming doubled, unaccented: Hop on left foot and raise and lower right with pawing motion (movement 2)
9. 4 counts—Drumming at one-fourth above tempo (hitting every fourth beat only): Make four hops to left, hopping on both feet, shaking head and snorting on each hop
10. 16 counts—Repeat 8
11. 4 counts—Repeat 9
12. 8 counts—Repeat 8
13. 2 counts—Repeat 9, making two hops
14. 8 counts—Repeat 8
Exit walking.

When the fast kick starts on No. 8 it continues for the 16 counts, then the four hops are made to the left to the very slow drumming, after which the fast kicks are immediately resumed. There are thus repeated changes in tempo and mood.

Yei-be-chi

There is sickness and much of grief and woe in the riverbeds, the valleys, and the low, damp places. Thus only can it be cured—by the medicine of nine-day Night Chant. Conspicuous in the routine of the potent Night Chant is the Yei-be-chi. (Pronounced yā'-be-che'.)

For this Navajo routine I am indebted to Julia M. Buttree whose kind permission permits me to take it from her *Rhythm of the Redmen*.*

THE DANCE

Sixteen to twenty dancers are needed. Each holds a gourd rattle in his right hand. There is no drumming, the shaking of the rattles setting the rhythm, although drumming should be used in practice and, if the dancers are inexperienced, may also be used in the dance to prevent the speeding up of the rhythm that invariably occurs in group dances without drumming. The rhythm is in medium tempo, unaccented. The step is a relaxed back trot (page 38).

* Julia M. Buttree, *The Rhythm of the Redmen*, page 33. New York: A. S. Barnes & Company, 1930.

The dancers are paired up as to size, the pairs arranged in a column, two abreast.

1. 22 counts—Enter with the back trot
2. 2 counts—Face front, thus forming two sidewise lines, one behind the other, all facing front
3. 4 counts—With feet still, flex knees and shake rattles in time
4. 3 counts—With a sudden sharp bend of the knee, bow forward and yelp, straighten up, and about face. The lines are now facing in the opposite direction.
5. 4 counts—Repeat 3
6. 3 counts—Repeat 4, facing in the original direction again
7. 10 counts—The back line trots forward and joins the front to form one line facing front
8. 4 counts—Repeat 3
9. 3 counts—Repeat 4
10. 4 counts—Repeat 3
11. 3 counts—Repeat 4
12. 10 counts—They form two lines again, the back line trotting backward to position, the front line turning around and facing the back line
13. The two at the head of the column trot forward to meet each other, turn and trot side by side down the aisle between the two lines, then take their places at the end, each again in his own line. The second column then goes down the aisle in the same manner, then the third, etc. The group continues to shake their rattles and to keep time by trotting in place.
14. When the last couple has gone down the aisle to position, all turn to form the original column and trot off.

In the above description 22 counts are specified for the entrance. This number of counts can, of course, be altered depending upon the conditions. If done on the stage they trot in from the wings to position and then turn front. If in the council ring the column enters at the Council Rock entrance and, going counterclockwise, trots all the way around the ring, then stops in front of the Council Rock and turns toward the fire, thus forming two sidewise lines facing the fire.

Sia Crow Dance

From a gentle, soft-spoken weaver of artistic belts at Sia this characteristic Pueblo dance was learned. Like all such here recorded it is a quiet number, pleasing but unspectacular.

Crow-like, the dancers are painted black from head to foot except for the face which is natural, and wear very small black breechcloths. There are four such crows in line with a guard at each end. For our use eight dancers give more body to the dance, and the guards can well be dispensed with, since they serve no purpose and appear out of place unless set off from the rest by special costuming. The dance can be done in ordinary dance costume without the black paint, a great convenience, especially if the dancers are to appear in other dances on the program.

THE STEP

There are two movements used in the dance.
In the first, the drumming is in medium-slow, accented two-time.

1. Jump on both feet bringing the left down about six inches farther forward than the right, taking the weight on the left and allowing the right to come down gently on the toe, the left knee soft and flexing to lower the body.
&. Keeping the right leg inflexible, straighten left knee to raise the body, then lower it again, thus raising the right foot and lowering it on the count.
2. Jump on both feet bringing the right foot down about six inches farther forward than the left, taking the weight on the right and allowing the left to come down gently on the toe, the right knee soft and flexing to lower the body.
&. Keeping the left leg inflexible, straighten the right knee to raise the body, then lower it again, thus raising the left foot and lowering it on the count.

It is a graceful, flowing movement without jerks or sudden motions. The secret rests in the soft knee and the graceful dip of the body caused by flexing the knee. The body is bent forward slightly and naturally at the hips and the arms hang naturally at the sides. As the left foot leads the upper part of the body is turned slightly to the right, and as the right foot leads it is turned to the left.

The second movement is a kick step with the right foot which is the same as that used in the Jemez Buffalo Dance, described on page 182, except that the right foot is kicked down each time the left foot hops, or on every drumbeat, instead of on every other one.

THE DANCE

Eight dancers are required, arranged in a single column. They walk in, take positions, and wait for the drum.

I. The drumming is in medium-slow, accented two-time, counted 1-&, 2-&, etc.:
    9 counts—Dance forward with Crow step as described

3 counts—The feet are still—stand with feet side by side and flex knees
to drum beats, lowering and raising body, looking skyward
and moving head on count

6 counts—Dance forward with Crow step, straightening up and raising
both hands overhead on 6th count, stopping

II. Drumming doubled in time, unaccented:

4 counts—Kick step in place

1 count —Kick step, throwing right arm overhead and lowering

1 count —Kick step, throwing left arm overhead and lowering

4 counts—Kick step

2 counts—Kick step, throwing right arm overhead and lowering on
each count

4 counts—Kick step

1 count —Kick step, throwing right arm overhead and stopping.

Repeat the entire series from beginning three times.

Part I is done in the slow, graceful, flowing motion of the Crow step.
When the feet are still and the knees flexed to lower and raise the body
the movement is without jerks and harmonizes with the general movement of the step itself. In Part II the fast kicks stand out in distinct contrast to the flowing movements of the first part. The second part is done
in place without making progress.

In each case when the arms are thrown overhead, whether in the first or
second part, the head and eyes are turned up.

The column moves around the stage or ring during the dance and when
finished the dancers walk off.

Chapter X

COMEDY DANCES

THE LOFTY BEAUTY of the council-fire ritual, the seriousness of purpose of the dances, the religion-like atmosphere that is conjured up—these set the stage for comedy in unmatched fashion. Against this background the comedy dance appears as wholly unexpected, particularly if not announced as such. The very dignity of the situation serves to heighten the comedy and to give it a ludicrous quality that otherwise it would not have.

But comedy dances must be used sparingly and tempered always with reserve, lest they unmake the tone and thereby defeat both themselves and the balance of the program. One to a program is usually sufficient, preferably in a spot near the end after a long build-up of other dances. The sparing use of them accounts for their fewness.

None of the dances in this chapter are authentic Indian numbers.

Big Small and Little Small

This is a take-off on the Tomahawk Dance, the solo described on page 103. It calls for two dancers, one of whom is a small edition of the other. Often a man and a boy will make the just right combination. Although not essential, it helps if they are similar in appearance and build, except for size. But this much is necessary—*they must move alike*, the little one being able to imitate exactly all dancing movements of the big one.

Big Small must be able to do the Tomahawk Dance—indeed, the present dance is usually developed around a dancer who has the Tomahawk Dance as a specialty. As he dances it, Little Small, cocky and impertinent, trails around behind him and imitates all his movements and, in the end, harasses him.

Big Small is in usual dancing costume, dignified and nicely ornamented with bustles and feather trappings. Little Small wears only a breechcloth and a white skull cap like that shown in Figure 74, copied after those worn by the Delight Makers of the Pueblos. It is made from a woman's white stocking. The two tassels are padded to give them body and hang down behind.

Figure 74. Hat Worn by Little Small

THE DANCE

Big Small enters dancing the Tomahawk Dance (page 103) going counterclockwise, and about six feet behind him Little Small follows. Little Small keeps his eyes on Big Small and imitates instantly every move he makes. Big Small's face is serious but Little Small's has an impish smile on it constantly.

When Big Small reaches X in Figure 75 he plants the tomahawk in the ground and continues on. Little Small immediately picks up the tomahawk and, following him, plants it at Z. When Big Small reaches Y he stops for his play on the tomahawk, Little Small remaining at W. A surprised look comes over Big Small's face when he discovers the tomahawk missing— he shades his eyes, lowers and raises his body to look from different angles . . . convinced it isn't there he scans the ring and sees it at Z. Thinking he made a mistake in placing it, he goes back around to Z and gets it, Little Small following, then repeats the routine, going around the ring again and placing it at X as before. Little Small picks it up again and puts it back at Z, then continues on around the ring behind Big Small, imitating his movements.

When Big Small stops at Y again and finds it missing he immediately looks to Z and sees it. Now he knows there is some deviltry afoot. He looks around and discovers Little Small standing at W, laughing and pointing at the tomahawk. Big Small points accusingly at him, dashes toward

him and chases him around past Z, then picks up the tomahawk and
goes straight over to X and puts it in position, then goes directly across to
Y, Little Small following and going to his position at W. Reaching Y
Big Small takes up his routine again and begins the play on the tomahawk.
Each move he makes is imitated by Little Small and each time he advances
to get the tomahawk, Little Small trails behind him.

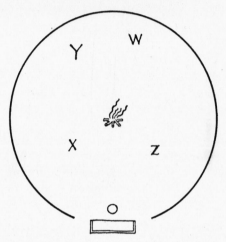

Figure 75. Diagram for Big Small and Little Small

When at last Big Small picks up the tomahawk and begins to dance,
holding it up and tossing it in the air, Little Small is right behind him
imitating every movement. Big Small continues on around the ring until
he is back at X, at which point he lowers the tomahawk and holds it at
his side for a second. Little Small dashes up and grabs the tomahawk out of
his hand, turns and dances swiftly around the ring in the opposite direction. Big Small whirls and starts after him but, seeing himself losing
ground, he stops dancing and starts running, raising his knees high in front
as though running hard but not covering ground very rapidly, and with
his face strained as though forcing himself to the limit. Little Small exits
with Big Small running frantically after him.

The Courtship of the Eagles

For this riotous dance I am indebted to Ernest Thompson Seton * who
originated it and with whose kind permission I include it here.

It is a burlesque best played by two large burly men. Make-up should
reflect its burlesque nature—bathing trunks instead of breechcloths, and a
blanket folded in triangular shape, tied at the neck and at the wrists, to
serve as eagle wings. On the head a dilapidated wig is worn with an old

* Ernest Thompson Seton, *The Birch Bark Role of the Woodcraft League of
America*, page 99. New York: Brieger Press, Inc., 1924.

bustle tied on top. The face is painted red with a yellow beak or nose, the body is not painted.

More comic results are often obtained if the men are not trained Indian dancers. They bend well forward with legs slightly straddled and dance in imitation of the flat-heel step as best they can.

The routine here given follows in the main that of Seton.

THE DANCE

Two small but strong packing boxes are placed on opposite sides of the ring near the edge. One is the mountain on which dwells the he-eagle and the other the mountain of the she-eagle. That of the he-eagle should be larger, just big enough for two to get their feet on it when squatting side by side.

The he-eagle enters and is followed presently by the she-eagle, both dancing over to their mountains, uttering softly "Kek Kek Kek." They settle on their mountains and spruce up their plumes with their beaks. The he-one is restless, flapping his wings and fidgeting. He utters a long, lonesome "Kek Kek Kek." Presently he discovers the she-eagle on her mountain, cocks his head and takes a good look, then utters a shrill "Kek Kek" and sails off his mountain over to hers. Meanwhile the she-eagle drops behind her mountain and hides. The he-eagle looks all around the mountain "Kek Keking" excitedly, fails to find her and gives up in despair, heading back to his mountain muttering repeatedly "Kak Kak."

The she-eagle climbs up on her mountain again, looks for a moment and then cries "Kek". He sails over again, loudly "Kek Keking" but she hides again and he misses her. He returns to his mountain as before, grumbling his disgust, "Kak Kak."

She climbs on her mountain and coyly calls "Kek." He pays no heed, his head down, brushing up his plumes. She rises higher, flaps her wings and calls "Kek." He answers "Aw, Kak Kak Kak." She jumps off her mountain, sails a few feet toward him and coyly trots back to her mountain. He grumbles "Kak Kak Kak." She advances again, this time halfway over to him and trots back. He turns his back and shouts loudly, "Aw, Kak Kak Kak." She "Keks" in vain from her perch, then sails over to the very foot of his mountain. He emits a long, excited "Kek Kek" and leaps for her. She flees and he pursues. In front of her mountain she goes around in a circle and cuts a figure-of-8 while he follows hot on her trail, both repeating excitedly "Kek Kek Kek". He turns suddenly and bumps her, both falling. They rise, he grabs her, they put their arms around each other, their beaks close together, and trot back to his mountain cooing "Kek Kek" softly to each other.

Together they squat down on his mountain, their arms around each other, their beaks close together. Quietly they perch there for a moment cooing, then, losing their balance on the tiny perch, both scream loudly

"Kek Kek" and fall over backwards on the ground. They arise and run off.

The Lost Drumbeater

The council fire opens with its usual dignity. The lofty ritual is completed, the opening dance announced. The Chief reaches for his drumbeater . . . it is not there! He looks around, casts a wary glance off stage, turns and begins beating the drum with his fingers. The Incense Bearers dance in to complete the opening ceremony.

There is much excitement off stage. Everyone is scurrying about for a drumstick. A spectator or two desiring to help arise and leave . . .

The solo dancer enters in the first dance to the feeble finger drumming and goes into his story dance, looking about the ground as if for tracks, searching here and there. Suddenly he drops to the ground and points across the ring—he arises, dashes over and picks up the lost drumbeater! He holds it in the air smiling, then trots over and gives it to the Chief. The Chief begins drumming with it and the dancer goes into brilliant solo.

So realistic can this be that it can be used repeatedly with the same group and still there will be an excited scurrying about for a drumbeater. The very formality and dignity of the Grand Council, its importance with so many spectators present, the intense desire of everyone to see it succeed, sets the stage for such a trick. But mark this well—not one soul except the dancer himself and the Chief can know the nature of the number, not even the other dancers on the program. It is merely listed as a solo.

THE DANCE

Place the drumbeater at the edge of the council ring and throw a little dirt over the wrapped end of it so that it cannot be recognized as a beater. It should be put in place before any spectators arrive and one man appointed to watch it constantly and to see that it is not moved.

When the Chief reaches for the drumbeater and finds it missing he glances about, looks down at the ground, appears confused for a second, turns and looks off stage with a worried expression as if asking for help, then begins drumming with his fingers.

The dancer enters, stops and looks back toward the Chief. The Chief nods his head and drums harder as if to say "Go ahead and dance". The dancer proceeds as in the story dances, looking about the ground, stooping as if to look under the benches, searching here and there, continuing thus with story-dance business for a circuit and a half of the ring. Suddenly he drops to the ground and points across the ring dramatically, holds his freeze for a moment, leaps to his feet and dashes across to pick up the drumbeater. He holds it high overhead, looks at the Chief and smiles. The Chief's face brightens up. The dancer trots across and hands him the drumstick. He takes it and begins drumming in fast tempo.

The dancer then goes into an exciting, dashing solo, circling the ring twice and exits.

Comedy Dances in Other Chapters

Three unsurpassed comedy dances appear in Chapter XI, "Mask Dances". They are: *The Ferocious Warrior, Laborers in Darkness* and *The Booger-men.*

A comedy number is also found in the Winnebago War Dance on page 130.

Chapter XI

MASK DANCES

MASKS HAVE played an important part in the dances of many tribes, particularly of the Southwest, the Northwest Coast, and the Iroquois in the eastern Woodlands. The Solid Face Society of the latter tribe was noted for the grotesque, eerie quality of its masks. The Cherokees of the Great Smoky Mountains, a tribe of the Iroquois family, also made much use of masks in their dances and indeed, retain to this day their mask tradition. There is good reason for this, for the evil spirits that cause disease lurk about in dark places, and only the spirit power of masks can rout them. Should a person fall victim to these spirits, the medicine of the masks is needed to free him.

These Cherokee masks lend themselves admirably for our use today and the various dances in the chapter are based upon them. Several are shown in the illustrations facing pages 182 and 183. It will be noted that they vary widely in type—some have a fierce, hideous, war-like expression, others are pleasant, and still others have a witless, imbecilic look. Mask dances allow considerable freedom of expression on the part of the dancer. Each mask should be studied for the type of character it represents in order to determine how this particular kind of person would dance. In this way the appropriate movements for each mask are created.

Making the Masks

The masks are made of wood but imitations of them can be fashioned from papier-mâché. The Cherokees make them of buckeye, using basswood as a second choice but only if buckeye cannot be had. They are hollowed out to fit the face and are held on by bands of strong elastic across the back. A piece of black cloth should be tacked to the top of the mask on the back edge to cover up the back of the head, tied under the chin by tapes sewed to the cloth.

The faces of the masks are painted a medium reddish-brown, the eyebrows and expression lines painted black. Sometimes black paint is used to represent hair and again pieces of fur are tacked over the top.

In making imitations from papier-mâché, particular care should be taken to copy the Indian originals accurately. Here as in all efforts at

Indian art it is better to copy than to improvise or attempt to improve upon the Indian original. In fashioning papier-mâché masks there is often a tendency to overdo the bizarre aspect, producing masks that would look more at home in a Halloween parade than in an Indian dance. It will be noticed that, bizarre as they are, the Cherokee masks are after all quite like the human face. These dances rely for effect upon this human-like quality.

One of these dances requires eight masks, all different, but the others call for only one or two.

Witch or Boogerman Dance

For sheer comedy the Boogermen of the Cherokees have no equal in the whole realm of Indian dancing. These eight old men are entertaining always, and more often than not, outlandishly ludicrous. Their power to induce laughter rests in their masks, for their quaint antics which so ably augment the comedy would go for naught without their wooden faces. These are the disease-healers who unexpectedly leap into the sick person's presence to startle them and thereby to drive the evil ones from him. But when they dance in public their purpose is naught but entertainment, pure and simple.

This is one of those rare dances that involves spoken lines.

Unfortunately the dance cannot be done without a mask for each dancer. Those in the illustration facing page 182 are typical Boogerman types. Among the Cherokees the Boogermen wear baggy suits of burlap or old rags. It is recommended, however, that they wear only breechcloth and moccasins. If anything this heightens the comedy, and is a great convenience since the dancers usually appear in other dances on the program in which the breechcloth is required, and they are thus saved the confusion of a complete change.

The descriptions here given is an exact representation of the dance as seen on various occasions among the Great Smoky Mountain Cherokees.

BOOGERMAN STEPS

These Boogermen are old—their legs are stiff, their joints full of creaks. Moreover, no two of them dance alike. There is a basic movement, however: To very fast, unaccented drumming, they shuffle the feet along without picking them up off the ground. With the feet kept flat they scuffle forward a few feet and stop, then scuffle sidewise on the spot, a foot or two in each direction, or keep the feet still and shake the knees sidewise with a trembling motion.

With this as the basic movement each Boogerman's mask is studied to determine the best movement for him, the mask creating a character that suggests appropriate movement. The aim is comedy always. The variations come chiefly when they stop and dance on the spot. The following are typical movements:

1. Shake knees sidewise rapidly to the drumming with a trembling motion, the feet stationary.
2. Shake body up and down with a trembling motion from head to foot, the feet stationary.
3. Move knees out and in slowly on every other beat of the drum, or on every fourth beat.
4. One knee is stiff, the other knee is moved from side to side slowly on every fourth beat of the drum.
5. Both knees are stiff and a cane is carried. The hand with the cane shakes back and forth to the drumming, the body quiet.
6. The head only is moved from side to side to the rhythm.
7. The feet are shuffled sidewise on the spot, stopping occasionally and shaking the knees.

With these movements as the general pattern, appropriate antics are worked out for each individual dancer.

There is a technique to handling the head that should be employed in all mask dances. When the dancer looks in a certain direction he should hold his head stationary for a moment to permit a good view of the mask; he moves his head to another direction and holds again. To move the head about as in normal looking does not give the mask a chance to take hold of the audience.

THE DANCE

Eight Boogermen are needed, each with a mask. Two benches are placed in the ring as shown in Figure 75.

After the dance is announced the Boogermen come walking in slowly and haltingly, their legs creaky and uncertain. They come from different directions, straggling in, one or two at a time. Each stops and looks over the situation, locates his seat, walks over and sits down. All enter thus except No. 1, whose place is vacant.

The Chief walks over to No. 3 and whispers to him. He shakes his head and points to the entrance. The Chief looks—No. 1 is coming in. After surveying the situation he hobbles to his seat. The Chief whispers to him, then looks up and announces:

"I ask him what manner of man he is. He says he is a Boogerman."

Repeats whisper: "I ask him where he is from. He says he doesn't know."

Repeats whisper: "I ask him where he is going. He says he doesn't know."

Repeats whisper: "I ask him if he will dance. He says sure."

The Chief whispers again and No. 1 points to No. 7. The Chief walks over and whispers to No. 7, who points across to No. 8. The Chief walks over to 8 and whispers, then announces:

"I ask him his name. He says he is a hoot-owl."

He whispers to No. 6. "I ask him his name. He says he is a skunk."

He continues in order for Nos. 4, 2, 7, 5, 3, and 1. Such names are given as *weasel, buzzard, jay bird, jack rabbit, pewee, bobcat,* and *wall-eyed pike.*

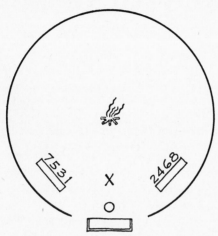

Figure 75. Diagram for the Witch or Boogerman Dance

The Chief returns to his drum and begins drumming in rapid unaccented tempo. No. 1 arises and shuffles up to the point marked X, faces the fire and begins his dance, using one of the appropriate movements described. He continues for a moment, then turns around and shuffles up to the drum. He stops on his right foot, swings his left leg forward slowly and brings the heel down with knee stiff, taking eight counts to make the kick. The drum stops with a loud thump as the heel hits. The Chief bends forward and the Boogerman whispers to him. The Chief announces:

"He says it's hot in here."

No. 1 then goes to his seat and No. 2 repeats. This continues until all eight have danced. The line whispered to the Chief changes with each dancer as follows:

No. 2—"He says his chin hurts." (Probably a fact with the mask on!)

No. 3—"He says he needs some air." (Again a fact behind the mask!)

No. 4—"He says he can't see." (Once more a fact.) He gropes his way back to his seat, assisted in sitting down by the Boogerman next to him.

No. 5—"He says he is all fagged out."

No. 6—"He says his back aches."

No. 7—"He says he can't find his seat." All of the Boogermen point to his seat.

No. 8—"He says he is feeling younger every day."

No. 8 carries a cane not over 15 inches long which he uses by bending far forward. He keeps his weight on the cane as he shakes his legs for his dance. As he goes to the Chief he swings his cane forward instead of kicking his legs.

When No. 8 has finished all walk up in line facing the fire and all dance, each using his own movement. The drum signals and all shuffle across the ring and line up on the other side facing the fire and repeat. The drum signals the exit and all shuffle out.

Laborers in Darkness

We see them in the illustration facing page 167. Their heavy task is to haul the short pieces of log on which they are leaning . . . and it is hard, oh, so hard. Often they must stop to rest as in the picture. . . .

This bit of pantomine is rich in comedy. The laborious antics to haul the logs that are obviously so light in weight and the stolid expressions on the immobile solid faces as they rest will create a gem of silent entertainment.

The success of the dance depends upon the masks. They should pair up together in type, yet each have a personality of its own. They must look the part of the dance. They should have a stolid, plodding expression, listless and weary of limb. The picture suggests the type better than words can do.

The dance is not an authentic Cherokee one as done by two men, but is built up from an oft-seen movement of hauling burdens in the antics of the Boogermen.

THE DANCE

In addition to the masks the dancers wear only breechcloths and moccasins. Each has a section of a small log three feet long, one of them six inches in diameter, the other nine inches. Dancer No. 1 has the smaller log.

The dance is a study in slow motion. The drumming is in two-time, very slow. They use a flat-heel step, stepping flat on the hard beat and raising and lowering the heel on the half-beat.

1. They place the logs on their right shoulders and steady them with both hands. They bend forward under the great weight. They enter dancing slowly, and once in, stop and look over the situation for a moment, then continue on to A in Figure 76.

2. Here they lower the ends of their logs to the ground, putting both arms around them and letting them down, slowly as though they had great weight. They lean with their arms on the logs and rest as in the picture. They must face the fire and hold their chins up to reveal the full face. They look the crowd over but hold their heads motionless for several seconds in each direction to let the audience get an unhurried view of the masks. All changes of position are done very slowly. Then they pick the

JAMES C. STONE

Photograph by the Author

Chippewa Dance House at Nett Lake, Northern Minnesota

logs up, putting both arms around them, bending far forward to get them on their shoulders again.

3. They continue over to B, lower the logs for another rest and repeat 2.

4. They continue on to C and repeat 2, but here No. 1 has trouble in getting his log on his shoulder—his strength is fast failing him. No. 2 lifts his up, looks down and sees No. 1 struggling to hoist his, reaches down with his left hand and helps him up with it.

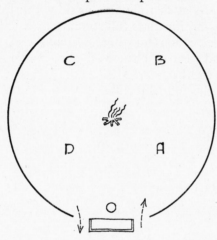

Figure 76. Diagram for Laborers in Darkness

5. They continue to D and rest again, repeating 2. This time No. 1 cannot raise his log at all. When No. 2 lifts his, No. 1 looks up at him and they exchange a long look. No. 2 lowers his log and lays it on the ground, takes hold of No. 1's log and together the two of them manage to get it up on No. 1's shoulder. Then No. 2 lifts his again and, putting his left hand under the end of No. 1's, they exit slowly.

The Ferocious Warrior

This is a comedy in which a ferocious warrior encounters an enemy he cannot handle—a burlesque on the fighting dances. The mask must be war-like, fierce, unrestrained in its fury. The one at the top right corner of the illustration facing page 183 indicates the type.

It is not an authentic dance of the Cherokees but is in full harmony with the unpredictable antics of the Boogermen.

THE DANCE

Two characters are needed, a large dancer to wear the mask as the ferocious warrior, and a very small boy, the smaller the better, wearing a bobbed Indian wig with a headband across his forehead to make him look as cute and harmless as possible. The warrior carries an ugly-looking tomahawk and the boy has a tiny bow about a foot long, made of a pealed twig and a string.

The drumming is medium-fast, accented in two-time. The step used by the warrior is a flat-foot run, bringing the heel down first.

The warrior hustles into the ring, running with a quick, jerky motion and goes counterclockwise a quarter of the way around, stops and looks across the fire, his knees widespread and pointing outward, his elbows sticking out to the sides at sharp angles, as shown in Figure 77. This pose he holds without moving for three full seconds, then jerks his head quickly to look in another direction for three seconds, etc., making four such looks; with each head turn he changes the angle of his tomahawk. Then he runs quickly to the halfway mark and repeats, and continues thus, repeating at each of the four directions.

Figure 77.

As he passes the Council Rock the little boy walks in and sits on the ground just to the left of the drum and begins playing with some twigs on the ground, childlike and unconcerned.

The warrior continues around until he is directly opposite the boy when he discovers him. He stops suddenly in his usual pose (Figure 77) and points. He pauses motionless for three seconds, knocks his knees together quickly and separates them widely again, repeating the pause and knee knock three times. At this point the boy sees him and stands up. The warrior's knees begin trembling, shaking sidewards violently in his nervousness. He shuffles sidewise, across and back several times to gain momentum, his tomahawk raised in the air, then dashes toward the boy.

The boy raises his tiny bow, pulls the string with his thumb and finger and shoots just as the warrior is abreast of the fire. The warrior grabs his stomach with both hands, leans far back and utters a long-drawn-out, loud, agonizing groan (very loud—the mask muffles it), then doubles up and staggers to his keep his feet, grunting and groaning audibly. A moment of staggering and he gets control of himself, raises his tomahawk and faces the boy, takes two steps toward him. The boy steps forward and raises his bow—seeing this the warrior throws both arms overhead, screams loudly, turns and dashes around the ring, screaming, and exits, the boy running after him with his tiny bow raised.

Smoky Mountain Spirit

This quaint solo dance is in the mood of the masked Witch Healers of the Cherokees, yet, unlike the Boogerman Dance, there is no deliberate attempt at comedy. It relies on the bizarre mask and appropriately bizarre movements, artistically done. Comedy will evolve willy-nilly, however, for masks resembling the human face make one appear freakish and queer, and the movements at once become humorous.

The appropriate mask is shown at the center of the illustration facing page 183. The dancer wears burlap clothes, a loose sack on each leg as leggings, a large sack with slits for head and arms pulled over the head, and a piece of burlap for a breechcloth. The baggier it fits the better. The burlap should be ripped in spots to be made to appear ragged.

THE STEP

The fundamental step is shown in Figure 44, done to slow drumming in two-time. The knees extend outward as shown, are well bent and remain so constantly.

1. Hop on both feet flat
&. Hop on left foot raising right
2. Hop on both feet flat
&. Hop on right foot raising left.

The foot is raised rather high as illustrated and the sole remains parallel to the floor.

The arms are bent at right angles as shown in Figure 44. It should not be assumed, however, that the position of the arms is changed with each step as in the illustrations. The arm illustrations merely show the various positions that the arms may take. For best effect the arms should be put in one of these positions and held there for three or four steps before changing to another.

THE DANCE

The dancer enters with the step described, moving forward slowly and deliberately. Once inside he stops, raises his arms in angular fashion, and sways up and down by flexing his knees to the rhythm, looking in this direction and that but holding his head motionless for a few seconds between each look. Each time he changes his head position he also changes the position of his arms. Next he spreads his knees widely apart, then knocks them together, repeating this several times in slow motion to the drumming.

He dances a quarter of the way around the ring, stops and repeats, continuing with stops at each of the four directions. As he reaches the

Council Rock to complete the circuit, he stops and repeats, then hops backward on both feet to the exit, with hands overhead, turns and dances out.

Reliance is put upon the bizarre appearance of the mask and make-up, combined with the angular motions of the legs and arms. When well-executed it can be an artistic and entertaining number.

The Masked Deer Hunter

The deer is the most inquisitive of animals . . . indeed, his curiosity is often his undoing. That which seems strange to him fascinates him and tricks him into standing and looking, wide-eyed and motionless. Capitalizing on this fatal trait, the hunter covers his face with a deer mask and carries a branch of a tree to camouflage the movements of his body. Then he sallies forth in search of the deer.

The deer mask is shown at the bottom right corner of the illustration facing page 183. The hunter wears a large burlap sack with slits for his head and arms, extending down almost to his knees. The sack should be ripped up one side and across the shoulder, then tacked together again very lightly so that it can be easily torn off. Beneath the mask he wears a wig and headband. He carries a branch of a maple or other broadleaf tree which has a spread of about two feet.

THE DANCE

The drumming is in accented two-time, medium slow.

The hunter enters with the toe-heel step, going counterclockwise. He carries the branch in his left hand covering his legs from the hips down. He goes a fourth of the way around the ring and stops, looking across at the fire, crouching a little and holding the branch in front of his waist. As in all masked dances he holds his head steady for two or three seconds, then changes the angle of his vision for another such pause. He repeats the stopping and looking at each of the four directions in going around the ring.

As he passes the Council Rock he looks to the ground and sees tracks, pointing at them and studying them as in the "I Saw" dances. He continues stealthily a quarter of the way around, then discovers the deer across the ring. He drops to the ground and freezes, holding his branch in front of him and slowly swaying it back and forth. He arises cautiously, drops the branch, raises his bow and shoots (see page 56 for method). He stands for a moment watching the effect of his shot, yanks his mask off with his left hand and rushes to the deer. He turns triumphantly toward the fire for a moment, grabs the bottom of his burlap shirt and gives it a sudden jerk to rip it off, and discards it; the drum increases in tempo and volume and he breaks into a dance of exultation, carrying the mask in his hand and holding it up overhead at times, circling the ring twice and exiting.

Chapter XII

HOOP DANCES

WHAT TRIBES dance the hoop dance? Well, almost all of them—from the sun-drenched mesa country to the broad expanses of the Plains and across through the eastern Woodlands. It is thought by some that in olden times the hoop dance was exclusively an art of the Indians of the northern Plains, but however that may be, it has been well-nigh universal in recent years. And there is a similarity to these dances as we go from tribe to tribe that is surprising. Body style may change in conformity to the style of dancing preferred by the tribe, but the hoop tricks are much the same.

Hoop dancing has brought far-flung fame to the dancing Indian. It has rare elements of challenge to any audience. To dance within and through the hoop is accepted as proof of great agility. There is strong eye-appeal in the hoop itself—it attracts attention to itself and to the part of the body around which it is manipulated, in much the same way that a circle catches the eye on a printed advertisement in a magazine. It frames the body, so to speak.

But be it known that hoop dancing is open only to those who have mastered the fundamental Indian steps and who are well past the clumsy stage, whose feet are agile and sure, and whose body is fluid and willowy from much dancing. There is nothing difficult about the hoop tricks, but to synchronize them with the dancing steps would be quite impossible unless the steps have become so much a part of one that no thought need be given them. The hoop tricks will be just tricks unless they are blended with the dancing movements into one graceful flowing whole. That takes practice.

Hoops

Dancing hoops may be purchased for a few cents from any of the mail-order theatrical-supply houses, or they may be made as the Indians made them.

A hoop 24 inches in diameter is recommended for a person of average size. If the hoop is too big the dance looks cheap, and if too small it cramps the dancer, prevents graceful movement, and handicaps him unnecessarily. A variation of an inch or two one way or the other from the 24-inch size should meet the needs of anyone.

To make the hoop a stick 7½ feet long is needed. The circumference of the hoop is 6½ feet and the ends must overlap for a distance of one foot. A long branch of a tree or a young shoot may be whittled down to uniform thickness of one-half inch and bent into the hoop, but much better results may be obtained if the stick is split from a log. White cedar is easily bent and makes a strong, light hoop. Split a six-inch log in half, then quarter it, and continue the splitting until a long straight-grained stick is secured. This is then whittled down to a thickness of one-half inch. If placed in water for a day it will become flexible enough to bend. By placing it over the knee and bending it a little at a time it can be gradually worked into a circle. The overlapping ends should be tapered down and bound tightly with wet rawhide thongs or adhesive tape. A more perfect circle may be obtained if it is bent around a barrel of proper size and let dry there.

Some of the trick dances in which two or more hoops are used at once require smaller hoops 18 to 20 inches in diameter, but for standard hoop dancing the size described will give the most pleasing results.

DECORATING THE HOOP.—The hoop may be painted or wrapped with brightly colored cloth. The Pueblo Indians usually paint them white but most of the tribes prefer the colored wrappings. Light colors are recommended for the sake of visibility. If a luster is desired, oilcloth may be used instead of cloth. The ends of the wraps should be left extending an inch or two as in Figure 78, then colored fluffies should be attached with thread here and there and allowed to dangle.

Figure 78. Dancing Hoop

Hoop-Dance Movements

The steps used in hoop dancing are the toe-heel, the crossed toe-heel, and the toe-heel-heel-heel. The latter step is much used because it slows down the foot action and permits time to handle the hoop.

In hoop dancing as in all dances there must be a basic movement which forms the foundation of the dance and which is returned to after each special movement or trick. This ties the dance together and makes possible smooth transitions from one trick to another. Movements No. 1 and No. 2 below serve this purpose, No. 2 being the most useful and the most frequently employed. Then follows the other movements that, when blended together into a routine, constitute the Hoop Dance.

1. BASIC MOVEMENT—BOTH FEET IN.—Hold the hoop as in A in Figure 79, in the right hand and in front of the legs. Step into it with the left foot, then with the right. The hoop is now in position shown in B—in front of the knees and behind the feet. Turn the hoop to the left, reversing its sides, and take it in the left hand as in C. It will now be in the position in D, in back of the knees and in front of the ankles. Note the string tied to the hoop in B—by following the position of this in C and D the movements of the hoop will be understood. With hoop as in D, step out of it with the left foot as in E and then with the right. The hoop is now behind the body held in the left hand. Take it in the right hand, turn it around reversing its faces as in F, and bring it around in front to the starting position in A.

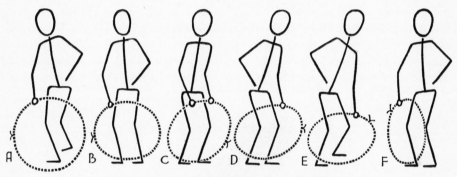

Figure 79. Movement No. 1—Both Feet In

Now to add the footwork: The step is the toe-heel-heel-heel. This requires four beats of the drum to each step (&-1, &-2) and thus gives ample time for unhurried handling of the hoop. Step in with the left, toe-heel-heel-heel, and follow with the right, toe-heel-heel-heel. As soon as the left steps in the hoop at A the right hand begins to revolve it slowly around so that by the time the right foot has completed its heel taps the hoop is in the position shown in D and ready for the left foot to step out. The left foot steps out and then the right, thus giving eight drumbeats to revolve the hoop and carry it around in back to A again. To complete the circuit requires four steps, or eight two-time counts, or sixteen drumbeats.

The hoop is revolved around and around smoothly and rhythmically, with the feet dancing in and out, in and out. Practice until the hoop can be revolved evenly and gracefully, unhurried to accommodate the feet, and conversely, so that the feet can dance in and out gracefully, unhurried to accommodate the hoop.

2. BASIC MOVEMENT—ONE FOOT IN.—This is more graceful and easier to do with nice effect than the preceding and is accepted by most dancers as their fundamental movement.

The step is the toe-heel-heel-heel but it is done in crisscross fashion like the crossed toe-heel, one leg crossing over in front of the other in stepping. Hold the hoop in the right hand as in A, Figure 80. Put the left foot through it and step toe-heel-heel-heel, at the same time turning the hoop to the left, reversing its sides and taking it in the left hand, as shown in B. While this is going on, swing the right foot around in front of the hoop and across the left and step—the feet are now in the position shown in B. As the right foot steps swing the hoop around behind the back, take it in the right hand as in C and bring it around in front in the position of A again. The hoop thus goes around and around the body but only the left leg enters it.

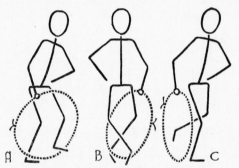

Figure 80. Movement No. 2—One Foot In

Remember that on each step the feet are crossed as in the crossed toe-heel step. The movement cannot be done gracefully otherwise. Indeed, the feet are swung far across, the left going over to meet the hoop and the right being swung equally far across as if to push the hoop around the left leg.

Do not attempt to make progress with it but concentrate on the swinging motion of the hoop and legs.

3. REVOLVING THE HOOP AROUND BODY.—Although the simplest of all tricks, it is nevertheless very decorative. The step is the toe-heel-heel-heel. Step inside the hoop and let it hang as in Figure 81. The legs stay inside the hoop all the time, the hoop being revolved around the body. Turn it to the left, reversing its sides so that the bottom edge is resting on the shins in front. Then turn it again, bring it back to the position in Figure 85. Pass it to the left hand in front, and back to the right hand behind.

It is revolved around the body once on each step, that is, once on each four drumbeats.

Figure 81. Movement No. 3—Revolving Around Body

4. GLIDES.—With the hoop in the position shown in Figure 82 do the backward glide or the forward glide. Note that the lower edge of the hoop is between the feet and that the upper edge is *behind* the legs. The best way to lead up to this movement is with movement No. 2, "One Foot In." In doing No. 2, step in with the left foot and cross the right over and you are in position for the glide.

Figure 82. Movement No. 4—Glides

Be sure that the hoop is placed symmetrically so that it frames the legs. It can be held by either hand or both hands. This use of the hoop gives a very nice effect.

5. GRAPEVINE.—It is illustrated in Figure 83. Holding the hoop in the right hand, put the right leg through as in A, raise the right knee high, bend forward, slip the hoop over the head as in B, taking the hoop in the left hand. Drop the hoop down below the hips. The hoop is still between the legs. Now raise the left leg and repeat. Continue thus alternating right and left legs rapidly.

Now to combine it with the foot action: The step is the toe-heel-heel-

heel. Place the right leg through the hoop. Step on the left toe, tap the heel as the hoop is raised over the head, and tap twice more as it is lowered below the hips. Then repeat the toe-heel-heel-heel with the right foot as the left leg is raised.

This is one of the major tricks on which the hoop dancer places his reliance for effect. It intrigues the audience and seems to baffle as to how it is done. Without time to analyze it, it is difficult to understand how one leg after the other can be raised to go on and on without stepping out of the hoop between times.

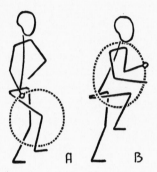

Figure 83. Movement No. 5—Grapevine

It can be done in double time, that is, with the toe-heel instead of the toe-heel-heel-heel step, and many Indians prefer to do it that way, but it is always better to do it gracefully rather than so rapidly that it becomes jerky. The rapid style is best used as a finale, starting with the slow movement as described and finishing with three or four fast movements.

6. SITTING IN THE HOOP.—This is another of the hoop dancer's best tricks. It is diagrammed in Figure 84. Hold the hoop in both hands behind as in A, squat and lean far forward as in B, revolve the hoop in the hands, slipping it up over the shoulders as in C and down over the head. The hands remain in the same position constantly and turn the hoop with the fingers.

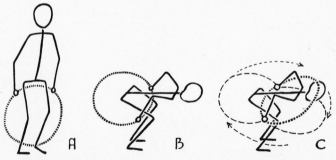

Figure 84. Movement No. 6—Sitting in the Hoop

Now to add the foot work: It is done with an eight-count heel tap, that is, with the toe-heel-heel-heel step continued for eight instead of four beats. When the hoop is at the lowest point in front, shown by the dotted circle in C, stand on the right foot and raise the left forward through the hoop. This is the point at which the count starts. Step on the left foot on 1 and raise the right, then tap the left heel to complete the eight counts, revolving the hoop around and down over the head as you do so. As the hoop comes down, extend the raised right foot forward through it and we are back at the starting point. Now step on the right foot and repeat. With very little practice it can be done rhythmically so that the hoop will not change its speed of motion and will swing around and around uniformly in the eight-count rhythm.

To do it in eight counts is really to do it in slow motion. When fully mastered in eight counts it should be learned in four counts, that is, with the toe-heel-heel-heel step. This is after all an unhurried rhythm to one who is well-drilled in the movement.

In the routine of the hoop dance this trick is done at the two speeds: The dancer starts by doing it in eight counts and repeats it six times, then doubles the speed of the hoop and does it in four counts for six times.

Some top-flight performers do this trick in two counts. This is difficult, requiring excellent co-ordination and long practice. While it makes a flashy spectacle, the slower motion done gracefully always pleases more than the fast one done in a jerky and frenzied manner.

This trick is also done by holding the hoop in front of the legs instead of behind them. The movements are otherwise the same.

7. CRISSCROSS STEP.—Of all the hoop-dance movements this one has the strongest appeal to the audience. Although really very easy, it appears to be exceedingly intricate.

The step is the toe-heel-heel-heel, done in crisscross fashion, as in the crossed toe-heel. Hold the hoop between the legs as in Figure 85. Cross the left through the hoop and over the right and step toe-heel-heel-heel. Then cross the right over the left and through the hoop, and step toe-heel-heel-heel.

Figure 85. Movement No. 7—Crisscross

Do this step several times, then change to the crossed toe-heel step, thus doubling the speed at which the feet step. At this point applause is sure to break.

When used as a finale, it is concluded with the backward glide without the hands touching the hoop.

8. BACKWARD GLIDE WITHOUT HANDS.—This is the best finale for the hoop dance and is used at the conclusion of the crisscross step just described. With the feet crossed in the hoop while doing the crisscross step take the hands off the hoop as in Figure 86. The hoop is securely locked in the legs and cannot fall. With the left foot in front of right, glide backward four counts, then withdraw the right foot from behind and place it in front of the left, without using the hands in the process. Then continue the glide backward for eight more counts and stop.

Figure 86. Movement No. 8—Backward Glide Without Hands

When used as a finale, the glide should be started from the center of the stage or ring facing the audience. The arms should be held out to the sides as in Figure 86. Glide straight backwards four counts, reverse the legs and continue back for eight counts, stop and bow forward with the hands still held out at the sides. Hold the pose for a moment and then walk off.

9. KICKING THE HOOP.—Hold the hoop in front of the body in both hands by pressing the fingers gently against the edges. Kick it straight up in the air with the right foot and catch it as it falls. If the hoop is held vertically when kicked it will go straight up in the air, but if held at an angle it may fly out of line. With full safety the hoop may be kicked six to ten feet in the air depending on conditions. While it is in the air the dancer continues to dance and as it falls, catches it in his right hand, swings it gracefully into position and immediately goes into the basic hoop-dance step again.

Such kicks are effective but not more than one should be used in the course of a dance. They are seldom employed by the Indians.

10. THROWING THE HOOP.—Every boy knows how to throw a hoop forward with a backward spin so that when it hits the ground it will roll directly back to him. The hoop dancer may use this in two ways: In the first he throws it forward, turns his back to it and dances away a few steps, then turns and dances back to meet it at the original spot, taking it in his right hand and going into the basic step again. The other is to spread his legs when the hoop comes back and to dance right on over it, allowing it to roll between his legs. Then he turns and pursues it again and dances over it, takes it in his right hand and goes immediately into the crisscross step.

11. IN-AND-OUT CRISSCROSS.—In the crisscross described above, the hoop was held between the legs. In this step it is held at the right side as in Figure 87. The step is the regular toe-heel-heel-heel done in crisscross fashion, but only the left foot enters the hoop. Step in with left toe-heel-heel-heel, then step over the left leg with the right foot, toe-heel-heel-heel.

Figure 87. Movement No. 11—In-and-out Crisscross

This is continued for three or four steps leading up to the next and more interesting movement: When you step into the hoop with the left foot, swing the right leg up over the hoop and down to its usual position for the next step. As you swing the right leg up the right arm holding the hoop will, of course, be in the way—let go of the hoop with the right hand, then as the leg passes over it grab it again before it falls. Repeat about four times.

This in-and-out crisscross is a minor movement of less significance than those described above.

12. TAPS THROUGH THE HOOP.—Hold the hoop at the right side as in Figure 88. It is done in four counts:

1. Cross left over right and tap through hoop
2. Hop on right, withdrawing left
3. Cross left behind right and tap in hoop
4. Hop on right, withdrawing left.

Repeat several times.

Figure 88. Movement No. 12—Taps Through the Hoop

13. HANDLING THE HOOP.—An excellent transition from one trick to another may be achieved by swinging the hoop in the hand without stepping in it. Hold the hoop in the right hand with the arm relaxed and swing it around in front, take it in the left hand and continue the swing around behind. After two such graceful revolutions of the hoop around the body while dancing, hold the hoop straight out to the side at arm's length as in Figure 89, extend the left hand across in front of the chest as shown with fingers extended and pointing toward the hoop, and turn the head and look at it. Hold it stationary in this position for four steps, then pull it in and go into the next trick.

Figure 89. Movement No. 13

14. WHIRLING THE HOOP.—An interesting flourish is achieved by hanging the hoop over the right wrist and whirling it around the forearm by revolving the arm in the air. When whirling raise the right arm perpendicular overhead and let the spinning hoop drop over the head; it will continue to spin as it drops around the body until it is stopped by spreading the legs, where it is grabbed by the hand again. This stunt is easier with a smaller hoop.

The Hoop Dance

The hoop dance is a solo. The movements have all been described. The task remaining is to fit them together into a routine.

Hoop dances are done with various tempos from medium-slow to very fast. The Southwest Indians, for example, are noted for their very fast tempo. Rather than speed, the goal should be to bring out the full grace and beauty inherent in the hoop movements. As a rule slower tempos facilitate this grace and fast tempos detract from it. Very fast tempo tends to give it a trick aspect as if to show how fast the dancer can go through the hoop. It is recommended that medium to medium-fast tempo be used, depending on the skill of the dancer.

It must be remembered that the two basic movements (Nos. 1 and 2) go on throughout the dance, the dancer returning to one or the other of them again after each special trick or movement. These basic steps weld the various tricks together into a dance. The following routine indicates the special movements only, assuming that interspersed between them the basic movements will carry on.

The hoop is laid on the ground near the fire, or in the middle of the stage, as the case may be. The dancer enters with the double toe-heel step and immediately spots the hoop. With eyes fixed on it he dances back and forth, shading his eyes with his hands and uses all the business of playing on an object (page 52). He advances to the hoop by throwing his arms toward it, taps his right foot in the middle of it, turns and retreats from it with the fear step. This he repeats twice and on the third time he places his right foot in the middle of it, pivots around it by hopping on his left foot, stoops and picks it up with his right hand. He is now ready to start his hoop routine.

A. Basic Movement—One Foot In (Step No. 2)
B. Revolving Hoop around the Body (Step No. 3)
C. The Glides (Step No. 4), forward and backward
D. In-and-out Crisscross (Step No. 11)
E. Taps through Hoop (Step No. 12)
F. Grapevine (Step No. 5), repeating eight times in succession
G. Basic Movements with Glides
H. Sitting in the Hoop (Step No. 6), six times in eight-count rhythm
 I. Kicking the Hoop (Step No. 9)
 J. Throwing the Hoop (Step No. 10)
K. Crisscross (Step No. 7)
L. Backward Glide without Using Hands (Step No. 8)
    Exit.

Should the hoop be dropped *the dancer must not admit the error but make it appear to be a part of the dance.* To grab up the hoop quickly is a plain admission that dropping it was accidental. He should capitalize on the mistake by letting it lay and dancing away from it a few steps, repeating the business of looking at it as at the beginning of the dance, then picking it up and continuing as though nothing happened.

At the beginning of the dance and wherever it is dropped, the hoop may be picked up by the feet and raised up the legs without the use of the hands if desired, as described under the Double Hoop Dance.

Variation.—Another type of hoop dance common among the Indians of the Plains and Southwest differs in that there are no basic hoop movements to unite it. There is no dancing in and out of the hoop with the feet. Only the more spectacular tricks are used and between them the dancer merely dances with hoop held in hand. These tricks are done with speed and flash, then the tempo of the dance quiets down until the next trick starts.

Burning Hoop Dance

The showmanship of fire and the use made of it by the Indians was referred to in connection with the Burning Torch Powwow. Most breathtaking of its uses is dancing in a blazing hoop.

Dangerous? Not at all! The dancer need not fear the slightest burn provided attention is given to the details of equipment and handling as here set forth.

Two things must receive attention—the costuming and the hoop.

The dancer wears breechcloth only, with no clothes or feathered bustles to ignite. Head ornaments are limited to a wig and beaded headband. This eliminates the only hazard for his body. His hands only contact the hoop directly and if the hoop is made as directed his hands are as safe as in any hoop dance.

MAKING THE BURNING HOOP

A regular dancing hoop 24 inches in diameter is used. For a distance of 24 inches, or about one-third its circumference, it is padded with burlap wrappings—this is the area that will be set afire. The burlap strips should be wrapped to a thickness of one inch and wired in place with flexible wire—do not use string, it burns. Then the entire hoop is wrapped with white cloth. Adhesive tape is then wrapped around the hoop at each end of the burlapped section for a distance of six inches to prevent the fire from spreading.

The burlapped section is rested in a shallow pan containing about two inches of kerosene and allowed to remain there at least two hours. It should be moved a time or two so that all sections of the burlapped area contact the kerosene. The adhesive tape prevents the white cloth from soaking up kerosene beyond the burlapped area. A half hour before the dance the hoop should be removed and placed with the soaked part on the ground to allow the excess kerosene to drip.

Photograph by Paul Boris

JAMES C. STONE

Photograph by Arthur C. Allen

ROBERT MEEKER

THE DANCE

When the hoop is lighted the flame rises only to a height of four or five inches from the soaked area so that the remainder of the hoop can be freely handled. The trick in manipulating it is to keep it moving. When in motion the flame is drawn away from the hoop itself. Whenever the hoop is near the legs all the dancer has to do is to dance in the opposite direction and the flame will be pulled away from him.

The dance opens as in the regular Hoop Dance with the hoop lying on the ground in the ring. After picking it up the dancer dances with it as in the Hoop Dance for a moment, then dances up to the central fire, holds the hoop at arm's length in it and dances around the fire, circling it completely. The hoop is now ablaze.

A. Swing the hoop in front of the body in a figure-of-8 motion.
B. Swing the hoop around the body (Step No. 13).
C. Holding the hoop down in front, hop on the right foot and tap the left foot in it several times in succession.
D. Step into the hoop and raise it up around the body and over the head, repeating several times in succession.
E. Taps through the Hoop (Step No. 12).
F. Bring the hoop down over the head and step out of it, repeating several times.
G. Roll the hoop with a reverse spin so that it rolls back (Step No. 10).
H. Kick the hoop and catch it as it falls (Step No. 9).

Avoid "Sitting in the Hoop" (Step No. 6). This might be done safely enough except for the possibility of singeing the hair of the wig, but it is not needed—a brilliant spectacle will result using the above routine without resorting to extreme measures.

Two-man Hoop Dance

Although a departure from the typical solo pattern of the Indians, one of the most interesting forms of the hoop dance is with two good dancers doing it at the same time. For best results they should resemble each other in size, appearance and movement. The routine follows that of the Hoop Dance just described, with each dancer performing independently but both doing the same general movements at the same time, except for the added feature of throwing the hoops across from one to the other at frequent intervals, thus exchanging hoops. This throwing is the most spectacular feature of the dance and is the only new movement over those already described.

To throw the hoop turn the shoulders to the right and hold the hoop at a full arm's length out to the right and behind: keeping the arm stiff, revolve the upper body to the left, sending the arm forward and sailing the hoop so that it floats across in a horizontal plane. It is thus not thrown by an arm motion but by a turn of the body; this tends to float the hoop, and lends itself to more graceful movement and better control. When both are to throw their hoops at the same time they hold them out at arm's length, then take four steps before throwing, thus permitting them to time their throws together. In catching the hoop, it is taken in the right hand and the body spun around to the left so that the motion of the hoop is not broken suddenly.

Lay the two hoops on the ground on opposite sides of the ring or stage. The dancers enter as in the Hoop Dance, advancing to and retreating from the hoop and finally picking it up. They move to opposite sides of the ring and remain directly across from each other at all times. Each stays in his own area in performing the following routine, without making progress around the ring unless so directed.

Between each of the following movements it is assumed that the basic steps will be employed to make the transitions.

A. Basic Movements (Steps Nos. 1, 2, and 3).
B. Glides (Step No. 4).
C. Grapevine (Step No. 5) repeating six times in succession.
D. Dancer No. 1 tosses his hoop to No. 2 who catches it in his left hand, spins around and in the same motion throws his own hoop over to No. 1. This is repeated four times.
E. Crisscross (Step No. 7).
F. They throw their hoops *simultaneously*, moving around the ring counterclockwise, repeating the throws in intervals of eight steps until they have completed the circuit and are back to position again.
G. Each kicks his hoop in the air and catches it himself.
H. They roll their hoops on the ground across to each other.
I. They roll their hoops with a backward spin so that they go half-way across to the other dancer, then return to the thrower. They spread their legs, let the hoop roll through, turn and pursue it.
J. They throw their hoops high in the air to each other, sending them up in a *vertical* plane instead of with the usual horizontal throw.
K. They throw their hoops high to each other but give them a back-ward spin. The hoops are not caught but are allowed to hit the ground and roll back to the throwers. They spread their legs, let the hoop roll between, grab it and immediately start the Crisscross (Step No. 7).
L. They dance to the far side of the ring from the exit, advance to-ward each other, tossing their hoops to exchange them, turn toward the exit and, two abreast, prance across. As they pass the fire they throw their hoops over the Council Rock and out of the ring, prancing out after them.

A dance of this type, of course, takes good teamwork between the two performers. Through practicing together they come to understand each other and to move in harmony. They take their cues from each other for the various movements. If one misses the hoop and drops it, the other instantly drops his, then they repeat the business of picking them up as at the beginning of the dance.

Beginners sometimes find that the hoops collide in the air when they are thrown simultaneously. This could not happen if the hoops are thrown correctly as described. When on opposite sides of the ring, if each turns his shoulders to the right and holds the hoop at arm's length to his right and behind, they are facing in opposite directions when the hoops are thrown. From this position the hoops will pass several feet apart.

Every effort must be made to do the dance gracefully and artistically, as a dance and not as a trick performance. The tempo and the rhythm of the movements remain constant throughout. The hoops are thrown, move through the air, and are caught at a speed of motion in harmony with this tempo and rhythm.

Double-hoop Dance

This dance was first encountered at the Nett Lake reservation of the Chippewas on the northern edge of Minnesota, danced by a middle-aged Indian who was the only one in that territory able to do it, and later was seen again at the Bad River settlement of the Chippewas on Lake Superior in Wisconsin.

In it two hoops are used and, as if that were not enough, the hoops are not touched with the hands in the course of the dance. It is a stunt type of dance and anything it may lack in grace and beauty as compared to the usual type of hoop dancing is compensated for by its uniqueness.

Such an intricate dance as this one is suitable only for an expert performer, thoroughly experienced in hoop dancing. There will be no need, therefore, to describe the movements in minute detail. A reference to the nature of the movements will be sufficient to permit experimentation, and it is only by experimentation that the dance can be worked out.

Two small hoops are needed, just large enough to permit the dancer to manipulate them about the body. One must be very slightly smaller than the other so that, by a tight squeeze, it can be forced through the other. For a person of average size diameters of 20 and 21 inches respectively should be about right.

The dance is in two parts, the first using one hoop only. The step is the double stomp, or at times just a jarring of the heels up and down. It is done on the spot, without progress.

The hoops are laid a few feet apart and the dance opens as in the Hoop Dance, the dancer concentrating his attention on one hoop and advancing and retreating from it. He picks it up without the use of the hands: He steps on it with one foot so as to raise the far side enough to shove the other foot under it. With both feet under it the legs are spread to press against the edges of the hoop. Now by jarring the heels up and down and keeping sufficient pressure against the hoop it can be worked up the legs to hip level. Here the arms are put through it and pressed against it and the hoop worked up to neck level, where it is allowed to hang around the neck and down in front against the stomach. The jarring of the heels is kept up constantly as the basic step.

The dancer then leans forward parallel to the ground and raises his arms forward fully extended thus lifting the hoop to the level of his back. Assisted by the jarring motion the hoop is worked backward until it is lying on the back, during which process it is prevented from falling off by extending the elbows out to the sides, parallel with the back. From this position it is worked backward very gradually until it drops over the rump, hanging on the back and resting on the thighs behind. The dancer then quickly shoves his head down between his knees and jars the hoop down over his head, straightening up suddenly to have it circling his legs again.

This maneuver is then repeated until the hoop is lying on the dancer's back again. He works it backward over his rump as before but this time he raises his arms fully extended behind and lifts the hoop up to the level of his back, thereby working it back up on to his back and over his head so that it is hanging around his neck. He puts his arms through it and lets it drop to waist level where it remains while he picks up the other hoop for the second part of the dance.

With the first hoop around his hips and held by straddling his legs, he steps into the second hoop and raises it as before until the two are together. He shoves an arm through each of the hoops, holding them in the crooks of his elbows, lifts his left foot out of the two hoops and inserts it in the one held on his left arm, then lifts his right foot out and inserts it in the right hoop. There is now a hoop around each leg, held up by the arm. He does the Grapevine trick with his right leg, putting his head through the hoop and letting it hang over his left shoulder. He must bend far forward now for the hoop is around his neck and under his right thigh. Then he repeats the Grapevine trick with his left leg, putting the hoop in the same position over his right shoulder. The hoops now overlap each other in front by about a foot. He shoves his arms and head through this foot-wide space, spreading the hoops as he does so with the result that the smaller hoop slips through the larger; then he straightens up and the hoops slip down around each leg as at the start. This maneuver is then repeated as often as desired.

DANCES USING SEVERAL HOOPS.—The Southwest Indians do hoop dances with three hoops, four hoops and even six hoops. With the foundation of the Hoop Dance and the Double-hoop Dance, one is equipped with the necessary knowledge to experiment with three or more hoops and to work out the possibilities. In such dances the hoops are handled by the hands, however.

Chapter XIII

CONTEST DANCES

THE DANCES IN this chapter are all built around a competitive element. The dancing is incidental to a contest. Rather than to call them dances it would probably be more accurate to say that they are contests placed in a dance setting.

They are more enjoyed by the participators than the spectators. For the entertainment of an audience most any other dance would serve the purpose better, but few other dances are as entertaining to the dancers themselves. Boys are particularly fond of them. They do much to add interest to practice periods.

Dancing the Scalp

This is the third episode in the Chippewa ceremony of Dancing the Scalp, described on page 115. After the ever-popular Scalp Dance is over the scalp is placed on a stick in the center of a circle and a contest held by the dancers for the possession of it. Either of these two episodes may be lifted out and used as a separate dance. The Scalp Dance is described on page 115. The following description has to do with the contest.

THE DANCE

Draw a 10-foot circle on the ground or floor. Set up a stick in the middle about one foot high and place the scalp on top of it. A bundle of horsehair will serve as the scalp. The dancers form around the edge of the circle and dance around and around it, their eyes fixed on the scalp. When the drumming stops they all dash for the scalp, the one wins who succeeds in getting possession of it.

The drummer attempts to trick the dancers into stepping over the line too soon, in which case the guilty ones are eliminated and withdraw. The drummer skips beats occasionally, changes the volume of the drumming from very loud to very soft, and otherwise tries to give the impression that the drumming has ceased. He aims to stop at the most unexpected time.

Once the scalp has been secured a powwow follows.

Fluffy Dance

In this playful little dance of the Cheyennes the dancers vie with each other in the picking up of fluffies off the ground with their teeth. The fluffies are the small downy plumes of the type used to embellish the bottoms of feathers in a war-bonnet. The longer ones should be selected, at least four inches in length.

As done by the Cheyennes it is indeed a difficult feat, for the fluffy is stuck in the ground and the dancer required to pick it up with his teeth *without touching the ground with any part of his body except the feet and without stopping dancing!* If he touches or breaks rhythm he fails. Only much practice on the part of exceedingly limber dancers will make this difficult feat possible, but until such ability is developed through considerable practice the following adaptation will provide a most interesting pastime dance.

Place as many fluffies as there are dancers at various points around the ring by sticking them in the ground so that they stand upright. The dancers walk in, each taking his position beside his fluffy. The drumming starts and each begins dancing around his fluffy, circling it, dancing away from it and back to it, his eyes fixed on it, shading his eyes with his hands, retreating from it and advancing by throwing his arms toward it (see "Playing on an Object," page 52. When the drumming stops each drops to his knees, *folds his arms in front of his chest*, bends down and attempts to pick up the fluffy in his teeth. The one wins who first gets to his feet with the fluffy in his mouth.

The drummer attempts to trick the dancers into thinking the drumming has stopped by skipping beats, changing accent, changing volume from loud to very soft. Should a dancer drop to his knees before the drumming has stopped he is eliminated.

Once the feathers are picked up a powwow follows.

Falling Eagle Nest

A favorite sport of the Blackfoot boys was to shoot down an eagle's nest from a tree with their arrows, then dash forward to touch it as it fell, the honor going not to the one who shot it down but to the one who touched it first.

This is an adaptation of the sport in the form of a dance contest.

THE DANCE

Cut and trim a sapling that it will stand up 15 or 20 feet when planted in the ground. Tie together a bundle of twigs and straw to represent the eagle's nest and tie it to the top of the pole with an ordinary string. Tie a rope around the nest that will hang down the length of the pole. Set up the pole near one edge of the dancing ring and draw a line on the ground near the opposite side behind which the dancers must stay.

A chief holds the rope at the foot of the pole and the drumming starts. The dancers dance behind the line with their eyes fixed on the eagle's nest, using all of the looking devices such as shading the eyes with the hands, etc. The chief at the rope feints at pulling it down repeatedly and finally yanks it. The dancers dash forward and dive for the nest, the honor going to the one who touches it first. The chief at the rope indicates the winner by slapping him on the back. The drum picks up again and a powwow follows.

Should any dancer step across the line before the eagle's nest is actually pulled loose he is eliminated and withdraws.

Chapter XIV

THE GIVE-AWAY DANCE

THE NIGHTS ARE many that I have danced in Indian roundhouses, moccasins afoot and bells on ankles, joining in the exulting powwows, giving and receiving gifts in the festive give-away dances, accepted as one of the people. And many are the times I have reproduced the give-away dance among city-dwelling folk, always to have it endorsed as an occasion long to be remembered.

Not a dance for the entertainment of spectators, it is solely for the enjoyment of the dancers. Its deep-rooted appeal grows out of two factors —the compulsion of the primitive rhythm, and the Christmas spirit of the giving and receiving of gifts.

Vividly fixed in mind is my first acceptance as a dancer in a native Indian dance. It was years ago in an ancient roundhouse near the Canadian border in Minnesota. The dance had been going on for better than an hour as we sat on the sidelines watching. The rhythm of the booming drum was irresistible, its urge to action overpowering.... We went out to the car and got moccasins and bells, returned and put them on. Reluctant to intrude where we were not sure we were wanted, we sat by and hoped for some means to break the ice. It was not long in coming: a dashing young dancer came up and handed me a quarter—I stepped up beside him in the line of dancers and sidestepped around the ring with him in the accepted fashion. Then a feeble old woman went to my companion and gave him a beaded bracelet and he, too, joined the circle. On the next dance I went over to the young dancer and gave him my pocket-knife, and my companion to the old woman and gave her a small mirror. Instantly a chorus of shouts broke out around the hall, "Ho, Ho" and "How, How." Now they knew that we were of their kind in spirit, that we understood the etiquette of the dance.

Among the northern Woodland and Plains peoples these give-away dances take place in an evening of dancing in which they are alternated with powwows, first a series of one, then a series of the other. The unalterable rule is that when a gift is received, a gift of approximate value must be returned, for the gift is given as a token of friendship and regard, and the giving of one in return signifies that the friendship feeling is mutual, a fact often misunderstood by early travelers who failed to return gifts to their would-be Indian friends and thereby created a situation in which the Indian's personal dignity demanded that he ask for the return of his gift. Hence the term "Indian giver" which we toss about so glibly in current slang today.

The gifts exchanged are many and varied in type, but there is one item more often used than any other—*calico or printed cloth*. Years of tradition dating back to the old treaty days have established this as a token of friendship, as a symbol of sincerity with the result that five- or ten-yard pieces are freely exchanged in the dances. Although rare today, another such symbol is a peace-pipe bowl of catlinite. In addition to these there is much exchanging of blankets and patchwork quilts, of items of dancing costume such as beaded vests and leggings, of items of ordinary clothing such as woolen shirts, etc. It was not unusual for a dancer in the old days to "dance away" his entire dancing costume, piece by piece to his friends, since it was not customary to wear the same costume longer than one year. Most prized of all gifts in the olden times was a pony, but the pony itself did not enter the dance hall—a stick or a match was given to the recipient which told him if he would call the next day a pony would be his.

The give-away dance has great potentialities as a recreational feature today. For the closing days of a summer-camp season it is a delightful and most appropriate event, giving the campers who have spent happy weeks together a chance to recognize their particular friends by the exchange of gifts. In that situation it carries the name of "Friendship Dance."

Indeed, there are several names by which this type of dance is called. In addition to *Give-away Dance* and *Friendship Dance*, it is called a *Woman's Dance* or *Squaw Dance*, this being the term most often used in the literature on the subject. Again, the Chippewas call it a *Powwow* since it is an evening of dancing comprised of both powwows and give-away dances. Most often, however, they call it a "dance." Other dance occasions are referred to by their names but this, the most common of dancing events, is usually spoken of as just a "dance."

The Chippewa Give-away Dance

Let us see what actually happens in the Indian give-away dance and then describe how one of these dances can be adapted for use today. And for setting let us take a dance in a Chippewa village of northern Minnesota, although it could well be in any of the neighboring Woodland tribes, or in a Sioux village on the Plains to the westward, for the routine would be essentially the same.

In the morning we go to the Head Man of the dance and give him two packages of tobacco, thereby calling a dance. During the day he visits each lodge in the village and leaves a pinch of the tobacco, thus inviting the household to the dance. No spoken word of invitation is necessary, merely the statement, "Tonight at seven in the roundhouse."

The snows and winds of many northern winters have left the round-house with but a fragment of its original glory. The weary hands of the old men can no longer keep it trim and their lean purses do not permit of good repair. But its time-battered frame belies the strength of the spirit that dwells within, for it is still the vibrant life-center of the people, its mighty drum the pulse beat of the village.

As it stands today it is seen in the photo facing page 199. The floor plan is shown in Figure 90.*

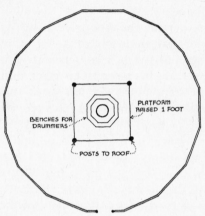

PLATFORM
RAISED 1 FOOT

BENCHES FOR
DRUMMERS

POSTS TO ROOF

Figure 90. Plan of the Dance House

At seven o'clock the drum voice begins to boom, heard in the remotest corners of the village. We hurry to the scene, joining women whose dresses ring out from the hundreds of tin tinkles that adorn them, and men whose coming is heralded more loudly still by the sleigh bells on their ankles. Many have jugs of drinking water in their hands and all have packs on their backs containing gifts for the dance.

The drumming and singing bring no response for a while, but ere long the women begin going around the ring with the characteristic squaw step, the tinkles on their dresses responding noisily to their vibrating bodies, soon to be joined by the men, and within a half-hour the powwow dances are going full-blast, the men leaping with fullest vigor, the twelve drum-mers uniting to make the big drum boom, their weird chanting welling louder and louder.

---

* The roundhouse is 16-sided, 45 feet in diameter. The floor is of hard-packed earth. Benches are built around the edges. The only obstruction is the drum altar in the center with four posts at the corners rising to the square cupola at the apex of the roof. The drum altar is a platform 13 feet square, one foot high, in the center of which the drum is hung, with benches built around it in the form of an octagon measuring seven feet across. These benches accommodate the 12 drummers who "belong to the drum."

The Head Man of the dance arises to silence the hall, and addresses the drum. In his hand he holds the two packages of tobacco we gave him upon arrival at the dance. He invokes the blessing of the One Above and offers the tobacco to the drum. He calls upon an elderly man of high standing to pass the tobacco. A pinch is given to each person present.

Then comes *Everybody's Dance*. Not everyone is able to dance in the strenuous powwows, but all can take part in Everybody's Dance. The head men start it, standing in line facing the drum and side-stepping around the ring to the left. Others join and soon all are in the circle, or perhaps in several circles one behind the other. Many times they repeat the dance without leaving the floor.

Everybody's Dance heralds the first give-away dance. Someone arises with a piece of calico or perchance a beaded vest in his hand, walks around in front of the benches and hands it to a friend. The giver stands facing the drum, the recipient takes his place to his right, and together they begin side-stepping or squaw-stepping to the left, or if they are youthful men, perhaps moving sidewise with the toe-heel step. Proud of his gift, the recipient holds it up in his hand so all can see and perchance yips at times to call attention to it. Others give gifts and presently there is a long line moving around. A man desires to give a gift to a person who has already received one and is dancing—he goes up to him and presents the gift, then steps between him and the person who gave the first gift.

Four of these give-away dances follow one another in a series, during which the recipients "pay back" or perhaps have still more gifts bestowed upon them.

A group of powwow dances comes next. During one of these a man goes up to another and gives him a blanket. It was given in a *powwow*— that means no gift is to be given back in return. If it were a give-away dance, he would be duty-bound to "pay back." Such giving of gifts in a powwow is rare and is done only as a very special token of regard.

Then more give-away dances and more powwows. About the middle of the evening the Waboos or Rabbit Dance takes place (pages 141 and 146), after which still more powwows and give-aways. And so it goes far into the night.

How does one tell what dance is being drummed, whether a powwow or give-away? The song identifies it. If one does not know the songs or understand the language he has no choice but to ask or to wait and see.

In all of these dances, whether Give-away, Powwow, Everybody's or Waboos, the dancers move around the ring in a clockwise direction. In the powwows a dancer is more or less on his own and occasionally may reverse his direction for a few steps, but by and large the motion is always clockwise.

CONDUCTING A GIVE-AWAY OR FRIENDSHIP DANCE

It should be announced several days in advance to give everyone a chance to prepare. Its nature should be carefully explained, with the friendship theme played up as central. It is well to place a limit on the amount to be spent for a gift, emphasizing that it is not the value but the thought that counts. It should be suggested that the gifts be left unwrapped and assembled in a bag to be carried to the dance.

The dance is best conducted indoors, permitting the drum to be placed in the center of the circle—if outdoors, the fire, of course, must occupy the center. A large powwow drum is needed (see page 252). Arrange the chairs in a 24-foot circle and place the drum on the floor in the center. Four or more drummers sit on the floor around the drum, each with a "hard" drumbeater (page 253). One is the head drummer.

The exact procedure should be demonstrated before the program starts: The giver goes to the recipient and hands him the gift, then stands facing the drum. The recipient takes his place to the giver's right and the two side-step around the ring to the left, using the squaw step (page 40) if they know it, otherwise just side-stepping. The recipient holds his gift up with his right hand so that all can see. At the end of the dance each walks to his own seat.

The program consists of groups of powwow dances alternated with groups of give-away dances. A proportion of two powwows to four give-aways is about right. Each dance lasts about two minutes after which there is a rest when everyone sits down.

The signal for a give-away dance is four slow accented beats of the drum, after which the drumming starts for the dance. If no such signal is given the dance is a powwow.

In the powwows anyone may dance who chooses, but in the give-aways only those take the floor who are giving or receiving gifts. At the end of each powwow there is a brief "encore." The dance ends and the dancers start for their seats, then the drum picks up again for an "encore" of 8 to 16 counts. Indian etiquette demands that one stop dancing on the last beat of the "encore"—to ring one's bells after the drumming ceases is a social blunder. There is no "encore" after the give-away dance.

Near the end of the evening the number of give-away dances still to be conducted should be announced so that everyone can plan accordingly and see that their debts are paid. In case one does not have an appropriate gift with which to pay back, he should go to the person and tell him that he will see him tomorrow; then the two dance as though the gift had actually been given then and there. Should the program end before a person has an opportunity to return a gift, the situation should be explained and the person told that he will be seen tomorrow.

Should a dancer give a gift to someone without expecting a gift returned, he does so in a powwow number, not in a give-away number.

PART IV

STAGING THE DANCES

Chapter XV

THE DANCING RING

As HAS BEEN indicated so often in these pages the ideal setting for Indian dances is in the out-of-doors. There they are in their original element. They may be presented effectively enough on an indoor stage, and more often than not that is the only choice, but a certain atmosphere of appropriateness, of primitive flavor and of beauty can be developed outdoors that no amount of stage setting and skillful direction can quite match otherwise.

An outdoor stage, however, has little if any advantage over an indoor one. The unmatched setting is the outdoor *council ring*, the time-honored assembly place of the Indians, the age-old theater of the America that was. There, with the central fire in the middle and with the amphitheater of seats extending all around, we are in an arena that at once squares with tradition and provides the best practical arrangements.

Any institution that has opportunity to give repeated outdoor performances, such as a summer camp for example, will do well to build a permanent council ring with immovable seating arrangements. For a single show, a temporary one can be improvised following the same general plan.

Great care must be given to the plans for the ring, to its ornamentation, and to its related facilities.

Laying Out the Ring

In another book, *Woodcraft*, I have devoted a full chapter to the construction of the council ring and its adornment.* Complete details will be found there, making it necessary to discuss here only the essential features dealing with the adaptation of the ring to dancing and the dance program.

The dancing ring is a *circular* arrangement of benches around a fire, with no more on one side than on the others. The general layout is shown in Figure 91. The ring within the benches is level and unobstructed, except for the central fire which is *on the level of the ground;* there is no fire altar, nor is the fire surrounded by logs or stones, or protected in any other way.

* Bernard S. Mason, *Woodcraft*, Chapter XVI. New York: A. S. Barnes and Company, 1939.

A ring of the wrong dimensions can unmake the best of performances. The audience must be close enough to hear the speaking parts easily and distinctly—this means that it must be sufficiently small. The audience must be far enough away to gain prospective in viewing the dances—this means that it be sufficiently large. For dancing purposes *a diameter of 30 feet is recommended*. The standard size for a council ring used for storytelling and games is 24 feet but this is not large enough for effective dancing; the dancers do not have enough room and the audience is too close to see the

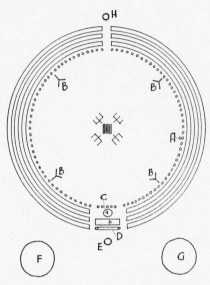

Figure 91. Layout of the Council Ring

A. Circle of white-washed stones
B. Tripods for incense bowls
C. Drum support
D. Council Rock with dancers' entrances either side
E. Thunderbird
F. Tepee for wood, fire supplies, tools etc.
G. Wigwam for costume changes, dancers' equipment, etc.
H. Totem pole behind spectators' entrance

dance as a whole. The 30-foot dancing ring makes speaking a little difficult but in dancing performances the speaking parts are always minor and incidental to the dancing. Camps or organizations doing much dancing will do well to have two adjoining rings, one 24 feet in diameter, simply constructed for general use, and the other 30 feet, elaborately ornamented for dancing. In the former the games and storytelling of Little Council can take place, and in the latter the dancing and lofty ritual of Grand Council.

An absolutely level piece of ground is needed, located in a beautiful

Photograph by Paul Boris

JAMES C. STONE

The Council Rock
and the Thunderbird

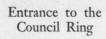

Photographs taken at Camp Fairwood

Entrance to the
Council Ring

spot, preferably solidly hemmed in by trees that form a green Gothic arch high above.

Around the 30-foot circle a row of whitewashed stones is placed (A in Figure 91), which stand out vividly at night, clearly indicating the edge of the dancing area. Close around this circle the benches are constructed, row after row as needed, elevated in amphitheater style so that all can see the entire circle.

Of greatest importance is the foundation of the ring itself. It must be absolutely smooth, free from roots, rocks and pebbles. A pebble of the size of a marble can make a stone bruise on a moccasined foot, and when stepped on can cause such sudden and unexpected pain as to force the dancer to break his rhythm. Pebbles cause dancers to lose confidence and worry about their footing. After the ground has been worked down to a level and hard-packed foundation, it should be surfaced with wet, black muck, if obtainable, to a thickness of four inches when rolled and packed solidly. If this surface is replaced once a year the ring will always have an excellent foundation for dancing, soft underfoot yet solid and firm. Before each performance the ring should be very carefully raked. If the muck dries out in hot weather it should be well-soaked at noon prior to the evening's performance. The earth should form a black, velvety carpet against the outline of the whitewashed circle of stones surrounding it.

There should be no more entrances to the ring than absolutely necessary. In a small ring one is sufficient, but in a dancing circle there should be two as indicated in Figure 91—one a double entrance at the Council Rock through which the dancers enter, and the other directly opposite it to accommodate the audience. Wide entrances break the circle of the ring and leave cold, empty spaces. Twenty-four inches should be a sufficient width, never more than 30 inches.

ADORNMENT OF THE RING

Ornamentations of many kinds, all in the Indian mood, adorn the ring. Circular plaques made of barrel tops and painted in Indian design are placed at intervals of every few feet around the edge, attached to poles and nailed to the backs of the benches. Symbolic eagle feathers of wood dangle from them. Totem poles of various types surround the ring, and tepees add their unique color. Above the Council Rock and dominating the scene is the Thunderbird, either painted on boards or carved from a log.

The making of all of these is described and illustrated in *Woodcraft.**

THE COUNCIL ROCK

While the term Council Rock refers specifically to the bench on which the Chief sits (D in Figure 91), it is used to mean the bench and the entire

* Bernard S. Mason, *Woodcraft*, Chapters XVI and XXIV. New York: A. S. Barnes and Company, 1939.

area around it—the focal point of the show, the center of the stage of the council ring. It is ornamented accordingly. Note the photograph of the Council Rock facing page 231—the entrances to either side through which the dancers enter and exit, the bench itself, the drum-frame in front of the bench, the "theater masks" in totem style either side, one laughing and the other scowling, and the Thunderbird rising above all overhead.

The entrance directly opposite the Council Rock through which the spectators enter is shown in the illustration facing page 231. The totem pole behind it is similar in design but shorter and smaller in size than the one behind the Council Rock. The location of this pole in relation to the entrance can be seen at H in Figure 91.

THE BLANKET RACK

Always a blanket or robe of some sort is hung behind the Council Rock to add an appropriate touch of color. Note the framework of poles above the bench in the illustration facing page 231 with the steer skulls on the corners—this is the rack on which the blanket is hung. There is a slender cross-pole just under the top log to accommodate the blanket.

An Indian blanket is always appropriate for the hanging, but most effective is a large hide painted after the manner of the old buffalo hides of the Plains.*

THE DRUM SUPPORT

The drum is located directly in front of the Council Rock and just at the outer edge of the circle of whitewashed stones, as shown at C in Figure 91. It is hung on a frame that elevates it to waist level, made as described in Chapter XVIII, "Bells, Drums and Rattles."

THE INCENSE TRIPODS

Four small tripods for the holding of the incense bowls are placed at the very edge of the ring in the four directions as shown at B in Figure 91. These are 15 to 18 inches high, made of rustic sticks as in Figure 92, with a spread at the top sufficient to accommodate the incense bowls. The bowls are cereal bowls painted red and black in Indian design.

The bowls are filled half-full of dry sand and into each four cubes of pine incense are placed. The bowls remain outside the ring and are brought in during the opening ceremony (see Chapter XVI).

* For the design and instructions for painting the hide, see Bernard S. Mason, *Woodcraft*, page 452. New York: A. S. Barnes and Company, 1939.

Figure 92. Tripod and Incense Bowl

THE CENTRAL FIRE

The central fire must be viewed from two angles—utility and beauty. Its first purpose is to illuminate the dances. It must do this unfailingly. It is tragic to have the fire bog down in the middle of a dance, leaving in darkness a scene into which so much time and thought has been put. Nothing is so discouraging to a dancer as to have his efforts lost in darkness. A specialized type of fire handling is necessary to safeguard against this contingency.

The fire should be built and in full readiness long before the audience arrives. It is built in log-cabin or crisscross fashion, this type of construction giving a maximum light. It measures 20 inches in width and 20 inches in height. It is made of finely split softwood throughout and then soaked with kerosene so that, when the Firemaker's burning tinder is touched to it, it bursts dramatically into a blazing torch of light. This opening fire is designed to last only through the opening ceremony. It fairly explodes with brilliance, filling the ring with a blaze of glory that dramatizes the spirit of the opening ritual.

The fire is built with minute precision so that, as it stands there awaiting the opening of the council, it contributes to the beauty of the setting. It must be shipshape and workmanlike in every respect. Each stick is carefully sawed to measure, and all are of approximately the same thickness.* An opening is left at one side for the Firemaker's tinder. Then the whole structure is soaked with kerosene.

Let no one raise the question of the lack of woodsmanship in using kerosene . . . the question is the lack of showmanship in not using it.

The fire is placed in the exact center as shown in Figure 91 and extending out from it in the four directions are the forks of the "sand painting" as originated by Ernest Thompson Seton. This arrangement is shown enlarged in Figure 93. The "sand-painting" design is made with lime, or as a possible substitute, corn meal. If the central fire is 20 inches square, these white forks of lime should be 24 inches in size, the lines 2½ inches wide. At the central intersection of each fork a tiny wigwam fire is built from

* For detailed instructions see *Woodcraft*, page 175.

split sticks, standing about 10 inches high, well soaked with kerosene. These are the four lamps of the opening ceremony.

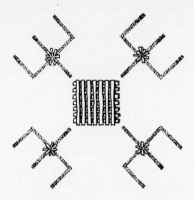

Figure 93. Sand-painting and Central Fire

Wood for replenishing the central fire is located outside the ring in two piles, one of softwood and the other of hardwood, with a bucket of kerosene standing alongside. After each dance the fire-tenders enter with a few sticks from each pile which they have dipped in the kerosene so that they will light immediately, the softwood giving quick illumination and the hardwood providing the staying power. The fire is never replenished during a dance.

TORCHES

Two long torches are needed for the Torchbearers in the processional and the opening ritual. These are made of green poles six feet long and two inches thick, around the ends of which burlap is wrapped to form a ball and then wired and securely nailed. Do not use string—it burns. A third and smaller torch of the size of a cane is also required.

These torches are inserted in a bucket of kerosene at noon on the day of the performance and are taken out about an hour before show time and placed with the soaked end on the ground to permit the excess kerosene to drip off.

BACK-STAGE ARRANGEMENTS

Two tepees or bark wigwams should be placed just outside the Council Rock entrances as shown at F and G in Figure 91. One of these is used for costume changes and for the equipment used by the dancers. The other is for the storing of wood and fire supplies and for keeping of the tools used by the custodians of the ring.

Outside the entrance also should be a tub of water into which the Torchbearers can souse their torches the moment they step out of the ring, thus cutting off the light instantly.

ORGANIZATION OF HELPERS

Two types of organization are needed to care for the preparations for a Grand Council or a dancing program. The first handles the preparation of the dancers, including their equipment, costuming and make-up. The second handles the preparation of the council ring and the mechanical arragements. Each of these require a division of labor among a number of people and a careful assignment of duties.

For the preparation of the ring and other mechanical arrangements, the following organization is needed:

2 custodians of the ring—to rake and prepare the ring, lay the "sand painting," and otherwise assume responsibility for its condition.

2 fire-tenders—to build the central fires, to prepare the reserve supply of wood, and to replenish the fire after each dance.

2 torch-makers—to make the torches, soak them in kerosene and have them at the appointed place at the proper time.

2 water boys—to water the ring during the day and to fill the tub in which the torches are to be extinguished.

1 incense lighter—to secure the incense, place it in the bowls and light it just before needed.

2 trail lighters—To build the fires on the Medicine Trail and light them just as the council closes (see next chapter).

Chapter XVI

COUNCIL-FIRE RITUAL

NIGHT AND the glamour of Council! The compulsion of atmosphere, the intrigue of ritual, the beauty of symbolism, the eternal youth of primitive dancing—all under the great canopy of the night, filled with the fragrant incense of the things that grow, vibrant with a thousand Voices that only the Faithful hear. . . .

A far cry, indeed, from the theater stage is the council ring in the woods. But the ring is, after all, only the place—the proper setting, the ideal locale. The peculiar advantage of Grand Council as a means of presenting Indian dances stems not only from the setting but from the ritualistic framework in which the dances are set forth.

The ritual holds much of importance. It establishes the tone, creates the mood. It sets the stage for beauty. It places the dances in their proper element. It lends to them a loftiness of purpose, a seriousness of meaning, a worshipful quality that is wholly appropriate and in harmony with their original background. It permits the dances to begin with the advantage of atmosphere already created. But the ritual is more than an atmospheric prologue, more than a springboard for the dances—it is in itself a lofty and inspiring spectacle, rich in beauty and symbolic in meaning. Indeed, it is in itself a dance, for the line of demarkation between ritual and dancing is hazy and fleeting. From the first drumbeat of the processional to the final word of the closing ceremony, the stuff of which dancing is made prevails, so that there is no impropriety in speaking of the whole Grand Council as a dance. The difference is merely one of degree—at some points dancing appears as more conspicuously such.

The ritual never changes. Each new performance presents new dances but always fitted into the same ritualistic framework.

It was Ernest Thompson Seton who first adapted the Indian council fire to modern use, and who more than anyone else has popularized it. The general concept of the ritual as here given is his, and the spoken lines in the opening ceremony are adapted from the laws of the Woodcraft League as originated by him.*

There are two kinds of council fires growing out of Indian custom—

* Ernest Thompson Seton, *The Birch Bark Roll of the Woodcraft League of America*, page 11. New York: Brieger Press, 1925.

Little Council and Grand Council. Little Council is largely devoted to games and is in the spirit of play.*

Grand Council is all in the spirit of beauty, devoted exclusively to dancing. It is the ritual for Grand Council that is here described.

Characters

Chief of the Council—the central figure who directs the council, handles the speaking parts, and does the drumming.

Herald—the soloist, a person with fine solo voice.

Second Chief—who assists the Chief in the spoken parts of the ritual.

Torchbearers—two well-built, attractive people who carry the torches.

Firemaker—who makes fire-by-friction in lighting the central fire.

Echo—a boy soprano who echoes the closing song from a distance.

The Processional

The crowd is all seated. The council ring is full of darkness. The scene awaits the distant drumbeat of the processional, the voice of the Herald....

Far back on the campus the processional forms. At its front are the two Torchbearers, each with a six-foot torch held up in front as a flag-bearer would hold his flag. Behind them is the Herald (soloist) holding a small hand-drum. Next in line is the Chief of the Council and behind him the Firemaker. Then comes the dancers two abreast. All are costumed for the dancing, the Chief in full Indian regalia, all others breechclothed and feathered for action, the dancers wearing their dancing bells.

The signal comes from the head usher that all is in readiness at the ring. The torches are lighted.

YO-O-O EE YO HO   YO HO   O   HO-O-O

Zuni Call to Council **

The Herald begins to drum and the column moves forward, walking at normal pace. The drum is struck on every other step. After eight beats the Herald begins singing the Zuni Call to Council to the slow tempo of the drumming. The song finished, he walks on for eight drumbeats and then repeats it, continuing thus, repeating at intervals of eight drumbeats.

The processional does not go directly to the council ring but rather circles far around it, following the course indicated in Figure 94. To the

*For description see Bernard S. Mason and Elmer D. Mitchell, *Social Games for Recreation*, Chapters 12 to 15. New York: A. S. Barnes and Company, 1934.

**From Ernest Thompson Seton, *The Birch Bark Roll of the Woodcraft League of America*, p. 10. By permission of the author. New York: Brieger Press, 1925.

audience seated in the ring the lights of the torches are visible through the trees, the singing and the drumming clearly audible. This lengthy processional is excellent stagecraft. Its effect is profound.

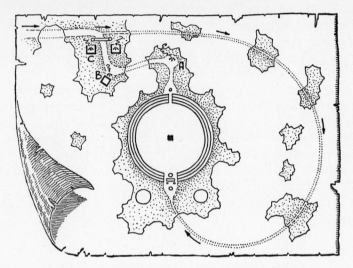

Figure 94. Approaches to the Council Ring

As the column nears the council ring the tempo slows down gradually, the loud drumming used at the distance is softened. When within 50 yards of the ring the song is repeated for the last time.

The processional comes up behind the Council Rock as shown. The two Torchbearers enter through the two entrances either side of the Council Rock and stand just inside, quiet and statue-like, their faces immobile and expressionless. The Herald, the Chief and the Firemaker stand behind the Council Rock shielded from view by the blanket. The dancers remain in column, their feet stationary to silence their bells.

The only light in the ring is that from the two torches.

From "Zuni Sunrise Call" as transcribed and harmonized by Carlos Troyer, copyright 1904 by Carlos Troyer, and published by Theodore Presser Company.

Opening Ritual

With the two Torchbearers in position, the Herald walks in slowly and quietly and takes his position directly in front of the Council Rock and behind the drum (Figure 91). He stands silently for a few seconds, his eyes looking beyond the ring into the distance. Then he sings the beautiful Zuni Sunrise Call using the Indian words, at the end repeating the first two measures, finishing with the soft echo.

The Chief enters with slow and measured step, walks inside the ring proper and stops directly in front of the drum. With deep religious feeling, his words measured in harmony with the tempo of his step, he says:

"Let there be silence. We stand in the presence of the One Great Spirit."

He takes two steps forward toward the fire and stops:

"Now light we the Council Fire after the manner of the forest children, even as Wakonda Himself doeth light His fire, by the rubbing together of two trees in the storm wind, so cometh forth the sacred fire from the wood of the forest."

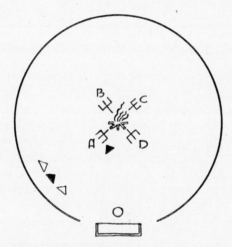

Figure 95. Diagram for Opening Ceremony of Grand Council

The Chief turns his back to the fire and stands facing the Council Rock, his eyes on the Thunderbird above. The Firemaker enters at the left of the Council Rock and walks slowly, quietly, and unostentaciously to the central fire, kneels at the left side of it, and makes fire by the rubbing-stick method.* He makes no undue fuss or commotion about the fire lighting, performing quietly and without flourish. His tinder lighted he inserts it under the central fire, arises and walks quietly out. Saturated with kerosene as it is, the fire instantly bursts into brilliant blaze.

* For description of fire-by-friction see Bernard S. Mason, *Woodcraft*, page 135. New York: A. S. Barnes and Company, 1939.

As the Firemaker exits the Chief turns and faces the fire, speaking with greater vigor and increased tempo:

"Now know we that Wakonda, the Great Spirit, has been pleased to smile upon His children, has sent down the sacred fire. By this sign know we that He will be with us in council, that His wisdom will be present."

The Chief turns and walks back to the Council Rock against which his small torch of walking-stick size is leaning, picks it up and walks back toward the fire. As he does so the Second Chief enters and takes his position between the two Torchbearers. The two Torchbearers and the Second Chief then move around the edge of the ring and take positions directly opposite the fork marked A, as illustrated in Figure 95. The Chief himself stands facing this fork as shown. He lights his torch in the central fire and with it lights the little fire on the fork.

Chief: "From the Great Central Fire I light this, the lamp of *beauty*. From it are these three rays (he places his torch on the first prong of the fork): Be clean."

Second Chief: "Both yourself and the place you live in."

Chief, placing his torch on the second prong: "Be strong."

Second Chief: Understand and respect your body. It is the Temple of the Spirit."

Chief, placing his torch on the third prong: "Protect all harmless wild-life."

Second Chief: "And be ever ready to fight the wild fire in the woods."

The Torchbearers and the Second Chief move around until opposite to the fork marked B, and the Chief takes his position beside that fork. Ceremoniously he puts his torch in the central fire then lights the little fire at B: "From the Great Central Fire I light this, the lamp of *truth*. From it are these three rays (he places his torch on the first prong): Speak true."

Second Chief: "Word of honor is sacred."

Chief, placing his torch on the second prong: "Play fair."

Second Chief: "Foul play is treachery."

Chief, placing his torch on the third prong: "Be reverent."

Second Chief: "Worship the Great Spirit and respect all worship of him by others."

They move to the fork marked C, repeating the ceremony.

Chief: "From the Great Central Fire I light this the lamp of *fortitude*. From it are these three rays (he places his torch on the first prong): Be brave."

Second Chief: "Courage is the noblest of all attainments."

Chief, putting his torch on the second prong: "Be silent."

Second Chief: "It is harder to be silent than to speak but in the hour of trial it is stronger."

Chief, putting his torch on the third prong: "Obey."

Second Chief: "Obedience is the first law in the woods."

They move to the fork marked D.

Chief: "From the Great Central Fire I light this, the flaming lamp of *love*. From it are these three rays (he places his torch on the first prong): Be kind."

Second Chief: "Do at least one act of unbargaining service each day."

Chief, putting his torch on the second prong: "Be helpful."

Second Chief: "Do your share of the work."

Chief, putting his torch on the third prong: "Be joyful."

Second Chief: "Seek the joy of being alive."

They move to directly in front of the Council Rock, the Torchbearers and Second Chief lining up facing the fire, the Chief standing between them and the fire.

Chief: "This is the law of the woods." He throws his torch beside the Central Fire.

The Torchbearers and Second Chief exit, the Torchbearers dousing their torches in the bucket awaiting them outside, thus cutting off the light instantly.

The Chief takes his position behind the drum, removes the blanket from it, picks up the drumstick, and begins drumming.

Into the ring come the Incense Bearers carrying their lighted incense bowls. They perform the routine of the Incense Dance as described at the end of this chapter.

This concludes the opening ceremony and the program of dances start.

The Program of Dances

The mood has been set by the opening ritual. The dances follow one after the other. Each is announced by the Chief, who steps forward in front of the drum in doing so. Each requires a descriptive sentence or two to indicate its nature and its meaning. The story dances require longer descriptions presenting the essential facts of the story that is to be enacted. In each case no unnecessary words are used. The lines are carefully prepared in advance, designed to create the atmosphere of the dance in question. They are spoken with dignity and reserve, in harmony with the mood and tone of the Council as reflected in the opening ceremony.

The Closing Ritual

The last dance over, the Chief walks slowly and quietly to a spot midway between the Council Rock and the fire. The Herald solemnly walks to a point on the other side of the fire, directly opposite the spot where the Chief is standing and faces him.

Chief, with head turned upward and in prayerful mood: Recites the words of "The Last Song" by Hartley Alexander (page 133).

Herald, slowly, gravely, solemnly, hymn-like: Sings the Omaha Tribal Prayer (page 242).

Echo (a boy soprano): Echoes the Omaha Tribal Prayer from the distance.

Chief, pronouncing the benediction: "And now may the Great Spirit put sunshine into all of your hearts."

They exit slowly.

From Alice C. Fletcher, *Indian Story and Song from North America*, page 29. By permission of Hale, Cushman and Flint, publishers.

The Medicine Trail

As the audience leaves the brightly lighted ring, the trail through the woods is dark, doubly dark by contrast. It must be illuminated, appropriately illuminated in the Indian way—by fires. But this illumination is to serve a higher purpose than mere safety and convenience—*it is to focus attention on the symbolism along the trail*. At the curve of the trail at A in Figure 94 is a little fire throwing light on a totem that stands behind it. At the curve marked B is another tiny fire made of pitch-pine chips illuminating a little Red God, patron saint of the out-of-doors. At C there are two fire-altars made of logs, four feet square and three feet high, the framework filled with rocks and gravel, on the top of which fires are burning illuminating the medicine arch over the trail and the Red God perched on top of it. Farther along, as the trail leaves the woods, there is a 20-foot rustic tower on the top of which a fire is blazing.[*]

Thus as the audience wends its way along the trail they remain in the atmosphere of the council, the illuminated symbols continuing to preach its gospel—the gospel of beauty, of imagination, of romance.

These various trail fires are lighted by the two Trail-lighters who take their positions during the closing ritual of the council and light the fires just as the last word is spoken.

Incense-bearer's Dance

This is the Incense-bearer's Dance that forms a part of the opening ceremony.

Four incense bowls, each containing four pieces of pine incense are

[*] For pictures of these symbols and instructions for making, see Bernard S. Mason, *Woodcraft*, Chapter 24. New York: A. S. Barnes and Company, 1939.

needed. Four prayer-sticks are also required as illustrated in Figure 96, 24 inches long, wrapped with colored cloth, with dangles of six-inch ribbons, and a tuft of fluffies on the end. These properties for the Incense Bearers are permanent equipment, used at the opening of each Grand Council.

For Incense Bearers four well-built boys are needed, attractive in appearance, light of foot, and as near alike in size as possible.

Figure 96. Prayer stick used by Incense Bearers

They take positions just outside the Council Rock, two at each entrance, as shown in Figure 97. The incense is lighted by an assistant who hands the bowls to the Incense Bearers just before they enter. They hold the bowls in both hands at chest level in front.

The step is the forward trot, done lightly and with prancing effect.

1. They enter one behind the other and start in opposite directions around the ring (Figure 97). They make the complete circuit of the ring and as they meet in front of the Council Rock they stop, face the Chief at the drum and bow deeply, marking time for eight counts.

2. They continue on around as before. When Nos. 2 and 4 come abreast of tripods 2 and 4, Figure 97, they stop, face the tripods, and mark time while Nos. 1 and 3 continue on around to tripods 1 and 3, where they stop and face the tripods. The drummer hits an accented beat, they mark time for four steps, stoop down and place the incense bowls in the tripods.

3. Nos. 1 and 3 mark time until Nos. 2 and 4 come up behind them, then all continue on around the ring as before until they meet in front of the Council Rock, where they turn and face the drum, marking time.

4. The drumming changes to a fast accented two-time and the dancers change their step to the flat-foot. An aid comes in with the four prayer-sticks across his left arm and presents them to the Incense Bearers, who hold them with the right hand at chest level, the sticks upright in front of the face.

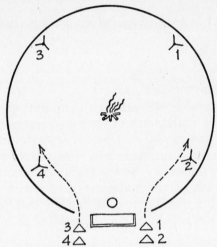

Figure 97. Diagram for Incense-Bearer's Dance

5. They turn and continue around the ring, each pair going in its original direction and stopping as before, each at his own incense stand.

6. The drum hits an accented beat, they mark time for four steps, then in unison shake the prayer-sticks forward four times in rhythm by turning their wrists downward, once on each of four steps.

7. They mark time for four steps, turn round and face the fire.

8. They mark time for four steps and shake the prayer-sticks toward the fire four times as before.

9. They dance forward to the fire and stop, mark time for four steps, then shake the prayer-sticks forward over the fire four times.

10. They mark time four steps, then turn toward the side of the ring opposite the Council Rock and dance over to the edge of it. Here two start around the ring in one direction, and the other two in the other direction, their faces turned outward toward the audience in the seats around the ring, their right hand with the prayer-stick extended outward toward the audience. On each step they shake the prayer-stick toward the audience as though invoking a blessing upon them. They continue thus around to the Council Rock where they exit, two on one side and two on the other, shaking their prayer-sticks over the head of the Chief at the drum as they do so.

It will be noted that they mark time for four steps before each new move is made—this is necessary to insure that all movements will be made in unison.

Chapter XVII

EFFECTIVE DANCE PROGRAMS

WHEN AUDIENCE appeal is the primary consideration, as it always is in presenting dances for entertainment, certain principles must govern the construction of the program. These are in no wise different for dancing than for any other type of entertainment. They apply alike to the concert, the vaudeville show, the circus, or the Indian council ring.

From the standpoint of the audience there are three considerations— *variety*, *build up*, and *a suitable finale*. From the standpoint of the dancers there must be added the important consideration of *protection against over-exertion*.

Variety and Balance

Good showmanship would never permit the scheduling of several dances of the same type in succession. To do so would run the risk of monotony and would jeopardize the effectiveness of each dance. The elements of appeal in any dance are given greater strength if they contrast with other types of appeal.

There is such wide opportunity for variety that any Indian program can be kept fresh and intriguing to the final drumbeat. Some dances are noisy and others quiet, some dashing and others reserved; some are group dances and others solos or duets; some rely on the appeal of dancing only, others add the dramatic element of a story; some are warlike in theme, some are built on hunting, others are religious in nature, and still others are based on imitations of nature. Dances also differ in the steps employed, in which respect they are divided into two main categories—those using toe-heel and similar free-moving steps, and those calling for the more restrained stomps and trots.

Toward the end of balance and variety, therefore, a dancing program should contain each of the following:

1. Powwows or strong dancing numbers.
2. Dramatic story dances (group).
3. Quiet chorus dances.
4. Solos and duets.

Care should also be taken not to overdo any one theme or motif, and so, to approach it from a different angle, the program should contain as many of the following as possible, and not too many of any one:

1. Dances involving the war theme.
2. Dances involving the hunting theme.
3. Dances in imitation of nature.
4. Dances of pure celebration.
5. Dances of a religious sort.

Build Up

Once the dances are selected, careful attention must be given to arranging them into a program that will build up to higher and higher levels as it goes along and reach its peak in the finale.

Were it not for other considerations, the ideal situation might result if the dances could be arranged in the order of their appeal, each stronger than the preceding, but this is seldom possible in handling Indian dances. To do so would mean to bunch the more vigorous and spectacular dancing numbers at the end, since these hold greatest audience appeal, and to group all quiet numbers early in the program. The need for variety argues loudly against this, as does the equally important need of the dancers for rest between vigorous numbers.

The technique that is used, therefore, is to arrange the dances into groups or units, each with a climax of its own. These are then fitted together in a program so that three or four peaks of interest are achieved. After each peak quiet dances are employed in building up to the next. The program thus moves in waves, each wave gaining in momentum to its climax and each succeeding wave reaching a higher point of interest than the preceding one. There is thus a crescendo of interest in each wave, and the waves together give a crescendo to the entire program.

If nine or ten dances are to be used, which is the usual number for a program to last an hour to an hour and a quarter, they should be arranged in three groups or waves. If twelve are scheduled, four waves may be used.

This arrangement becomes clear in these two sample programs:

Program I

1ST WAVE

Quiet Opening:	1. *Aleo*
"I Saw" Dance:	2. *Discovery Dance (Solo)*
Strong Dancing Number:	3. *Chippewa Scalp Dance*

2ND WAVE

Quiet Filler:	4. *Chippewa Deer Dance*
Stomp Dance:	5. *Cherokee Snake Dance*
Strong Dancing Number:	6. *Plains War Dance*

Photograph by Paul Boris

JAMES C. STONE

Photograph by Ralph Haburton

ROBERT RAYMON

The Sti-yu Step

3RD WAVE

Dramatic Number:	7. *Apache Devil Dance*
Artistic Solo:	8. *Spear and Shield Dance*
Strong Dancing Number as Finale:	9. *Burning Torch Powwow* (Spot Powwow if indoors)

Program II

1ST WAVE

Quiet Opening	1. *Comanche Buffalo Dance*
Stomp Dance:	2. *Cherokee Ant Dance*
Strong Dancing Number:	3. *Sioux Buffalo Dance*

2ND WAVE

"I Saw" Dance:	4. *Chippewa Deer-Hunter Dance* (*Solo*)
Dancing Number:	5. *Oto Rabbit Dance*
Strong Dancing and Dramatic Number:	6. *Zunzi Mundi*

3RD WAVE

Artistic Duet:	7. *Pueblo Dog Dance*
Dancing Solo:	8. *Chippewa Tomahawk Dance*
Strong Dancing Number:	9. *Banda Noqai*

SENTIMENTAL FINALE

10. *Passing of White Dog*

The Finale

An adequate finale should accomplish two purposes: It should climax the show, eclipsing all other dances in color and spectacle, and secondly, it should present again, in individual roles if possible, the leading dancers so that the audience may have a final glimpse of their favorite performers. For example, the Burning Torch or Spot Powwow which serves as the finale in Program I, presents the leading dancers both individually and collectively. That is the traditional nature of finales.

There is another type of closing dance sometimes used which is the direct opposite of this—a quiet dramatic number with strong emotional appeal, usually sad in nature. While this seems to violate a basic principle of showmanship, it finds justification in this case in the fact that the tragic ending seems somehow peculiarly appropriate in an Indian setting. An example is found in Program II which closes with The Passing of White Dog. When such a sad ending is used it is important that it be preceded by a dashing spectacle that brings the show up to a climax and serves the function of the usual finale. The brilliant Banda Noqai occupies that position in Program II. A climax of noise and color is essential always, and if not in the closing spot, should be next to closing. To follow it successfully, a sad ending must be very well-done.

Of the two, the rousing spectacle is safer and more certain of success. If the dances take place in Grand Council, the closing ceremony which follows can be relied upon to supply the religious note.

Protecting the Dancers

One final consideration affects the building of the program. When the dances have been selected so as to insure variety, and arranged in the best order to achieve the proper build-up, the program must be studied carefully to see that no dancer is overtaxed by being scheduled in too many strenuous numbers in a row. It is toe-heel and flat-foot dancing that is most fatiguing. Following a strong dance of this nature a filler of some sort is called for, during which the strong dancers may rest. Such a number is the Chippewa Deer Dance in Program I, a simple trotting dance for three people that can be done by lesser performers. Solos often serve this purpose also provided the solo dancer is kept out of the preceding vigorous dance. All the chorus dances in Chapters VI, VII, VIII, and IX are regarded as rest dances or "breathers," in that they do not require strenuous effort. A dancer could participate in two or three of these in succession but should not be asked to carry two two-heel or "dancing numbers" in a row. If it becomes necessary that he do so he should be given a long rest before and after.

Chapter XVIII

BELLS, DRUMS AND RATTLES

SOMETHING THAT one sees, something that he hears, something that he smells, something that he tastes, something that he feels—these are the inroads to consciousness. Good stagecraft employs as many of them as conditions permit.

There is much to see in the dances and their settings, much indeed. There is something to smell in the incense, even though it is fleeting and uncertain out-of-doors. This chapter deals with the things to hear in connection with the dances. And they are important.

These things to hear are the sounds of percussion only.

Dancing Bells

The ringing of bells is the voice of the dance. They make it articulate, they give it added animation, they increase incomparably its audience appeal.

To the dancer, bells are well-nigh indispensable. It has always been so among the Indians. They never like to dance without them, indeed, often refusing to participate if they do not have them. Bells on one's ankles reinforce the drum . . . they urge insistently to keep the rhythm. They are an incentive to dance, they stimulate and inspire to action. Once accustomed to them one finds it very difficult to dance without them. It is as if he tried to talk and made no sound. Beginners will find their learning days shortened by using them; old hands are much too wise to work without them.

A modern device? Ah, no! The type is new but the custom goes back for—we know not how long. Before the white man came the "bells" of the dancing Indian were the dewclaws made of hoofs, often attached to turtle shells for louder sound.[*] But once sleigh bells were to be had the Indians reached out for them avidly, taking them to themselves as their very own. Few things that the white man brought were received with such enthusiasm.

The ideal bells for dancing are brass sleigh bells. Novelty stores sell

[*] Bernard S. Mason, *Woodcraft*, page 473. New York: A. S. Barnes and Company, 1939.

small nickle-plated bells that make a sort of tinkling sound, woefully lacking both in volume and tone. Such as these are acceptable only if sleigh bells cannot be had. The best source of sleigh bells is second-hand stores and antique shops where a collection of old strings can usually be found which, when cleaned up, are apt to be better than any new bells that can be obtained today. Very few sleigh bells are being made nowadays.

The two common types of sleigh bells are illustrated at A and B in Figure 98. That shown at A is riveted to the strap and is not acceptable for dancing purposes because the bells rip loose and, once off, cannot be put back on. Bells worn around the ankles receive the hardest of usage; they are stepped on, kicked, battered against each other, and in general subjected to abuse that only the most substantial construction can withstand. The bell for dancing is shown at B—it has a flange that goes through the strap and is fastened in back by a piece of wire.

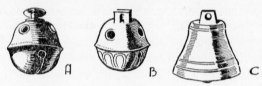

Figure 98. Types of Dancing Bells

To put old bells in condition they should be removed from the straps, thoroughly cleaned inside and out, and if very dirty and corroded, soaked overnight in a strong lye solution. Then they should be restrung on new leather of the best quality and wired in the customary way. To use the old leather will mean to lose the bells.

Two sets of bells are needed, one for ankles and the other for waist.

ANKLE BELLS.—Leg bells are sometimes worn just below the knee, supported by the calf of the leg, but it is more typical and much more desirable to wear them around the ankles. Figure 99 shows a set of ankle bells. Six to eight bells to a string is the usual number, with leather thongs at the ends with which to tie them around the ankle. Sleigh bells vary in size from No. 0 which are less than an inch in diameter, to No. 12 which are about three inches in diameter. Seldom are bells larger than the No. 5 size worn on ankles.

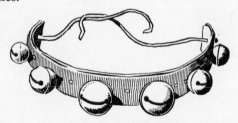

Figure 99. Ankle Bells

Most dancers wear just as many bells as they can carry conveniently without weighting down their feet unduly. Two strands of the type shown in Figure 99, worn one above the other, is customary for mature performers. In this case, one strand should be of the small sizes (Nos. 1 and 2) and the other of the larger sizes (Nos. 4 and 5).

Some Indians prefer to use bells with a slightly different tone on each ankle, thus giving each foot a sound of its own that can be readily recognized.

WAIST BELLS.—Larger bells are used around the waist because there the weight can be more easily carried. About twelve bells are customary, ranging from No. 6's to No. 10's, strung on one long strap with cloth strips attached to the ends for ties.

Each size of bell has a different pitch. The smallest ones are the highest in pitch, and as the size increases the pitch becomes progressively lower. A range of sizes from No. 1's to No. 5's on the ankles, and No. 6's to No. 10's on the waist make a delightful arrangement. But care should be taken to see that the various strands harmonize.

Open sleigh bells of the type shown at C in Figure 98 are also excellent for use around the waist because of their greater volume and their full, ringing tone. Unfortunately they are scarce nowadays. If full strings cannot be found one or two may be added to a string of round waist bells. Shaft chimes of the type that were attached to cutters or small horse-pulled sleighs are also excellent as waist bells.

Some Indians attach a long string of bells to their ankle and run it up the side of the leg to their waist bells. Most dancers find this arrangement inconvenient and hampering to free movement. These additional bells are entirely unnecessary. With an adequate number of ankle bells and a strand of larger bells around the waist, the dancer is amply equipped to make his dance heard.

BELL PROTECTORS.—Protection for the skin is necessary wherever bells are worn lest cutting and bruising result. The leather strap holding the bells can be wrapped with cloth to furnish some protection, but it is much better to use a padding of sheepskin with the wool still attached, obtainable at any harness shop.

Figure 100. Bell Protector of Sheepskin

Ankle pads are made as illustrated in Figure 100, the sheepskin cut 6 by 12 inches in size, with tapes attached for ties. They are wrapped around the ankle, with the woolly side next to the skin, before the bells are put on.

For the waist bells a strip of the sheepskin should be cut an inch wider than the bell strap and tied to the backside of it.

Drums

In another book, *Drums, Tomtoms and Rattles*, I have described how various types of dance drums can be made.*

Figure 101. Large Dance-drum

The drum best-suited for handling numbers of dancers is the large dance-drum illustrated in Figure 101, constructed over a wooden wash tub of cedar. This is a powerful drum with volume sufficient to be heard above

Figure 102. Hand-drum

the ringing of many dancing bells. The hand-drum shown in Figure 102 is adequate for solos but does not have the power to control group dances. Log drums of the Southwest type, as shown in Figure 103, also lack the

* Bernard S. Mason, *Drums, Tomtoms and Rattles*. New York: A. S. Barnes and Company, 1938.

volume and carrying power of the other type. Water drums are the least suitable of all because their boom, while capable of being heard great distances, is ineffective close at hand.

Figure 103. Southwest Log Drum

DRUM RACK.—The drum is suspended in the rack as shown in Figure 104, so that it hangs parallel to the ground at waist level. The Indian custom of hanging this type of drum just above the level of the floor will not serve our needs because it does not permit the drummer to stand, which he must do in directing the dances.

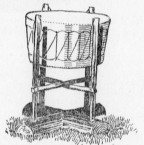

Figure 104. Drum Support

TUNING THE DRUM.—The drum should be carefully warmed before the program so as to tighten it and give it the proper tone. A blanket should then be heated and wrapped around it, and the drum placed in the rack just before the opening of the performance, with the warm blanket still over it. The blanket remains on until the Chief removes it to start the performance,

DRUMSTICKS.—The large dance-drum requires a hard drumbeater, either straight as illustrated at A in Figure 105, or curved as at C. The hard beater is the only one suitable for handling large numbers of dancers. Soft beaters muffle and soften the tone. The hard beaters give the loud, sharp, staccato boom that is needed to produce clean, sharp movement. The making of these is described in *Drums, Tomtoms and Rattles*.

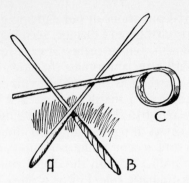

Figure 105. Hard Drumsticks

The Drummer and the Drumming

It is difficult to imagine anyone doing the drumming other than the director who has trained the dancers, who has conceived the details of interpretation, and who is responsible for their execution.

By no other means than drumming can the director exert control over the dancers during a performance. He cannot guide them by motions as an orchestra leader would direct his musicians. Audible controls are the only possibility. And the drum is a remarkably potent instrument to accomplish this.

As the result of rehearsals together, a feeling of rapport develops between the dancers and the drummer so that they understand each other and react unconsciously to each other. The drummer is able to make the drum speak a language the dancers understand. By the tone of its voice, by little subtleties of its intonation, the dancers come to know the feelings and desires of the drummer as he watches the performance. Moreover, deliberate drum signals are worked out to indicate the transitions from one figure or episode of the dance to the next. In many of the dances the time for these signals is left to the judgment of the drummer as he watches. To the Indian the accompanying song indicates the beginning and the ending of these episodes, but without the song the drummer's judgment is the only recourse. The drummer thus becomes the most important single individual in the cast, the one on whom all others rely for guidance, direction and inspiration.

If it is a solo rather than a group dance the dancer himself may take the initiative, set his own tempo, and make his own transitions, with the drummer following along, slowing down or speeding up the drumming as the dancer's bells seem to indicate. But even here it is the drummer's plain duty to do more than merely support, more than merely carry the dancer along —he must lift him to higher and yet higher levels, drawing forth from him that final bit of effort, that shade of artistry that is the difference between the commonplace and the outstanding.

Drumming occupies a more dramatic role in Indian dancing than is its usual custom. The metered pulsations of our dancing give way to a certain lawlessness. The rhythms change and change, seemingly oblivious to plan or preconceived arrangement, but in reality always following the dictates of the dance routine. With utter abruptness the slow, measured beat leaps into a rapid pulsation as startling as the sudden whir of pheasant wings in a peaceful meadow. And again a sharp, high-pitched staccato of exciting tempo sinks gradually away into a slow, deep throbbing. Yet again a booming crescendo suddenly ceases altogether in silent dramatic pause, to start anew with different time and accent. Obligatory upon the drummer, therefore, is a most intimate familiarity with the dance routines, for only then can he fully conceive his dramatic role. For he is more than mere drummer ... he is a vital part of the dance itself, if indeed, he is not its central figure.

In respect to the technique of drumming, just one suggestion will be needed by anyone who knows the rhythms: The wrist must be kept flexible and responsive to the drumstick. The beater must rebound freely from the drum. To use an arm rather than a wrist motion prevents the rebound and often results in faulty rhythm, blurred and deadened tone. No arm is quick enough of itself to lift the stick, but when the wrist is flexible the rebound lifts it automatically with a sharp, clear, full-toned boom.

Dance Rattles

The Indians made rattles from gourds, turtle shells, buffalo and steer horns, sea shells, rawhide, wood, and birchbark.

The gourd rattle is the one best-suited for practical use. It is attractive, light in weight, and loud in sound. These are very easy to make. As a substitute for gourds tin cans may be used. Indeed, rattles may be made from an assortment of things from pillboxes to ice-cream cartons.

For instructions for making rattles, both authentic and improvised, see *Drums, Tomtoms and Rattles*.

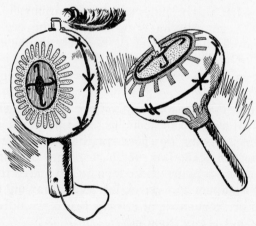

Figure 106. Gourd Dance Rattles

Chapter XIX

INDIAN MAKE-UP

ALL-OVER BODY paint and a breechcloth, with feathered ornaments added, is the dancing pattern for men. The gorgeously beaded dancing costumes that some of the tribes have used for dancing in recent years are less to be desired than the simple breechcloths of their ancestors. This is true both from the standpoint of the dancer and the audience, for the dancer has greater freedom of movement and finds the dancing less fatiguing, and the picture created is more appealing because of the visible muscular play. Moreover color effects can be obtained with body paint that cannot be matched by clothing.

When the body is painted all feeling of nudeness is relieved. To the audience the colored paint gives not the slightest impression of bareness and the dancer himself feels himself to be well-clothed.

If for any reason body paint is not desirable the alternative is to approximate it by wearing tights, made by dyeing heavy long underwear as described in Chapter XX.

Beaded dancing costumes are appropriate on the chiefs and dignitaries, and on elders who may dance, but not on the dashing, youthful dancers. They are recommended only for the Chief at the drum and others who may take part in the ritual only.

This chapter discusses paint make-up for the face and the body. Other costuming is covered in the next chapter.

In the case of women dancers, clothing is used as described in the following chapter, with face made up in the same way as for men.

Base Paint

A washable make-up is used, one that can be removed with soap and water. If only the face is to be painted grease paint will do, but for the painting of the entire body as is necessary if the dancer is to appear in breechcloth, it is quite out of the question. There are excellent washable make-ups on the market. Some of these come in powder form to be mixed with glycerin while others are prepared in paste form and packed in tubes. The latter are to be recommended.*

* One of the most satisfactory is Thespaint manufactured by Minor's Incorporated and marketed at most theatrical stores and make-up counters.

There is a crumbly rock obtainable in Texas popularly called Indian Paint Rock which is often used for Indian make-up. It is of the proper color and when finely powdered and mixed with water is quite satisfactory. Ordinary cocoa mixed with water is sometimes used. These are all makeshift methods, however, as compared to the use of standard theatrical preparations. For a smooth, finished, professional make-up the best grade of washable paint should be obtained. One may be sure these are entirely safe, an important consideration when the paint is to be applied from head to foot.

Face Make-up

Be it known at the outset that "war paint" is not recommended. The daubing of the face with an assortment of colors is neither typical of the dancing Indian nor conducive to a pleasing appearance. If used it must be applied with reserve and good taste. It is better to leave it alone entirely. It seldom adds and usually detracts.

The objective of the make-up is to achieve a natural, lifelike Indian face, as attractive and pleasing as it can possibly be made. Four colors are necessary to accomplish this:

(1) A base paint of Indian red
(2) Eye lavender, or dark brown, for the eyelids
(3) Black for eyebrows and eye lines
(4) Red for lips

Using a tube of washable theatrical make-up of the Indian shade, apply to the face with the fingers and rub until all streaks and blotches are removed and a smooth Indian-red complexion results. All areas of the face should be covered except the eyelids. Do not wet or dilute the paint but use it just as it comes from the tube.

Using lavender washable paint, apply a little to the end of the finger and rub it on the eyelids, covering the entire eyelids up to the eyebrows. This provides the eye shadow that puts life, sparkle and carrying power in the eyes.

The eyebrows are then lined with black washable paint. This should be applied with a pasteboard "stump" obtainable at theatrical stores, or with a matchstick. The eyebrows should be lengthened by extending them out to the sides. The photograph facing page 150 shows such a lengthened eyebrow.

With a tiny brush, the smallest obtainable, run a fine black line around the lower edge of the eye just below the lower eyelash; carry it far out to the side to enlarge the eye, then run a corresponding line up onto the upper eyelid to make the V. This V is then filled in with lavender paint and the eye make-up is finished.

A dark lip rouge is used on the lips.

Merely to paint the face red without using eye shadow, eyebrow lines and lip cream results in a ghastly, unhealthy face thoroughly lacking in personality, attractiveness and carrying power.

Body Make-up

Body paint is applied with an ordinary paint brush two inches in width. Squeeze a tube of washable make-up into a bowl, add just enough water to cover and paint from head to foot. With a two-inch brush the entire body can be painted in a very few minutes. Streaks and blotches are then rubbed out with the hands.

The Pueblo Indians are much given to painting the body in brilliant colors. By no other means can so much color be put into a dancing performance. If the rank and file of the dancers are painted in the usual Indian red, and each of the leading dancers painted in a vivid color of his own, a dramatically beautiful effect will result. But here again the aim is beauty, not bizarre effects or mere splashes of bright color.

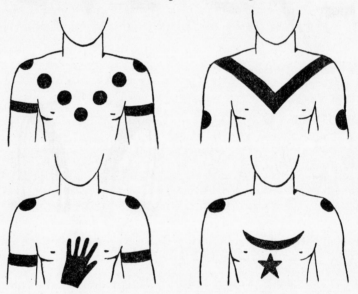

Figure 107. Designs for Chest and Arms

Of the beautiful shades available in washable make-up the following have given excellent results: *ultramarine blue, soft green, canary yellow, crimson, gray* and *white*. By the use of these, six dancers can be painted each in a different color, causing them to stand out vividly against the background of the dancers in Indian red. Such colors do not extend above the neck, however, for the face is always in Indian red.

After the dancer's body is painted in one of these colors it should be highlighted by designs in a contrasting color. It is on the body, and not as "war paint" on the face, that color designs should be used. The ultramarine blue may be highlighted with canary yellow, the canary yellow with black, the gray with yellow, the white with black, the crimson with white. The green is most effective if the natural color of the skin is used for highlighting.

Figures 107 and 108 show several appropriate designs for the chest and arms. It is also customary to paint a two-inch spot on the leg just above the knee. If these designs do not stand out vividly enough, as is the case when some colors are combined, they should be outlined with a very fine black line, best applied with a stump or matchstick.

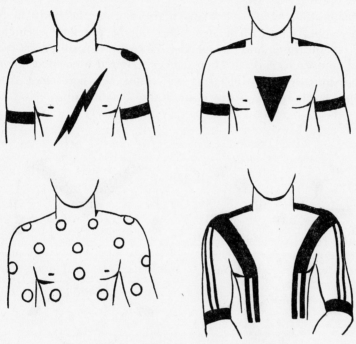

Figure 108. Designs for Chest and Arms

To repeat, the face is painted Indian red, regardless of the color of the body paint, and is made up naturally and without "war paint". The body designs as recommended should be used with reserve and good taste, their purpose being merely to highlight and add interest. They should never be allowed to become disproportionately large and conspicuous, gaudy or dauby.

Chapter XX

INDIAN COSTUMING

FROM THE photographs of dancers in this book it will be seen that aside from body paint the important items of costuming for men are (1) breechcloth, (2) head ornaments, (3) bustles, (4) leg wraps, (5) moccasins. These will be discussed in order. The making of tights is also discussed should clothing be preferred to body paint.

Women's costumes are treated later in the chapter.

Breechcloths

The typical breechcloth of the Sioux country of the northern Plains is illustrated at A in Figure 109. Beaded designs were seldom seen on breechcloths. They were usually made of the navy blue or red "list" cloth issued by the Government in the old days, and either left plain or decorated only by a contrasting hem and three or four ribbons sewed across the bottom edge as shown. Such breechcloths of heavy material are more appropriate when worn with a beaded costume than on a stripped dancer.

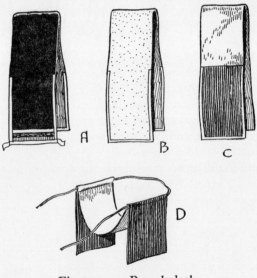

Figure 109. Breechcloths

For dancing purposes the breechcloth should be of soft, pleasing material in a color that looks well with the body paint used. Red, green and a medium shade of blue are much-used colors. The simplest type of breech-cloth consists of a long strip of cloth edged with a contrasting color as shown at B in Figure 109. For ordinary occasions outing flannel is a desir-able material, pleasing in appearance, soft to the touch, and launders well. Care should be taken not to make it overlarge lest it stand out undesirably and attract attention. A width of nine inches is right for a person of ordi-nary size, up to twelve inches for very large people. The length varies from 54 to 60 inches.

Such a breechcloth is held in place by a tie around the waist. A strip of any ordinary cotton material about three inches wide is commonly used for the tie.

Those doing much dancing will want a breechcloth made of better material, such as velvet or fine corduroy. When an expensive material such as these is used, it is customary to substitute a cheaper material between the legs where it is not seen. At C in Figure 109 a breechcloth of this type is shown, the corduroy measuring nine inches in width and eighteen inches in length, sewed onto ordinary cotton material such as gingham. When corduroy is used the cotton material may form a half-inch hem around the edge, but no hem is used on velvet.

A still more satisfactory type of breechcloth is shown at D, consisting of two pieces of velvet or corduroy nine inches wide and twelve inches long, with an open seam at the top through which the tie string is inserted. The middle section going between the legs is of a double thickness of cotton material.

The wide aprons used by the Chippewas in connection with their beaded dancing costumes are suitable only if tights or clothing are used. They are not a substitute for a breechcloth.

Head Ornaments

Everyone is familiar with the warbonnet, loved by all who know Indians and regarded by many as the most picturesque hat ever created. Indeed, so indelibly has the warbonnet been identified with the Indian that to the general public an Indian does not seem properly dressed without it. This is unfortunate in two respects—the warbonnet was the native head-dress only of certain Plains tribes, and secondly, it was not the characteristic garb for dancers even in the tribes where it is authentic. The older chiefs wore the warbonnet while the young dancing men preferred the hair roach.

For purposes of costuming there are advantages in the warbonnet be-yond its decorativeness. It covers the head completely so that no other paraphernalia is needed. It eliminates the necessity of using a wig. And it can be put on in a jiffy with no more difficulty than one encounters in putting on his hat. For the sake of convenience many dancers use it who might otherwise prefer a roach.

Instructions for making the warbonnet are to be found in *Woodcraft.**

ROACHES.—In the various pictures of dancers in this book it will be noted that in most cases the hair roach is worn instead of the warbonnet. This is always the preferred head ornament for dancers. It immediately makes one look the part of the dancer. It sets him up for action. It harmonizes with the breechcloth and body paint. The warbonnet is more at home on a heavily clothed person whose function is to walk around and be looked at.

Unhappily, roaches are not easy for inexperienced hands to make, and they are not as plentiful on the market as they once were, although most Indian craft shops handling Plains items can supply them. They are made of porcupine hair and of deer hair dyed red, with an eagle feather set up on top. They are held on the head by two ties of heavy black thread in front attached to a beaded headband, and in back by two tapes or thongs that carry around the neck and tie under the chin.

The roach, of course, requires the use of a wig.

WIGS.—The most appropriate wig for men is the bobbed type with a bang in front. It must be remembered that the dancing Indian is the younger Indian and the wig should be selected accordingly. Parted wigs may be used if preferred to those with bangs but either type is more practical and attractive if bobbed than if left long and braided. The bob should be cut about even with the chin.

A beaded headband makes an otherwise unruly and straggly wig look acceptable. Suitable wigs can sometimes be fashioned from rope dyed black. The best commercial ones are handmade of human hair. Machine-made wigs of human hair are very inexpensive as compared to the handmade ones, and mohair wigs are still less costly.

OTHER FEATHER ORNAMENTS.—Modern Oklahoma Indians make much use of the spectacular *feather roach* in dancing, a showy arrangement of feathers standing upright on the head and following the usual lines of a hair roach. Although most dancers prefer the hair roach, feeling it to be in better taste than these overlarge and elaborate ornamentations, a feather roach is a useful item to have in one's wardrobe for the sake of variety. They are less expensive than warbonnets in that they do not require good feathers, and are easy to make.*

Another similar feather headdress is the *feather crest* popular among the Chippewas in years past, a single row of eagle feathers standing upright and extending backward on the top of the head.**

When large numbers of dancers must be costumed, often the only

* Bernard S. Mason, *Woodcraft*, pages 481-489. New York: A. S. Barnes and Company, 1939.
** For instructions for making see Bernard S. Mason, *Woodcraft*, pages 489-497. New York: A. S. Barnes and Company, 1939.

Minataree Green Corn Dance

Powwow Concluding the Chippewa Scalp Dance

Photograph by Ralph Haburton

JOHN LANDIS HOLDEN

choice is to use a *single feather*. This is best used with a headband, either beaded or cloth, under which the quill of the feather is inserted. Another typical arrangement of this sort is the *wapeginicki*, a feather and fluffy arrangement stuck under the headband.*

SOUTHWEST HEAD STYLE.—To imitate the Southwest Indian head style, use a bobbed wig of the kind described above, with a silk or satin headband tied around it. The band should be eight inches wide and rolled to a width of two inches. Its length should be such that when tied around the head the ends will hang down six inches. It should circle the head parallel with the floor and be tied over one ear.

Bustles

Probably no item of costuming adds so much in decorativeness and does it so appropriately as do bustles. These circular arrangements of feathers come in many types, as the pictures of dancers in this volume will indicate. Those on the arms of the dancers in the photo facing page 23 are the traditional Plains type, made of many layers of feathers and fluffies one above the other. The dancer in the illustration facing page 22 is wearing another very decorative type, consisting of a single row of large, dark eagle feathers. Most spectacular of all are the elaborate Oklahoma bustles on the dancer in the picture facing page 86. Bustles are among the easiest of all feather ornaments to make (for instructions see *Woodcraft*, pages 500-510).

Three to four bustles are usually worn. One at least is important, indeed almost essential, worn on the middle of the back at waist level. This fills the hollow of the back and accentuates the dance style in the low positions. It is thought by some that it was originated to make the rump stand out still more conspicuously in the low crouches. The largest bustle obtainable should be worn here.

A smaller bustle is worn on each arm below the shoulder. These are not only most ornamental but give width to the shoulders, accentuate the shoulder motions, and cover up the arms in situations where they might otherwise attract attention undesirably.

The fourth bustle is worn on the back of the neck, impossible when a warbonnet is used but appropriate with a roach. This is of less importance than the back and arm bustles.

Very small bustles are sometimes used on the wrists. Hair bustles have a delightful effect here. They may be seen on the wrists of the dancer in the illustration facing page 166. Small feather bustles measuring about eight inches in diameter are also appropriate.

*For instructions for making see Bernard S. Mason, *Woodcraft*, pages 489-497. New York: A. S. Barnes and Company, 1939.

Arm Ornaments

In lieu of bustles for the arms an arm-band of some sort is needed to relieve the bareness. Many Indian tribes use a one-inch beaded band tied just above the elbow, often so constructed as to permit the ends to dangle. As a substitute for these *yarn wraps* will do very nicely, made as described in the next section, "Leg Ornaments".

Tin arm-bands are also a typical Indian arm ornament. These are three-inch bands of tin that circle the arm just above the elbow, from which strips of felt hang downward (*Woodcraft*, page 537).

Leg Ornaments

It is important that the lines of the legs themselves be fully visible and therefore but few trappings are desirable. Ornamentation should be confined largely to the upper part of the body. Bustles are out of place not only because they cover the legs but make the dancer appear bottom heavy. When used on the upper arms bustles give great width and brilliance to the shoulders where width is appropriate, causing the dancer's lines to taper down to his feet, wedge-like. This is destroyed by projecting leg decorations.

Two items only are desirable on the legs—*leg wraps* and *anklets*.

LEG WRAPS.—The simplest are those made of colored yarn, visible on the legs of the dancer in the photo facing page 6. Indians love yarn and use it in many unusual ways. It adds a primitive touch and an undeniable Indian flavor. Leg wraps of it are soft, reserved and wholly appropriate.

The wrap is illustrated in Figure 110. It is three feet long and consists of three to four dozen strands of yarn tied together as shown. The color should harmonize with the body paint. It is wrapped around the leg below the knee and above the calf, and tied either in front or at the side of the leg.

Figure 110. Leg Wrap of Yarn

Another type of leg wrap consists of a beaded band. The Chippewas use a band about three inches in width with yarn tassels at the ends for ties. The Oklahoma Indians use a band about an inch and a half wide with a circular beaded rosette attached in front.

Often a cluster of tiny feathers not over four inches long is attached to the yarn or beaded band so as to hang down in front of the leg. Again, three long quills are used, from which the web has been torn away and to the ends of which fluffies are glued. These may be attached to a cloth band 1½ inches wide. The length is such that when the band is worn the fluffies on the ends hang just above the moccasin. The quills are attached so that they curve outward, and are sewed to the band loosely so that they can move.

ANKLETS.—These are wraps of fur or angora worn just above the moccasin. They fan out above the feet and add much sparkle to the dancing steps. The traditional material, used whenever it can be obtained, is *angora goat hide* with its remarkably long, silky, white hair. As a substitute, any fur may be used but if it is of the short type a three-inch fringe of yarn should be attached to the bottom to fan out over the moccasin. Or the anklet may be made of yarn and cloth.

The construction of the angora anklet is shown in Figure 111. Cut a piece of canvas to the shape and size shown at A, then cut the hide to this pattern and sew onto the canvas, attaching tie tapes at the ends. The anklet is usually worn just above the moccasin with the ankle bells above it. If the angora is unusually long, however, it should be placed above the bells lest it be stepped on.

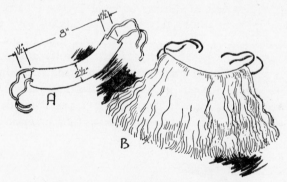

Figure 111. Anklets of Angora

To make a yarn anklet, cut a piece of cotton cloth 3 inches wide and 11 inches long. Cut the yarn 5 inches long, lay it along one edge of the cloth, extending up from the edge about an inch, fold the other edge of the cloth over it and then sew on a sewing machine. The cloth band is thus 1½ inches wide and the yarn fringe 4 inches long.

Moccasins

True Indian moccasins are the most essential part of a dancer's costume. Indian dancing is quite impossible with hard-soled shoes; indeed, the typical movements are difficult to achieve in any type of shoe or slipper other than moccasins. If moccasins cannot be had one should dance barefooted.

Some dancers prefer the soft-soled Woodland moccasin and others the hard-soled Plains moccasin. Indian-made moccasins may be purchased from Indian crafts shops or the dancer can make his own (*Woodcraft*, pages 427 to 440).

Tights

If tights are preferred to all-over body paint they should be made as the Indians make them, from a suit of long, heavy underwear. Such underwear tights are widely used among Woodland, Plains and Oklahoma tribes. Dye the underwear to the desired color and replace the white buttons with others of the color of the tights. One of the designs on page 258 may then be appliqued in cloth of a contrasting color.

At a distance of a few feet such tights are much neater in appearance than one might imagine. There is no danger of them being identified as underwear.

Costumes for Women

In making up women for Indian dances, conditions usually do not permit imitating the elaborately beaded or tinkled dresses of the Plains or Woodland women, nor is such effort necessary. Regardless of tribe, if authentic costuming is not to be had the best effect is obtained by using a simple slip-on dress in a neutral color, making no effort at authenticity but placing reliance on the dancing for effect rather than on the costuming. "Homespun" material or Osmaburg is very satisfactory. Such dresses can be quickly put together by cutting them to knee length, sewing up the sides and shoulders, leaving the arms bare. A tie will pull in the waist. Arms and legs should be painted as described in the last chapter.

A beaded headband is the only head ornament needed.

Index